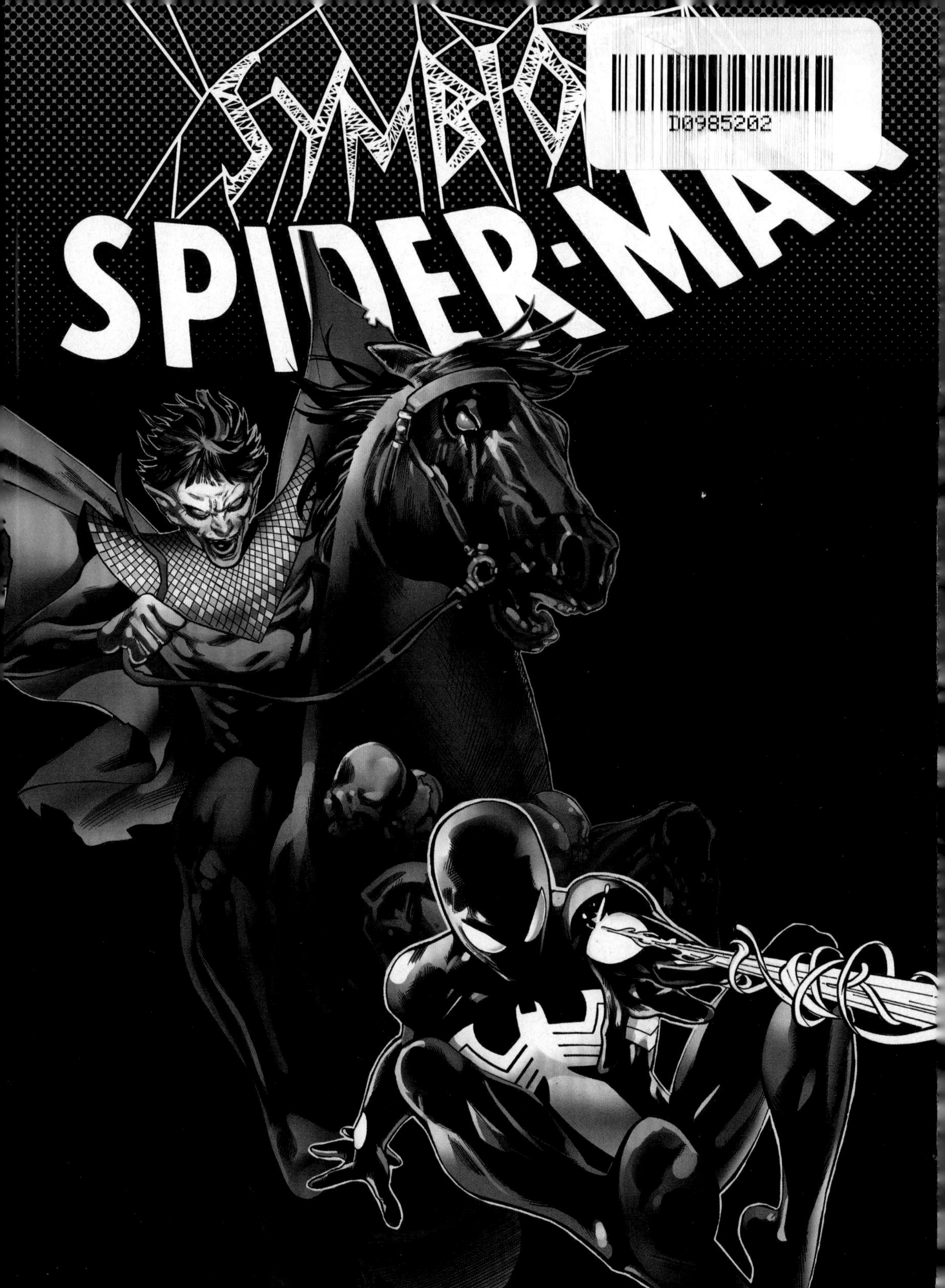
SYMBIO
SPIDER-MA

ALIEN REALITY

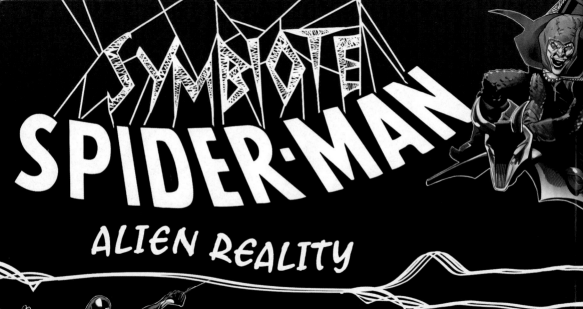

SYMBIOTE SPIDER-MAN

ALIEN REALITY

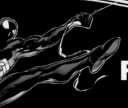

PETER DAVID
WRITER

GREG LAND
PENCILER

JAY LEISTEN
INKER

FRANK D'ARMATA
COLORIST

VC'S JOE SABINO
LETTERER

GREG LAND & **FRANK D'ARMATA** *WITH* **JAY LEISTEN** *(#1)*
COVER ART

DANNY KHAZEM
ASSISTANT EDITOR

DEVIN LEWIS
EDITOR

NICK LOWE
EXECUTIVE EDITOR

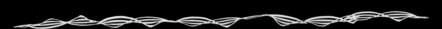

SPIDER-MAN *CREATED BY* **STAN LEE** & **STEVE DITKO**

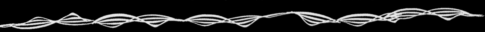

Collection Editor: JENNIFER GRÜNWALD
Associate Managing Editor: MAIA LOY
Associate Managing Editor: LISA MONTALBANO
Editor, Special Projects: MARK D. BEAZLEY

VP Production & Special Projects: JEFF YOUNGQUIST
Book Designers: STACIE ZUCKER WITH SALENA MAHINA
SVP Print, Sales & Marketing: DAVID GABRIEL
Editor in Chief: C.B. CEBULSKI

SYMBIOTE SPIDER-MAN: ALIEN REALITY. Contains material originally published in magazine form as SYMBIOTE SPIDER-MAN: ALIEN REALITY (2019) #1-5. First printing 2020. ISBN 978-1-302-92145-3. Published by MARVEL WORLDWIDE, INC., a subsidiary of MARVEL ENTERTAINMENT, LLC. OFFICE OF PUBLICATION: 1290 Avenue of the Americas, New York, NY 10104. **Printed in Canada.** KEVIN FEIGE, Chief Creative Officer; DAN BUCKLEY, President, Marvel Entertainment; JOHN NEE, Publisher; JOE QUESADA, EVP & Creative Director; TOM BREVOORT, SVP of Publishing; DAVID BOGART, Associate Publisher & SVP of Talent Affairs; Publishing & Partnership; DAVID GABRIEL, VP of Print & Digital Publishing; JEFF YOUNGQUIST, VP of Production & Special Projects; DAN CARR, Executive Director of Publishing Technology; ALEX MORALES, Director of Publishing Operations; DAN EDINGTON, Managing Editor; SUSAN CRESPI, Production Manager; STAN LEE, Chairman Emeritus. For information regarding advertising in Marvel Comics or on Marvel.com, please contact Vit DeBellis, Custom Solutions & Integrated Advertising Manager, at vdebellis@marvel.com. For Marvel subscription inquiries, please call 888-511-5480. **Manufactured between 6/19/2020 and 7/21/2020 by SOLISCO PRINTERS, SCOTT, QC, CANADA.**

10 9 8 7 6 5 4 3 2 1

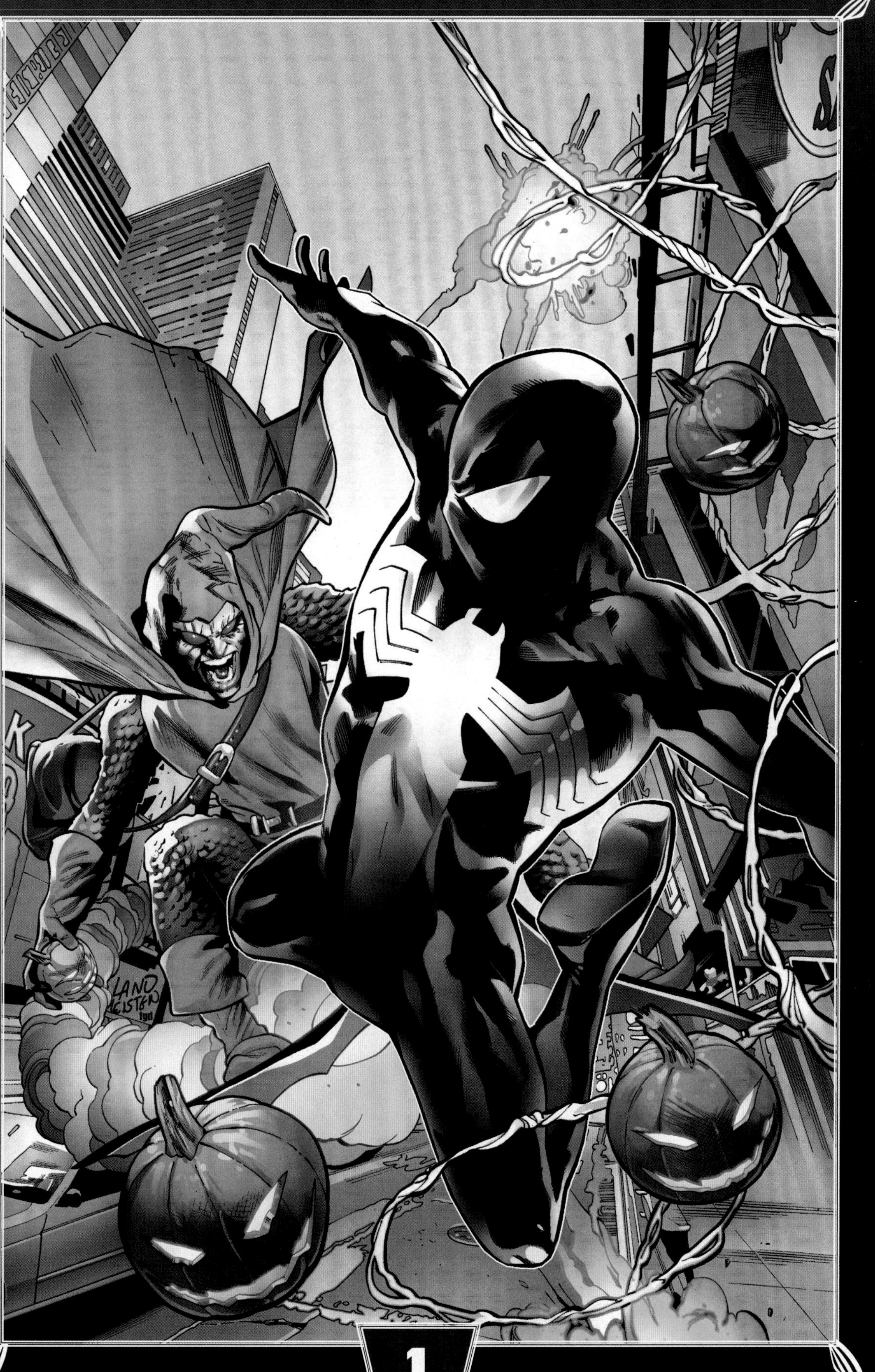

1

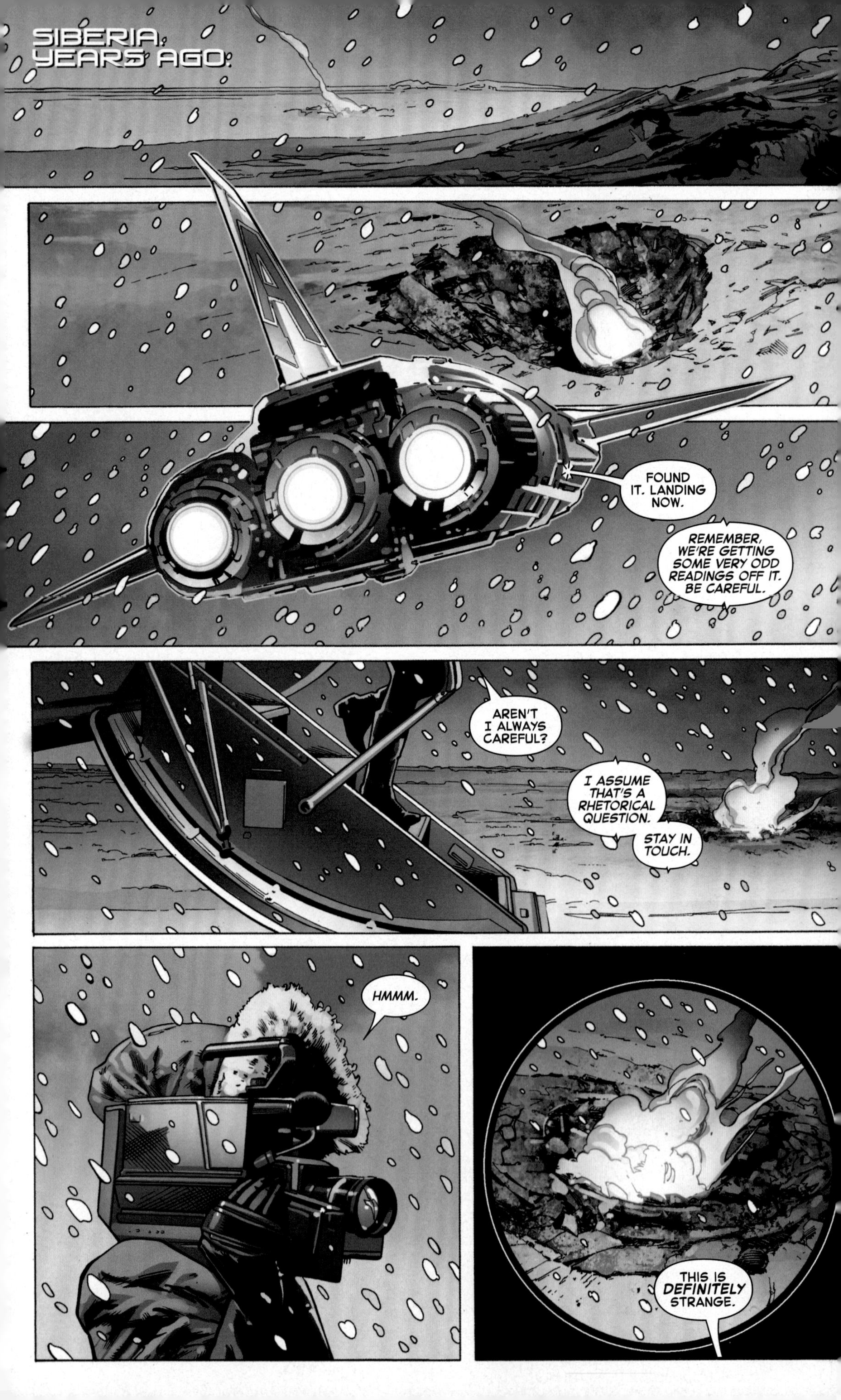
SIBERIA, YEARS AGO:
FOUND IT. LANDING NOW.
REMEMBER, WE'RE GETTING SOME VERY ODD READINGS OFF IT. BE CAREFUL.
AREN'T I ALWAYS CAREFUL?
I ASSUME THAT'S A RHETORICAL QUESTION.
STAY IN TOUCH.
HMMM.
THIS IS DEFINITELY STRANGE.

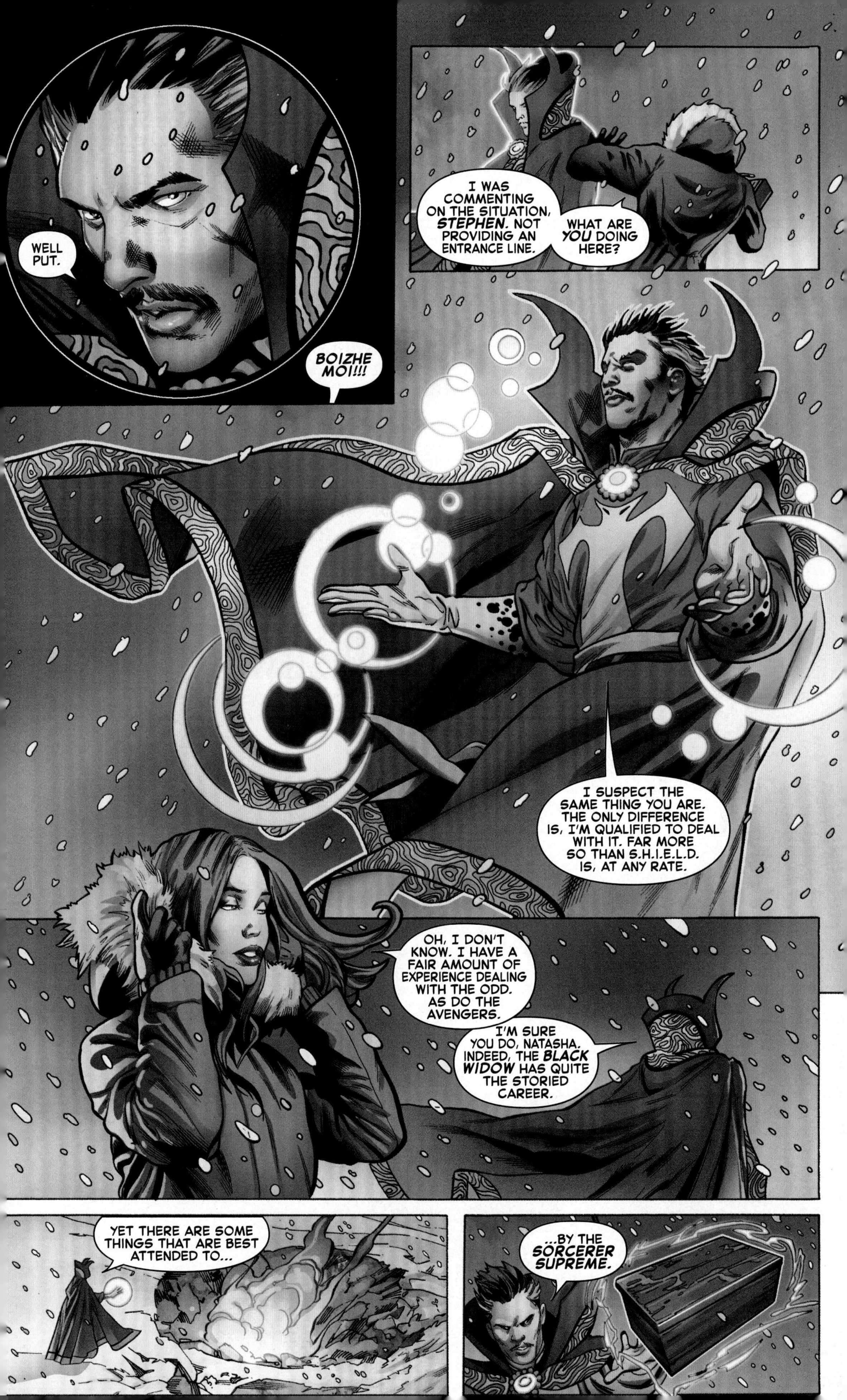
WELL PUT.
BOIZHE MOI!!!
I WAS COMMENTING ON THE SITUATION, STEPHEN. NOT PROVIDING AN ENTRANCE LINE.
WHAT ARE YOU DOING HERE?
I SUSPECT THE SAME THING YOU ARE. THE ONLY DIFFERENCE IS, I'M QUALIFIED TO DEAL WITH IT. FAR MORE SO THAN S.H.I.E.L.D. IS, AT ANY RATE.
OH, I DON'T KNOW. I HAVE A FAIR AMOUNT OF EXPERIENCE DEALING WITH THE ODD. AS DO THE AVENGERS.
I'M SURE YOU DO, NATASHA. INDEED, THE BLACK WIDOW HAS QUITE THE STORIED CAREER.
YET THERE ARE SOME THINGS THAT ARE BEST ATTENDED TO...
...BY THE SORCERER SUPREME.

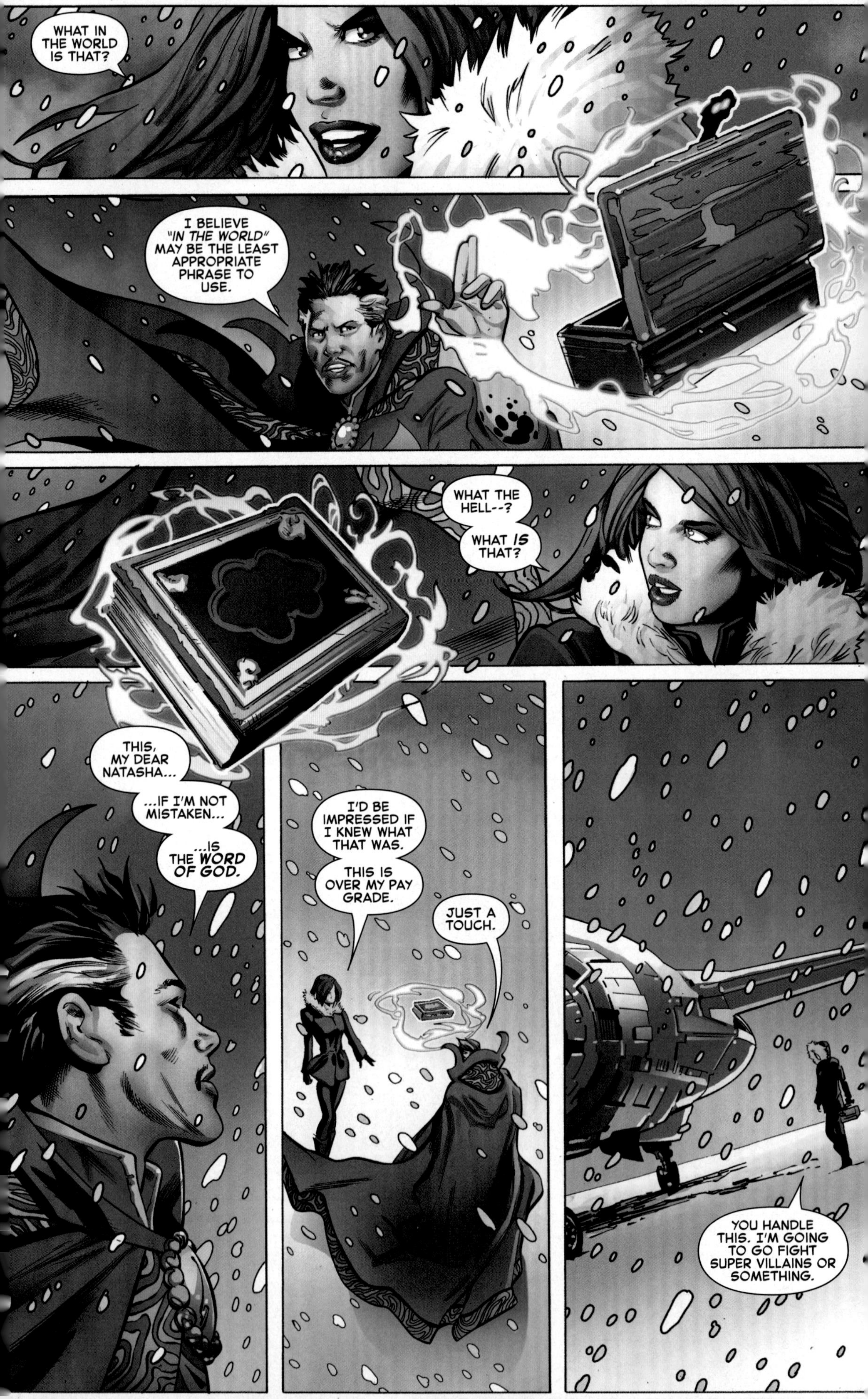
WHAT IN THE WORLD IS THAT?
I BELIEVE "IN THE WORLD" MAY BE THE LEAST APPROPRIATE PHRASE TO USE.
WHAT THE HELL--?
WHAT IS THAT?
THIS, MY DEAR NATASHA...
...IF I'M NOT MISTAKEN...
...IS THE WORD OF GOD.
I'D BE IMPRESSED IF I KNEW WHAT THAT WAS.
THIS IS OVER MY PAY GRADE.
JUST A TOUCH.
YOU HANDLE THIS. I'M GOING TO GO FIGHT SUPER VILLAINS OR SOMETHING.

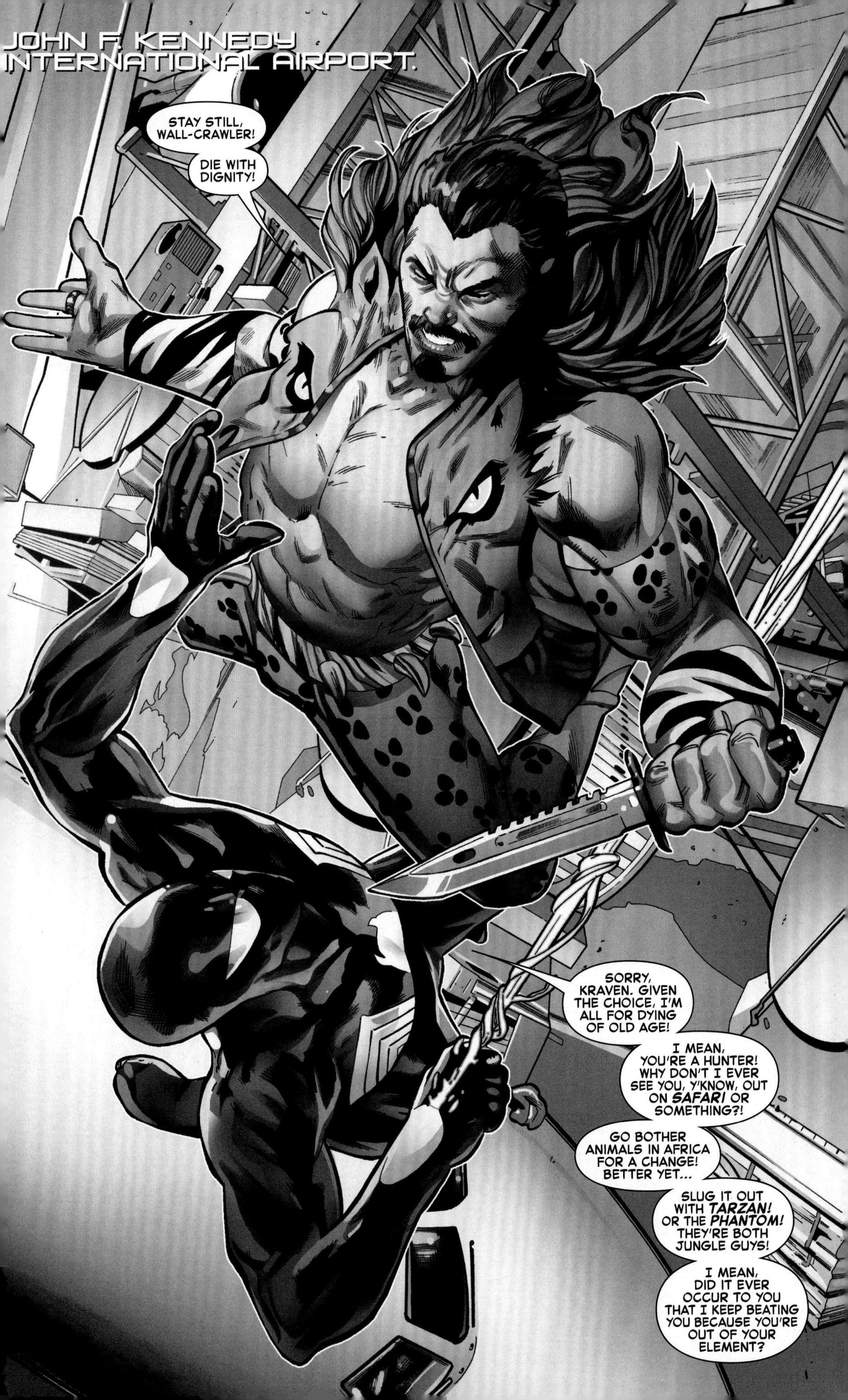

JOHN F. KENNEDY INTERNATIONAL AIRPORT.
STAY STILL, WALL-CRAWLER!
DIE WITH DIGNITY!
SORRY, KRAVEN. GIVEN THE CHOICE, I'M ALL FOR DYING OF OLD AGE!
I MEAN, YOU'RE A HUNTER! WHY DON'T I EVER SEE YOU, Y'KNOW, OUT ON SAFARI OR SOMETHING?!
GO BOTHER ANIMALS IN AFRICA FOR A CHANGE! BETTER YET...
SLUG IT OUT WITH TARZAN! OR THE PHANTOM! THEY'RE BOTH JUNGLE GUYS!
I MEAN, DID IT EVER OCCUR TO YOU THAT I KEEP BEATING YOU BECAUSE YOU'RE OUT OF YOUR ELEMENT?

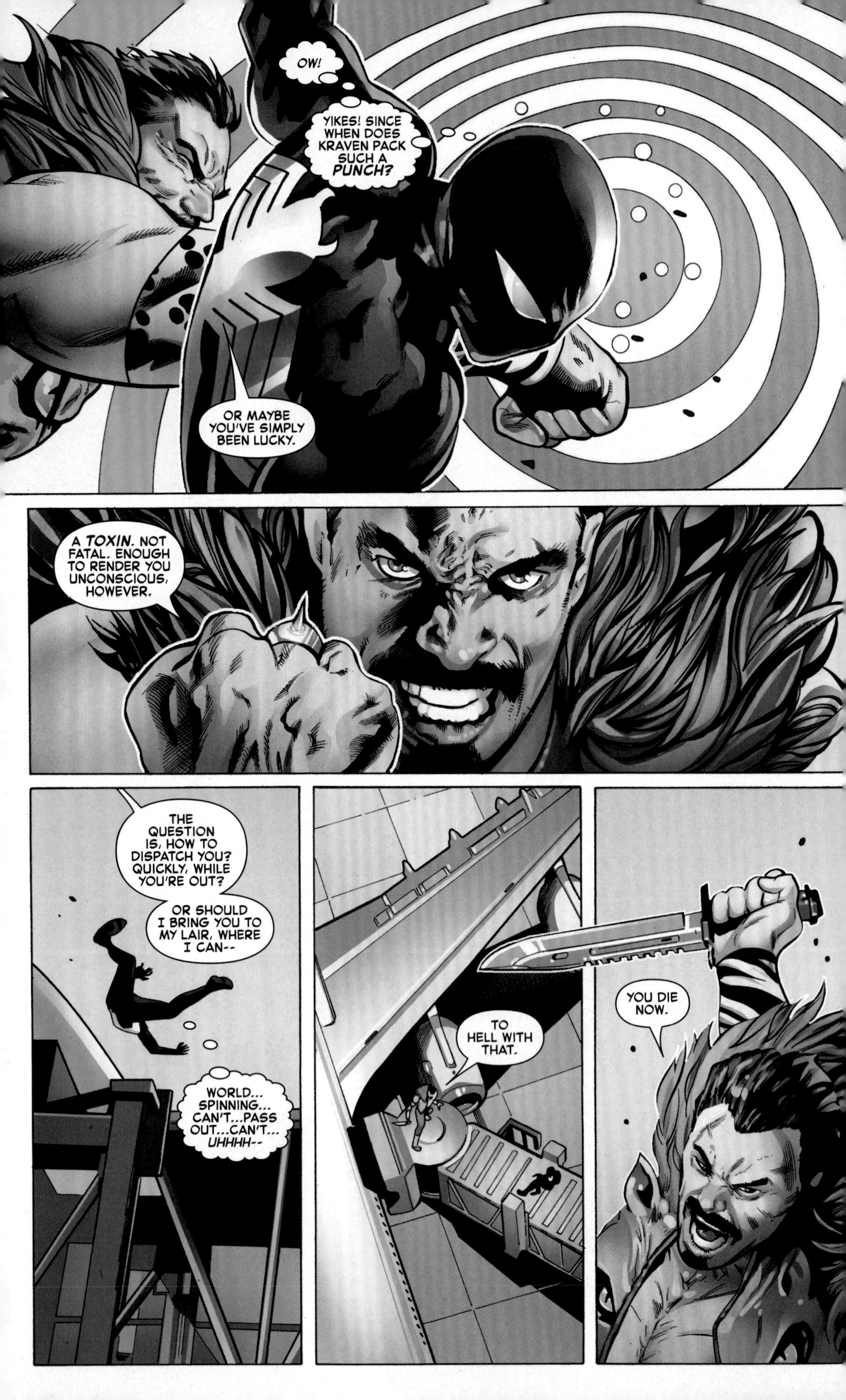
OW!
YIKES! SINCE WHEN DOES KRAVEN PACK SUCH A *PUNCH?*
OR MAYBE YOU'VE SIMPLY BEEN LUCKY.
A *TOXIN.* NOT FATAL. ENOUGH TO RENDER YOU UNCONSCIOUS, HOWEVER.
THE QUESTION IS, HOW TO DISPATCH YOU? QUICKLY, WHILE YOU'RE OUT?
OR SHOULD I BRING YOU TO MY LAIR, WHERE I CAN--
WORLD... SPINNING... CAN'T...PASS OUT...CAN'T... *UHHHH--*
TO HELL WITH THAT.
YOU DIE NOW.

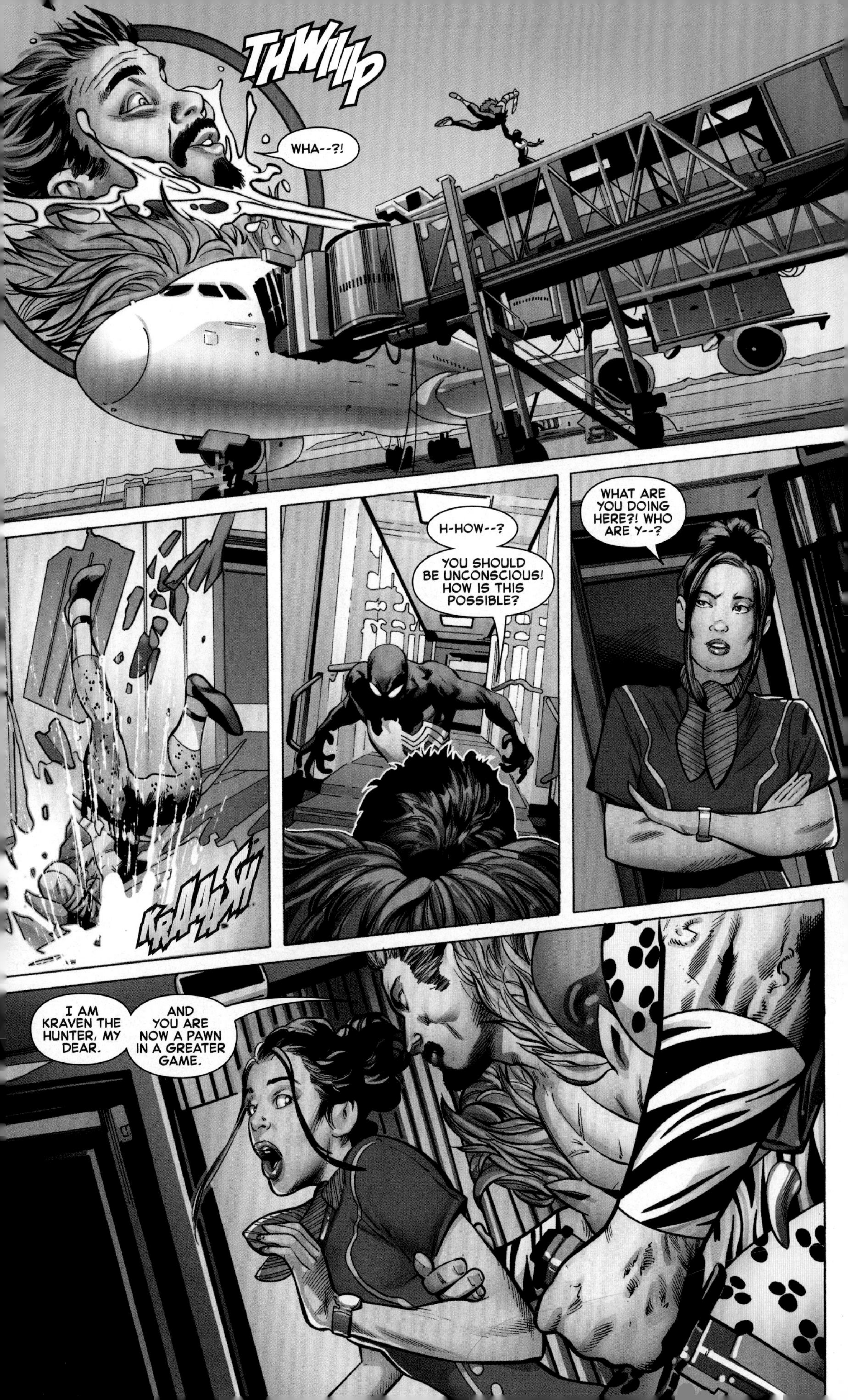
THWIIIP
WHA--?!
KRAAASH
H-HOW--?
YOU SHOULD BE UNCONSCIOUS! HOW IS THIS POSSIBLE?
WHAT ARE YOU DOING HERE?! WHO ARE Y--?
I AM KRAVEN THE HUNTER, MY DEAR.
AND YOU ARE NOW A PAWN IN A GREATER GAME.

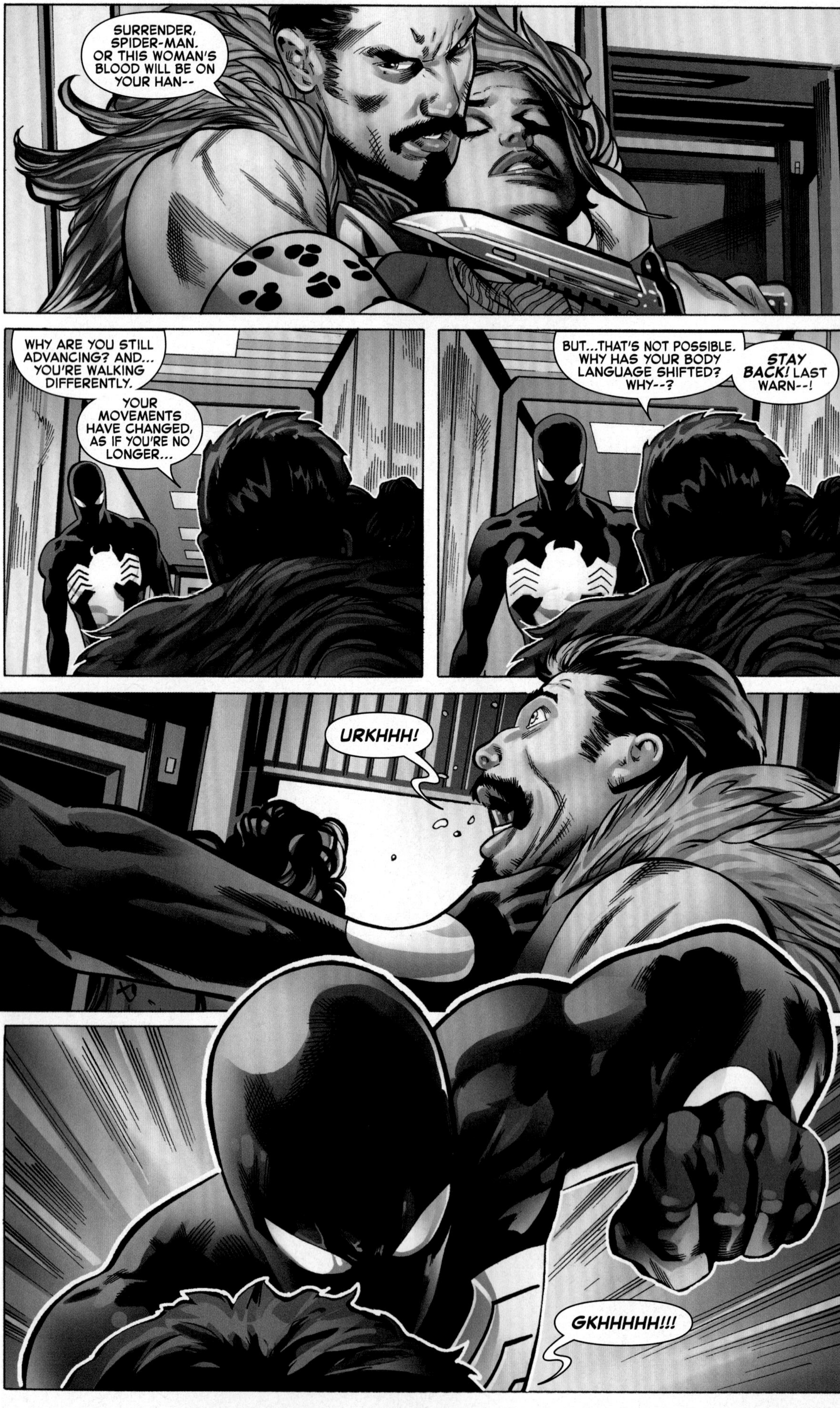
SURRENDER, SPIDER-MAN. OR THIS WOMAN'S BLOOD WILL BE ON YOUR HAN--
WHY ARE YOU STILL ADVANCING? AND... YOU'RE WALKING DIFFERENTLY.
YOUR MOVEMENTS HAVE CHANGED, AS IF YOU'RE NO LONGER...
BUT...THAT'S NOT POSSIBLE. WHY HAS YOUR BODY LANGUAGE SHIFTED? WHY--?
STAY BACK! LAST WARN--!
URKHHH!
GKHHHHH!!!

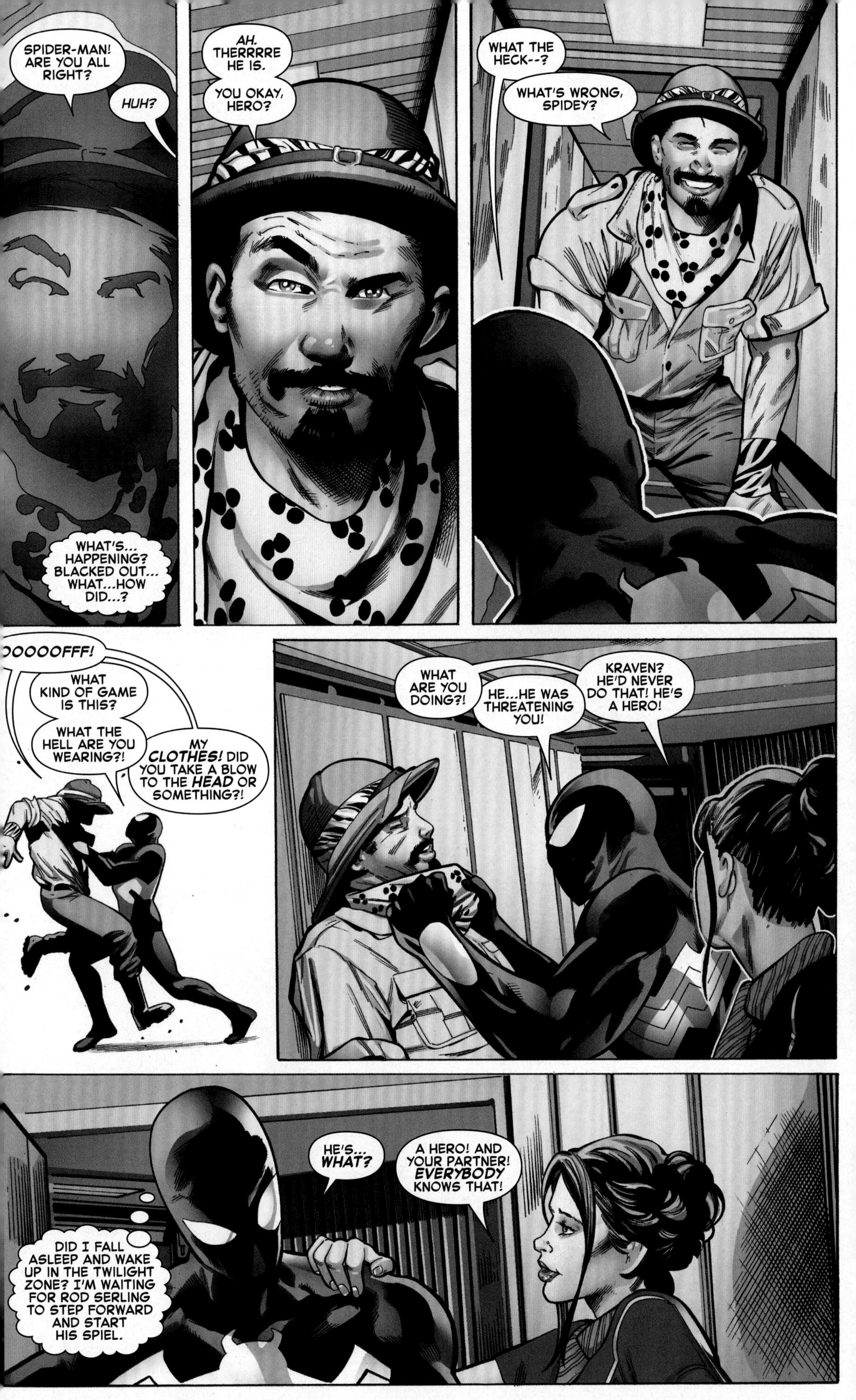
SPIDER-MAN! ARE YOU ALL RIGHT?
HUH?
WHAT'S... HAPPENING? BLACKED OUT... WHAT...HOW DID...?
AH. THERRRRE HE IS.
YOU OKAY, HERO?
WHAT THE HECK--?
WHAT'S WRONG, SPIDEY?
OOOOOFFF!
WHAT KIND OF GAME IS THIS?
WHAT THE HELL ARE YOU WEARING?!
MY CLOTHES! DID YOU TAKE A BLOW TO THE HEAD OR SOMETHING?!
WHAT ARE YOU DOING?!
HE...HE WAS THREATENING YOU!
KRAVEN? HE'D NEVER DO THAT! HE'S A HERO!
HE'S... WHAT?
A HERO! AND YOUR PARTNER! EVERYBODY KNOWS THAT!
DID I FALL ASLEEP AND WAKE UP IN THE TWILIGHT ZONE? I'M WAITING FOR ROD SERLING TO STEP FORWARD AND START HIS SPIEL.

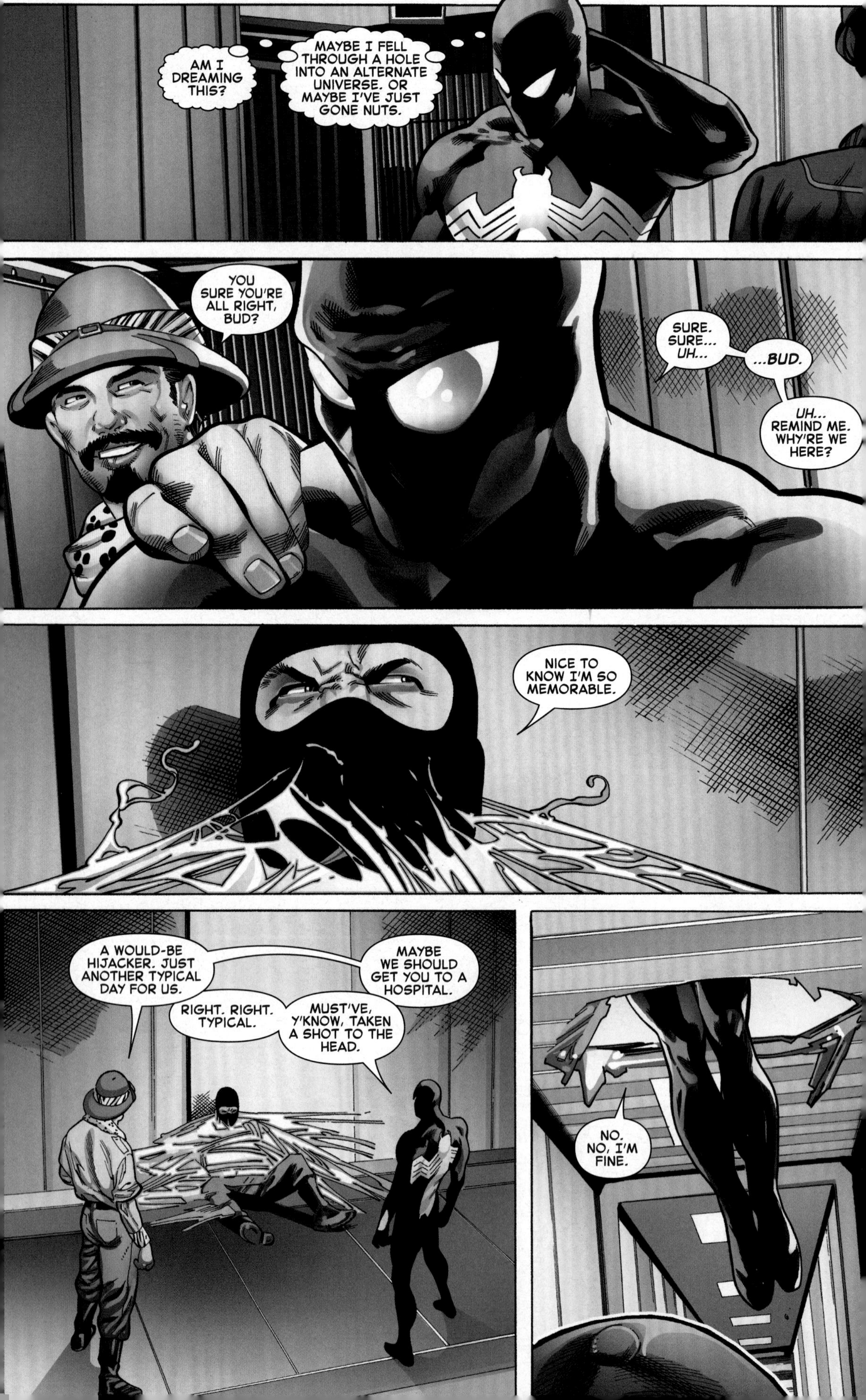
AM I DREAMING THIS?
MAYBE I FELL THROUGH A HOLE INTO AN ALTERNATE UNIVERSE. OR MAYBE I'VE JUST GONE NUTS.
YOU SURE YOU'RE ALL RIGHT, BUD?
SURE. SURE... UH...
...BUD.
UH... REMIND ME. WHY'RE WE HERE?
NICE TO KNOW I'M SO MEMORABLE.
A WOULD-BE HIJACKER. JUST ANOTHER TYPICAL DAY FOR US.
RIGHT. RIGHT. TYPICAL.
MUST'VE, Y'KNOW, TAKEN A SHOT TO THE HEAD.
MAYBE WE SHOULD GET YOU TO A HOSPITAL.
NO. NO, I'M FINE.

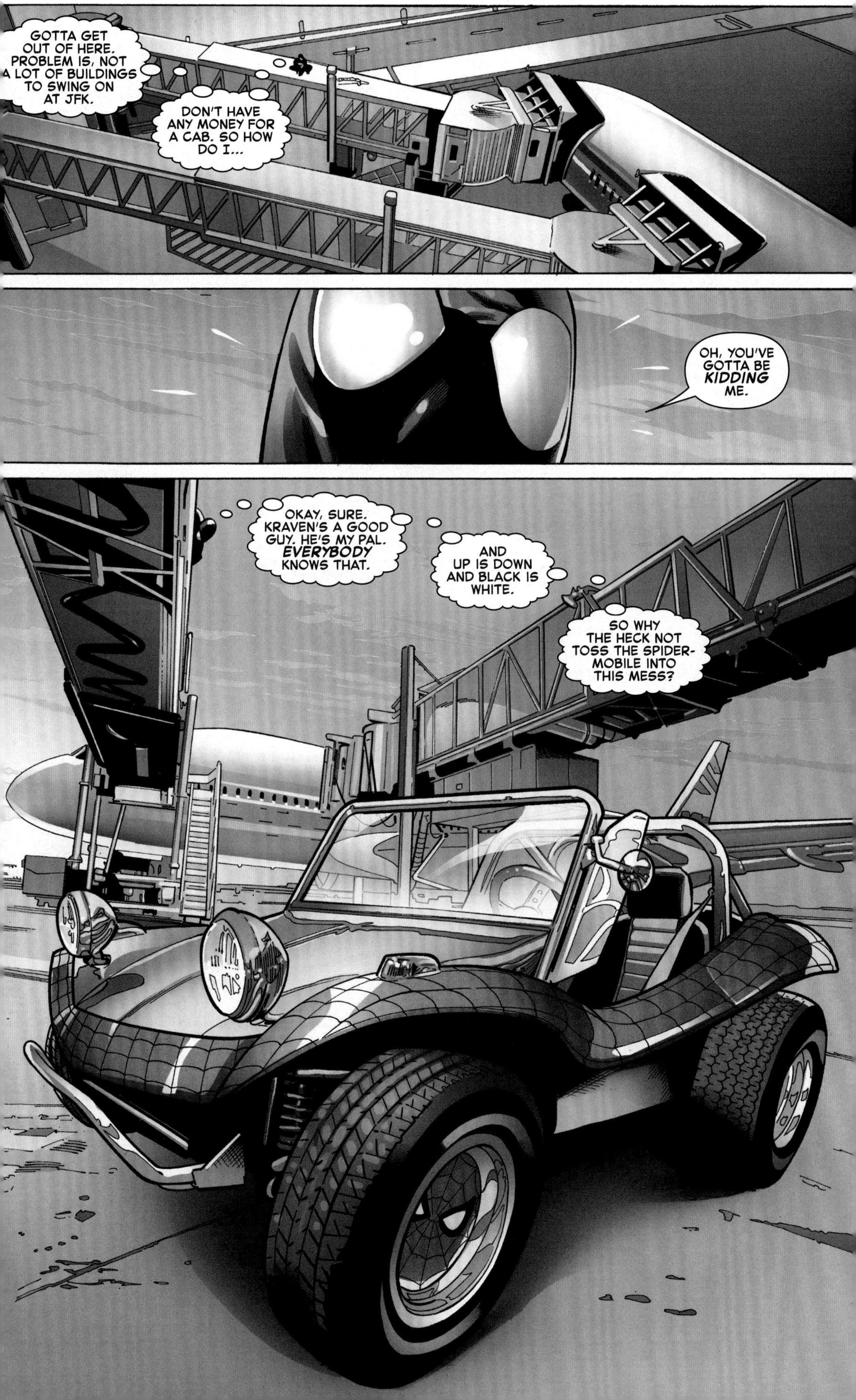
GOTTA GET OUT OF HERE. PROBLEM IS, NOT A LOT OF BUILDINGS TO SWING ON AT JFK.
DON'T HAVE ANY MONEY FOR A CAB. SO HOW DO I...
OH, YOU'VE GOTTA BE *KIDDING* ME.
OKAY, SURE. KRAVEN'S A GOOD GUY. HE'S MY PAL. *EVERYBODY* KNOWS THAT.
AND UP IS DOWN AND BLACK IS WHITE.
SO WHY THE HECK NOT TOSS THE SPIDER-MOBILE INTO THIS MESS?

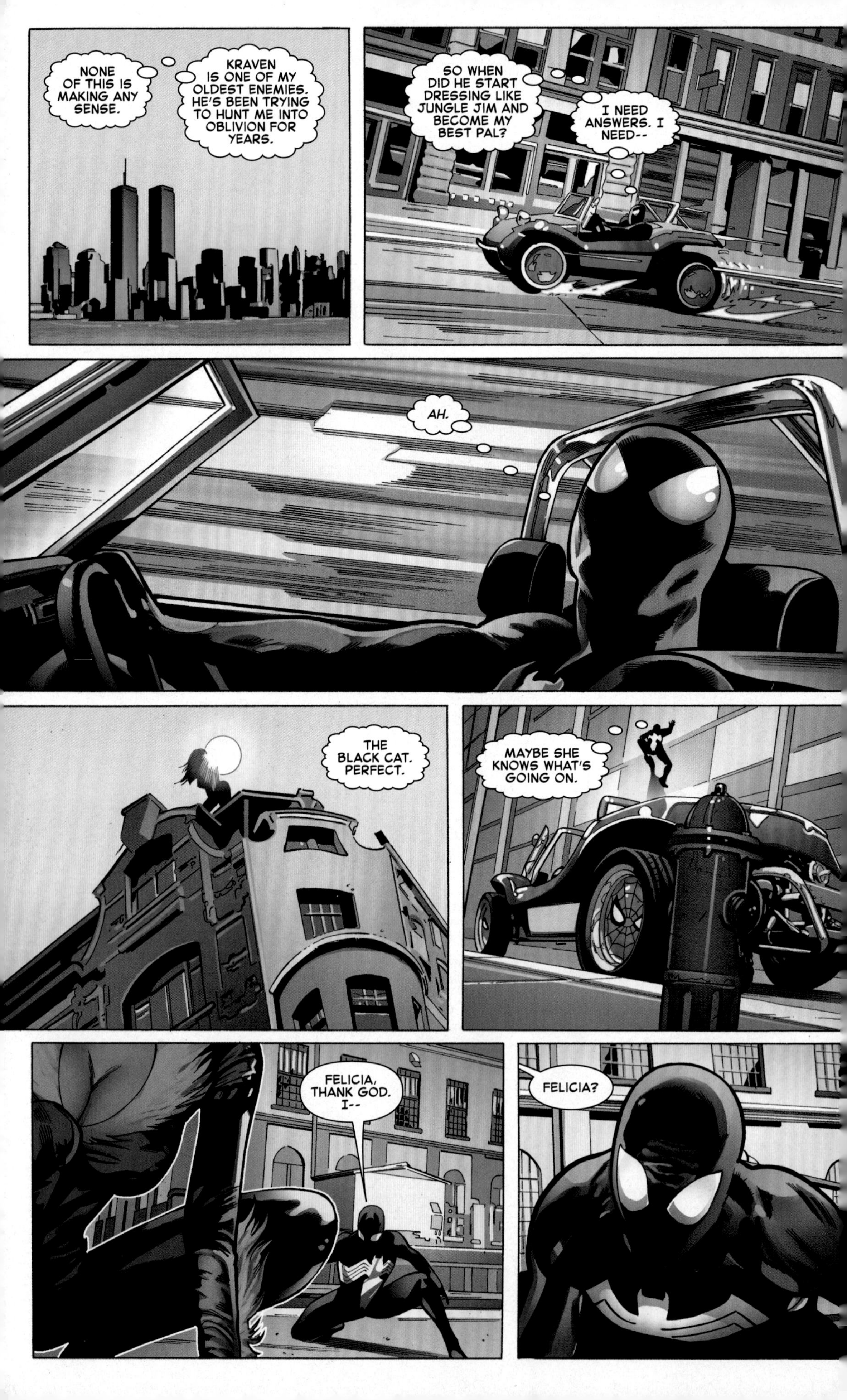
NONE OF THIS IS MAKING ANY SENSE.
KRAVEN IS ONE OF MY OLDEST ENEMIES. HE'S BEEN TRYING TO HUNT ME INTO OBLIVION FOR YEARS.
SO WHEN DID HE START DRESSING LIKE JUNGLE JIM AND BECOME MY BEST PAL?
I NEED ANSWERS. I NEED--
AH.
THE BLACK CAT. PERFECT.
MAYBE SHE KNOWS WHAT'S GOING ON.
FELICIA, THANK GOD. I--
FELICIA?

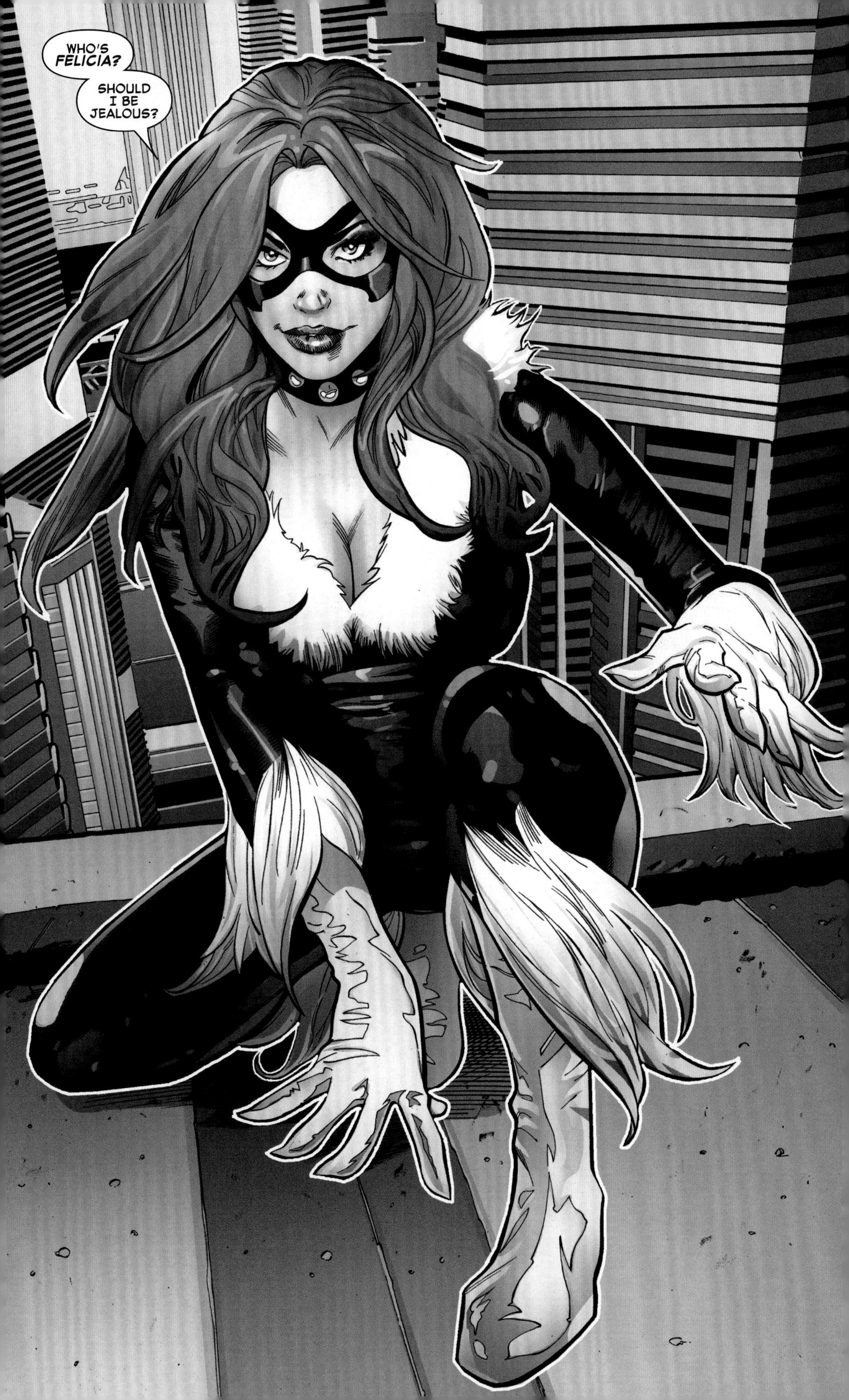
WHO'S *FELICIA?*
SHOULD I BE JEALOUS?

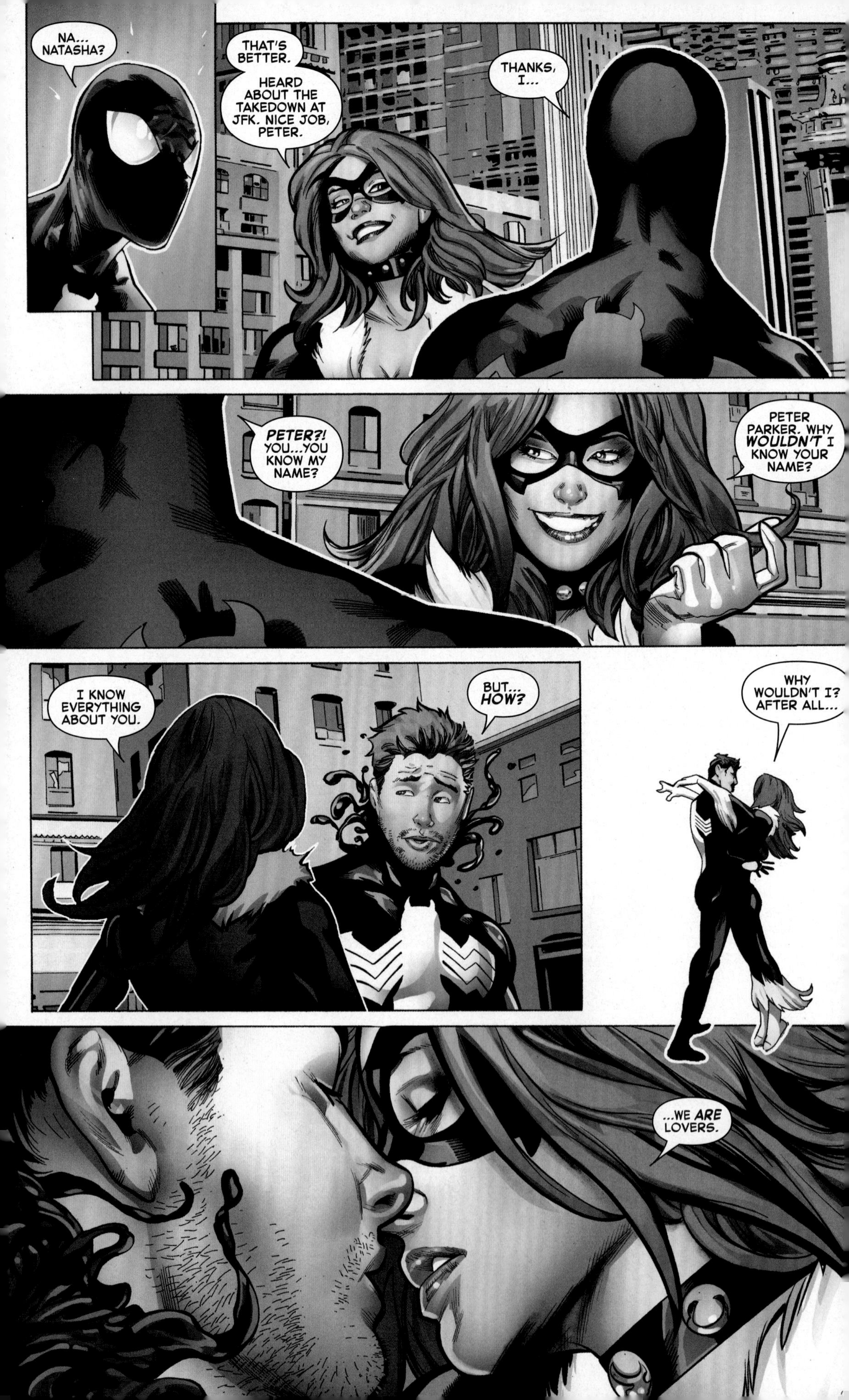

NA... NATASHA?
THAT'S BETTER.
HEARD ABOUT THE TAKEDOWN AT JFK. NICE JOB, PETER.
THANKS, I...
PETER?! YOU...YOU KNOW MY NAME?
PETER PARKER. WHY WOULDN'T I KNOW YOUR NAME?
I KNOW EVERYTHING ABOUT YOU.
BUT... HOW?
WHY WOULDN'T I? AFTER ALL...
...WE ARE LOVERS.

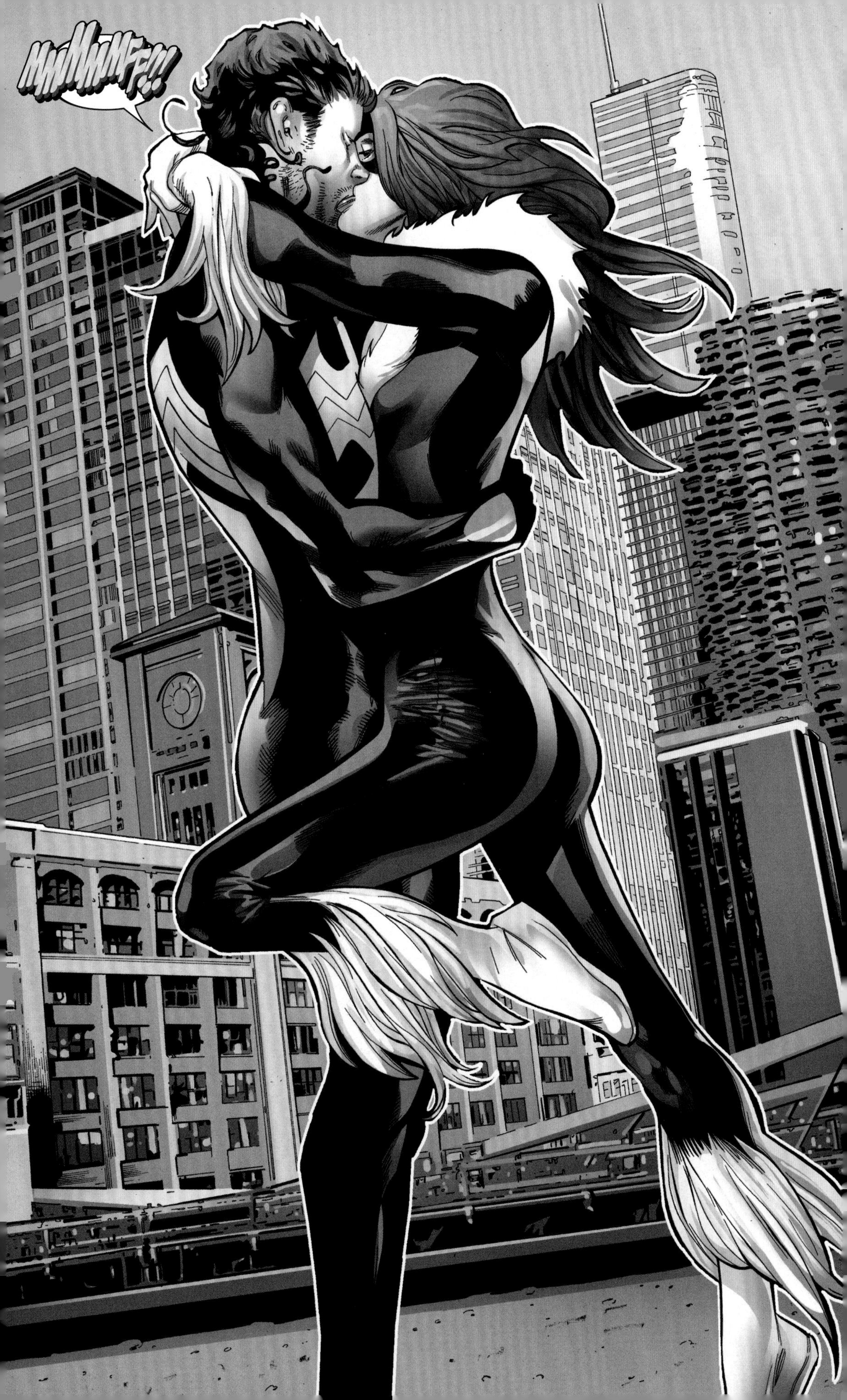
MMMMMMFF!!!

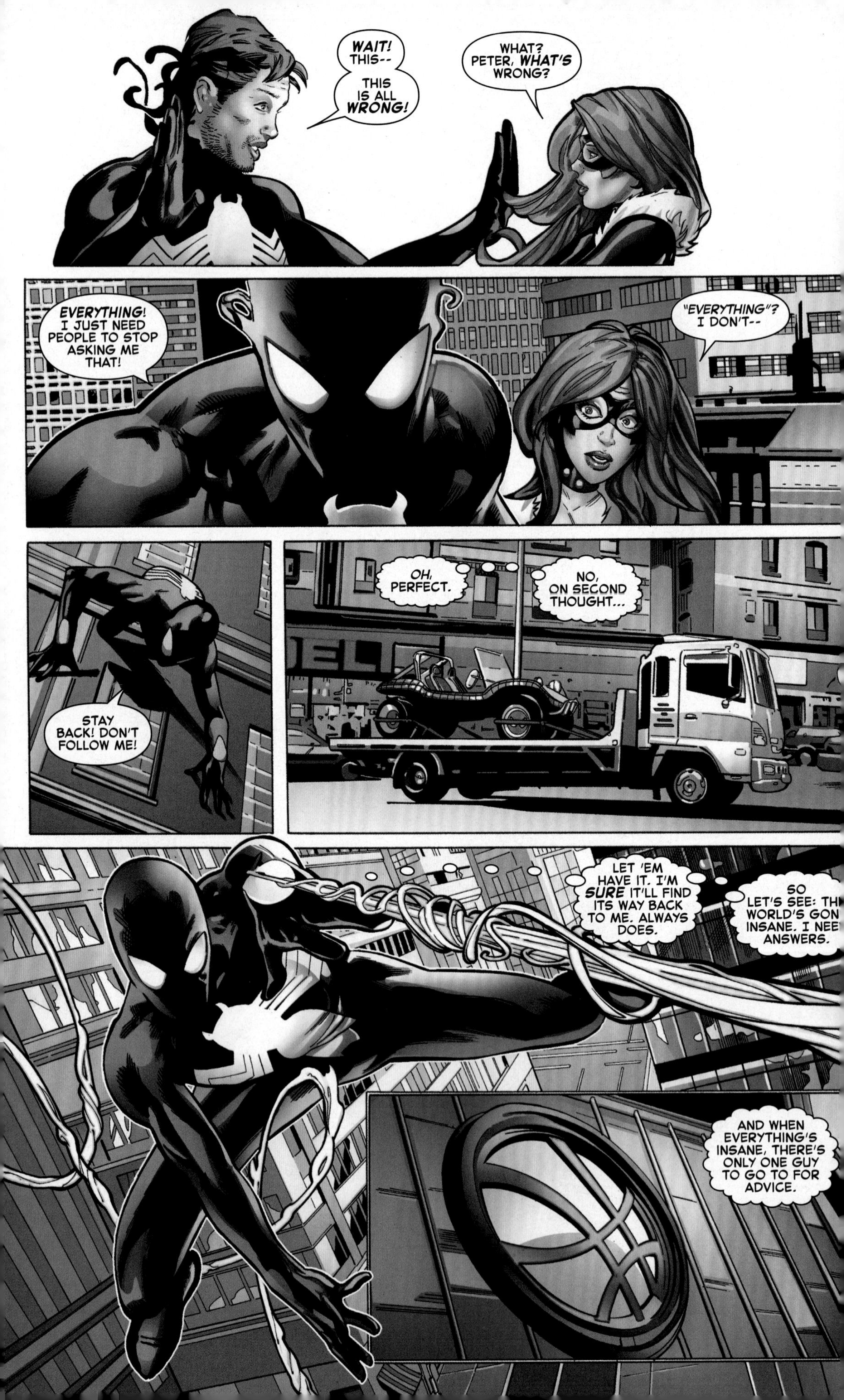
WAIT! THIS--
THIS IS ALL WRONG!
WHAT? PETER, WHAT'S WRONG?
EVERYTHING! I JUST NEED PEOPLE TO STOP ASKING ME THAT!
"EVERYTHING"? I DON'T--
STAY BACK! DON'T FOLLOW ME!
OH, PERFECT.
NO, ON SECOND THOUGHT...
LET 'EM HAVE IT. I'M SURE IT'LL FIND ITS WAY BACK TO ME. ALWAYS DOES.
SO LET'S SEE: TH WORLD'S GON INSANE. I NEE ANSWERS.
AND WHEN EVERYTHING'S INSANE, THERE'S ONLY ONE GUY TO GO TO FOR ADVICE.

SPIDER-MAN? WHAT ARE *YOU* DOING HERE?

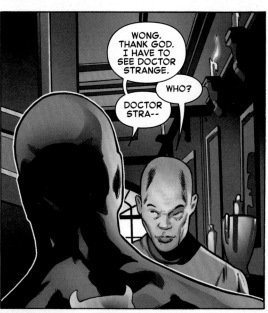

WONG. THANK GOD. I HAVE TO SEE DOCTOR STRANGE.

WHO?

DOCTOR STRA--

DOCTOR STRANGE.

I HAVE NO IDEA WHO THAT IS...

RIGHT, OF COURSE YOU DON'T. HE'S ONLY THE SORCERER SUPREME. WHY WOULD YOU KNOW HIM?

THE *SORCERER SUPREME* IS NOT HOME AT PRESENT. BUT HIS ACOLYTE IS AVAILABLE.

WOULD YOU LIKE TO CONVERSE WITH HIM?

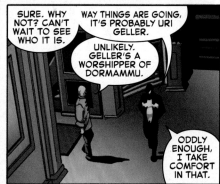

SURE. WHY NOT? CAN'T WAIT TO SEE WHO IT IS.

WAY THINGS ARE GOING, IT'S PROBABLY URI GELLER.

UNLIKELY. GELLER'S A WORSHIPPER OF DORMAMMU.

ODDLY ENOUGH, I TAKE COMFORT IN THAT.

TOUCH NOTHING.

THAT GOES WITHOUT SAYING. DON'T NEED CTHULHU TO SPRING OUT OF A COKE BOTTLE AND SWALLOW ME.

HE'S NOT IN A BOTTLE. HE'S IN--

I DON'T WANNA KNOW.

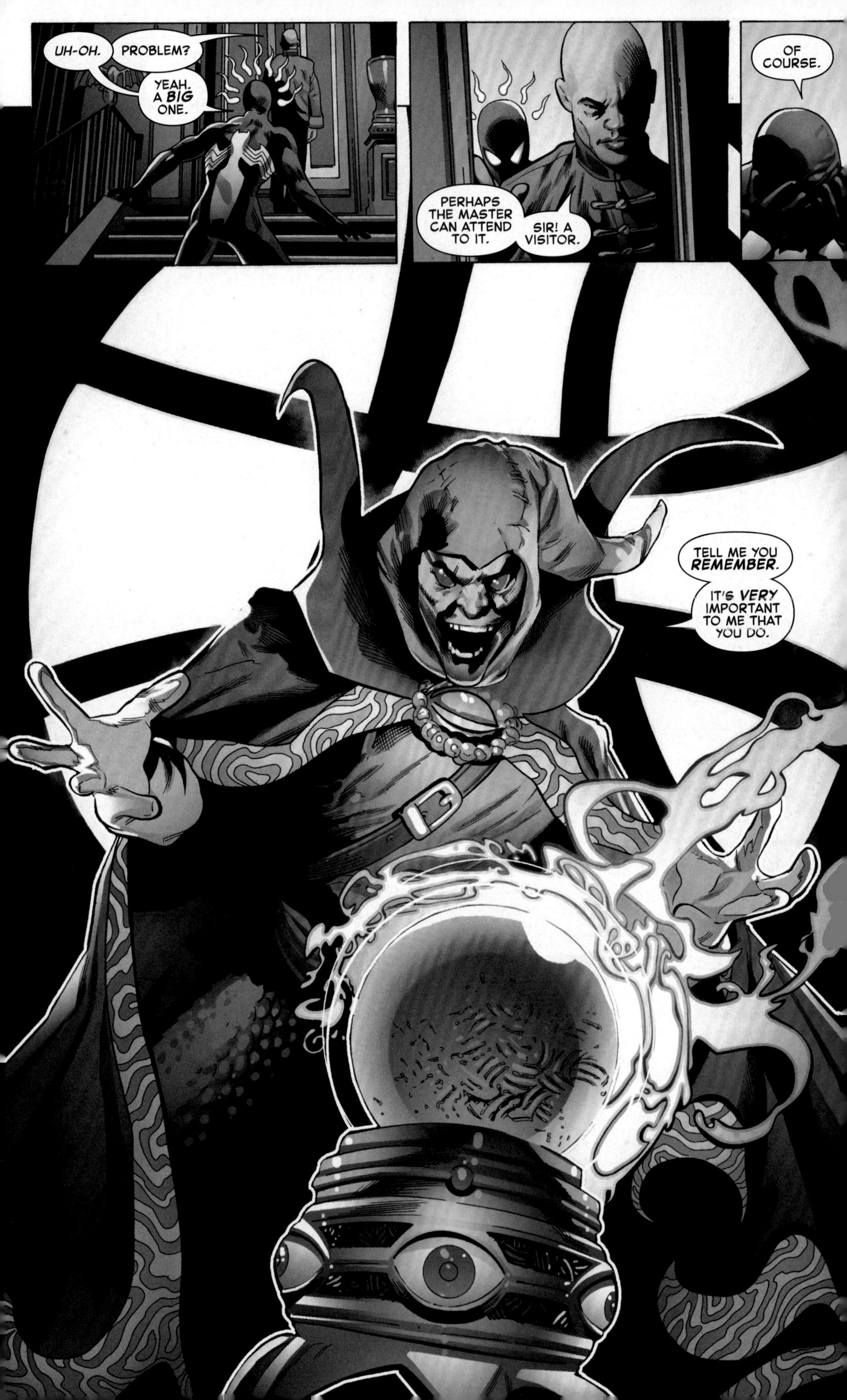
UH-OH.
PROBLEM?
YEAH. A BIG ONE.
PERHAPS THE MASTER CAN ATTEND TO IT.
SIR! A VISITOR.
OF COURSE.
TELL ME YOU REMEMBER.
IT'S VERY IMPORTANT TO ME THAT YOU DO.

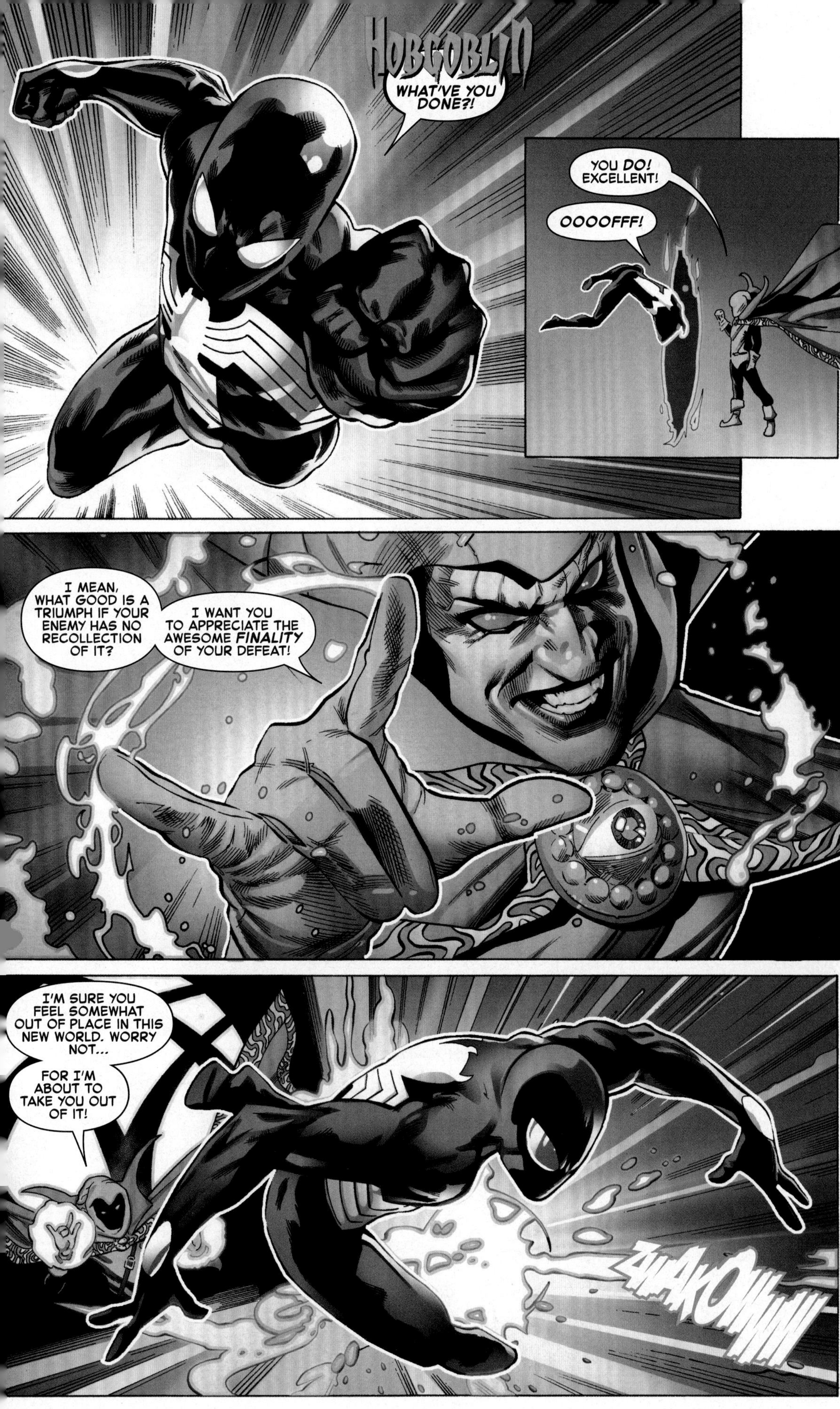
HOBGOBLIN
WHAT'VE YOU DONE?!
YOU DO! EXCELLENT!
OOOOFFF!
I MEAN, WHAT GOOD IS A TRIUMPH IF YOUR ENEMY HAS NO RECOLLECTION OF IT?
I WANT YOU TO APPRECIATE THE AWESOME FINALITY OF YOUR DEFEAT!
I'M SURE YOU FEEL SOMEWHAT OUT OF PLACE IN THIS NEW WORLD. WORRY NOT...
FOR I'M ABOUT TO TAKE YOU OUT OF IT!
ZHAKOWWW

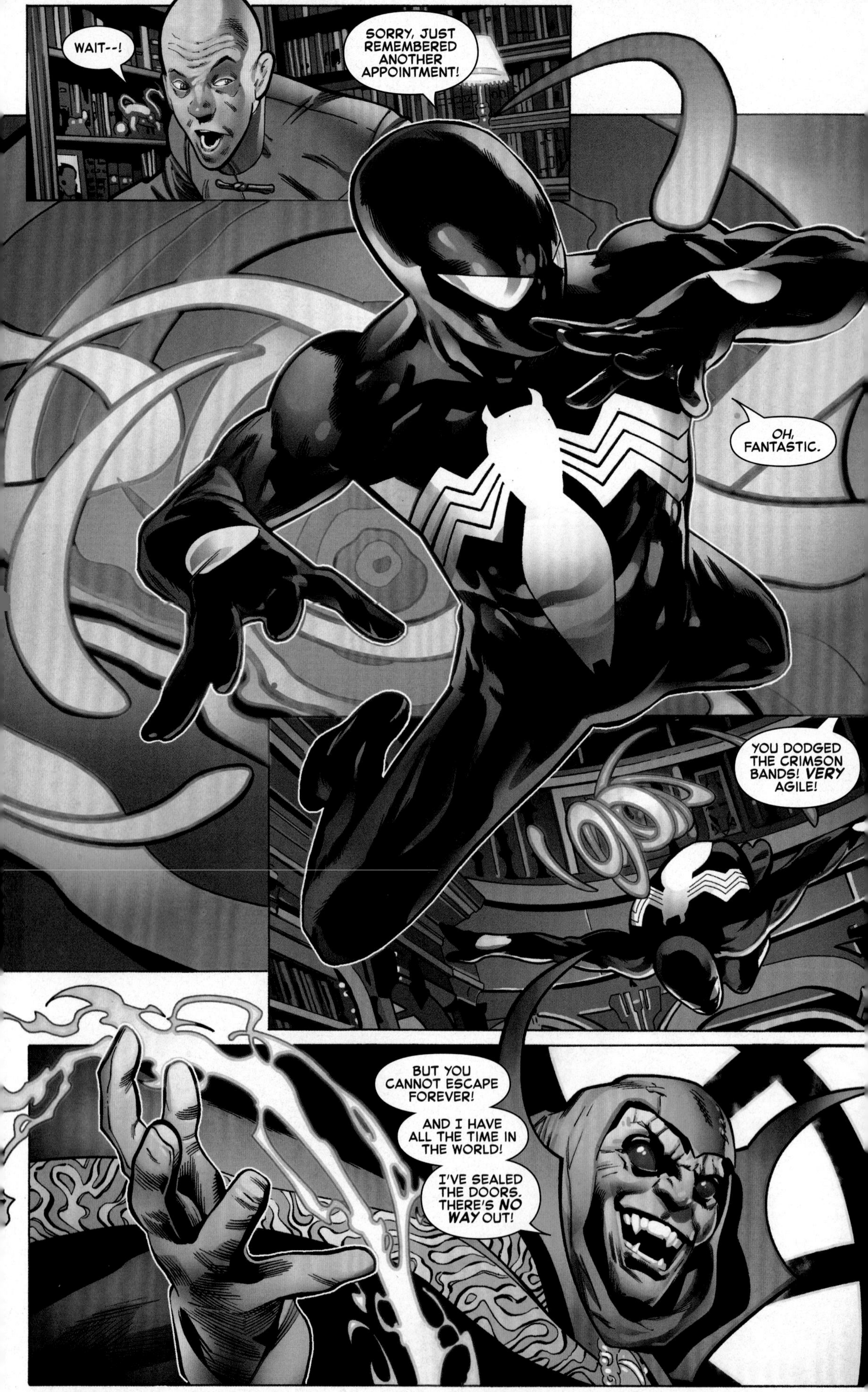
WAIT--!
SORRY, JUST REMEMBERED ANOTHER APPOINTMENT!
OH, FANTASTIC.
YOU DODGED THE CRIMSON BANDS! VERY AGILE!
BUT YOU CANNOT ESCAPE FOREVER!
AND I HAVE ALL THE TIME IN THE WORLD!
I'VE SEALED THE DOORS. THERE'S NO WAY OUT!

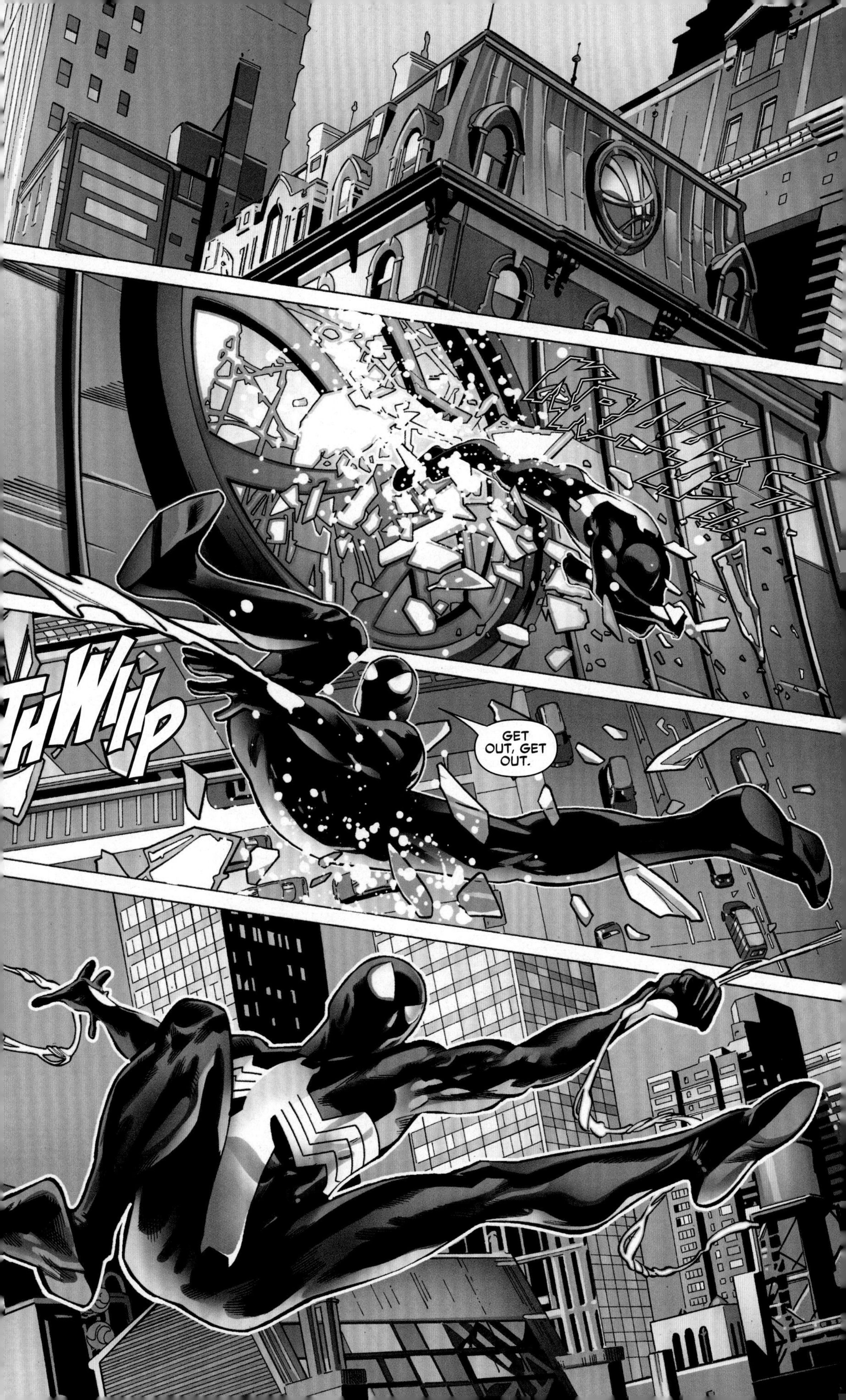
THWIIP
GET OUT, GET OUT.

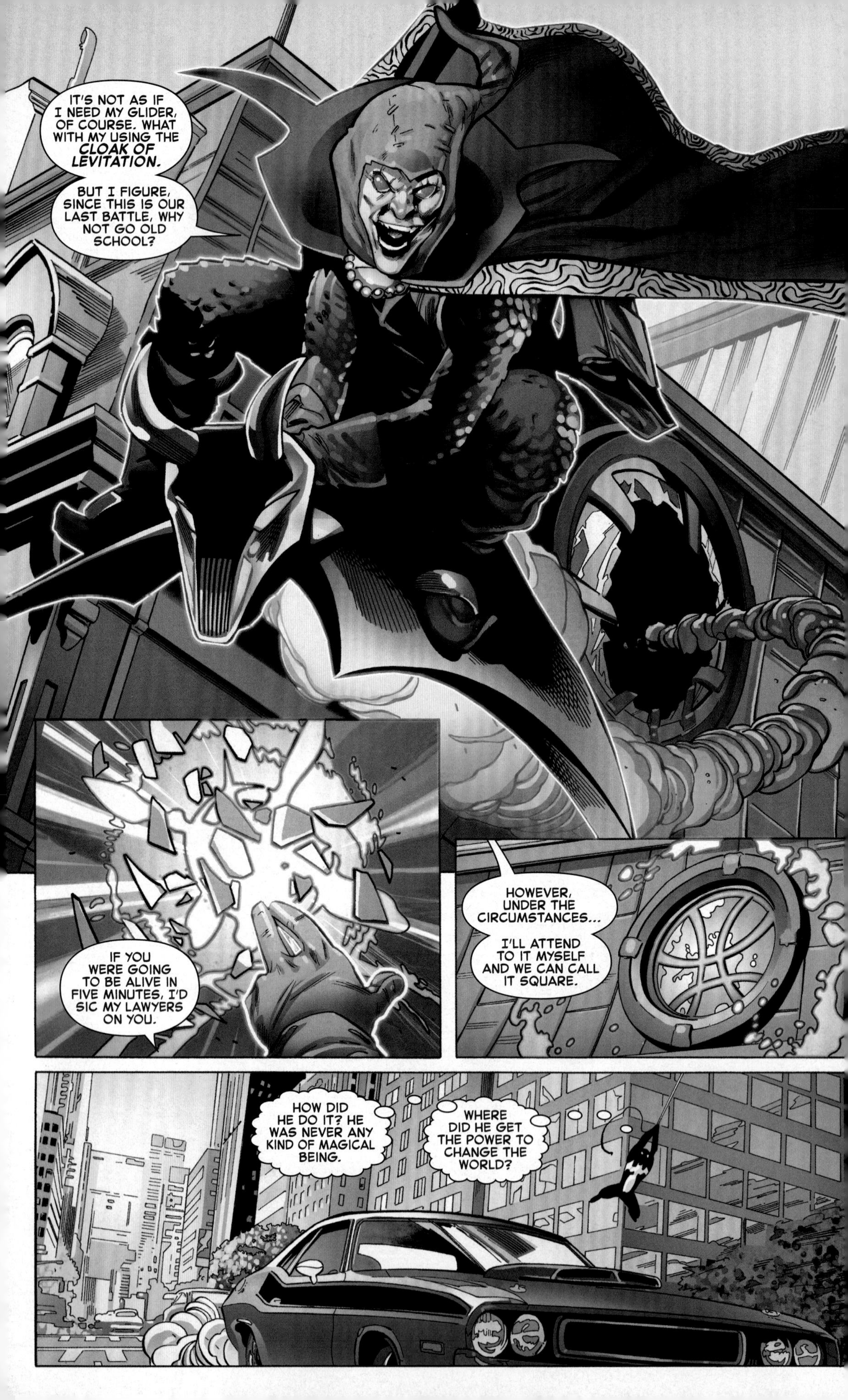
IT'S NOT AS IF I NEED MY GLIDER, OF COURSE. WHAT WITH MY USING THE CLOAK OF LEVITATION.
BUT I FIGURE, SINCE THIS IS OUR LAST BATTLE, WHY NOT GO OLD SCHOOL?
IF YOU WERE GOING TO BE ALIVE IN FIVE MINUTES, I'D SIC MY LAWYERS ON YOU.
HOWEVER, UNDER THE CIRCUMSTANCES...
I'LL ATTEND TO IT MYSELF AND WE CAN CALL IT SQUARE.
HOW DID HE DO IT? HE WAS NEVER ANY KIND OF MAGICAL BEING.
WHERE DID HE GET THE POWER TO CHANGE THE WORLD?

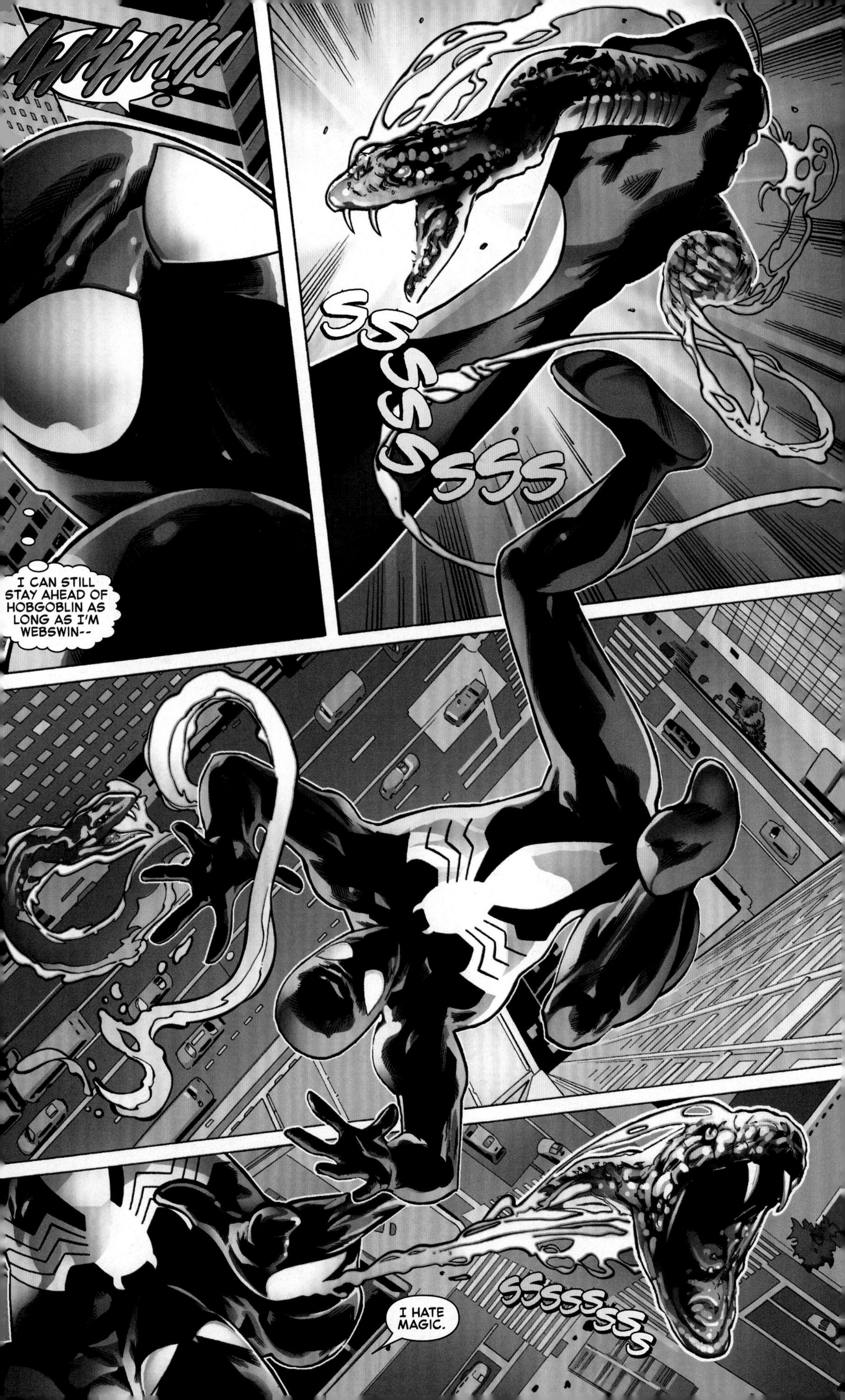
AHHHHH!!!
I CAN STILL STAY AHEAD OF HOBGOBLIN AS LONG AS I'M WEBSWIN--
SSSSSSSSS
I HATE MAGIC.
SSSSSSSSS

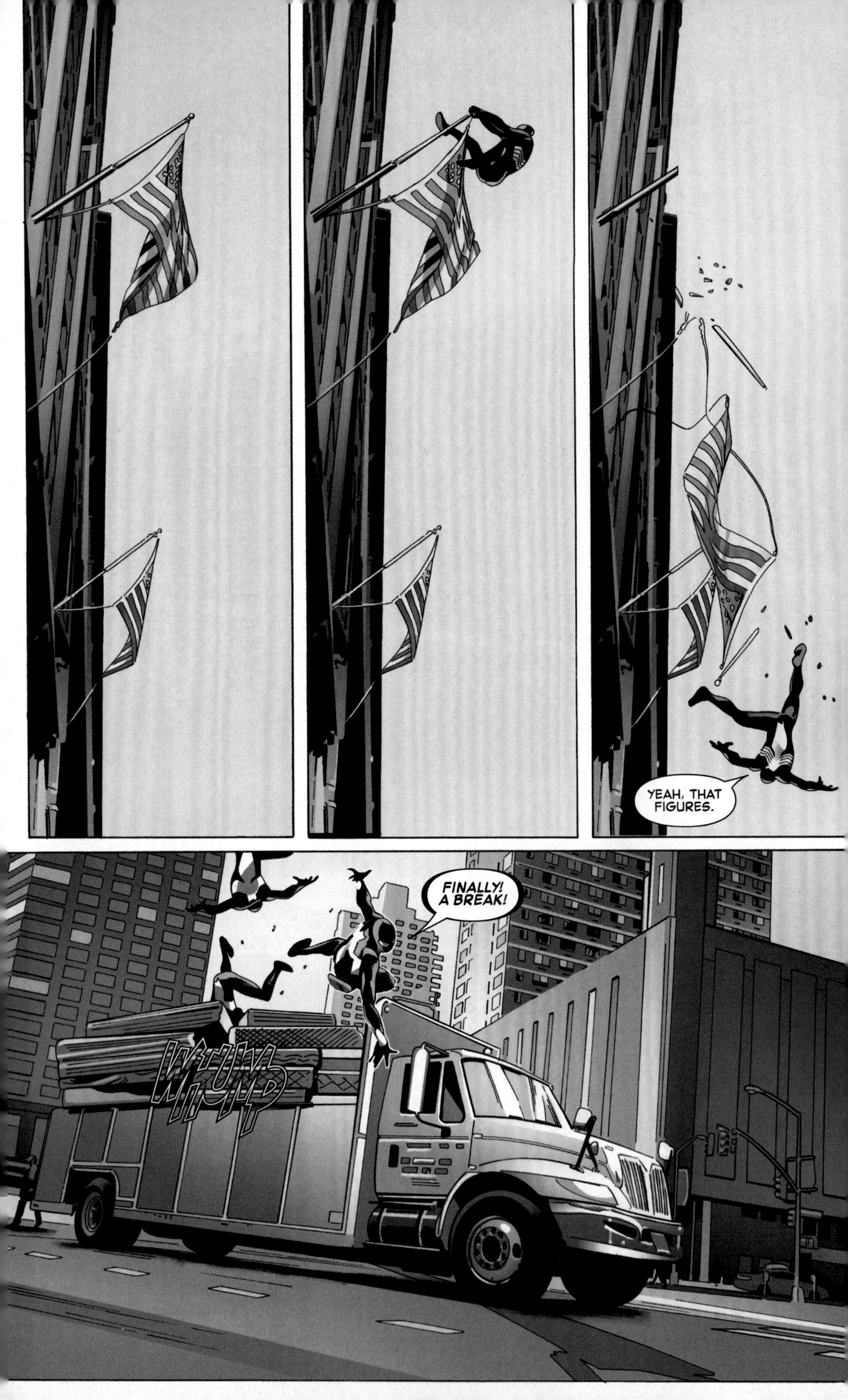
YEAH, THAT FIGURES.
FINALLY! A BREAK!
WHUMP

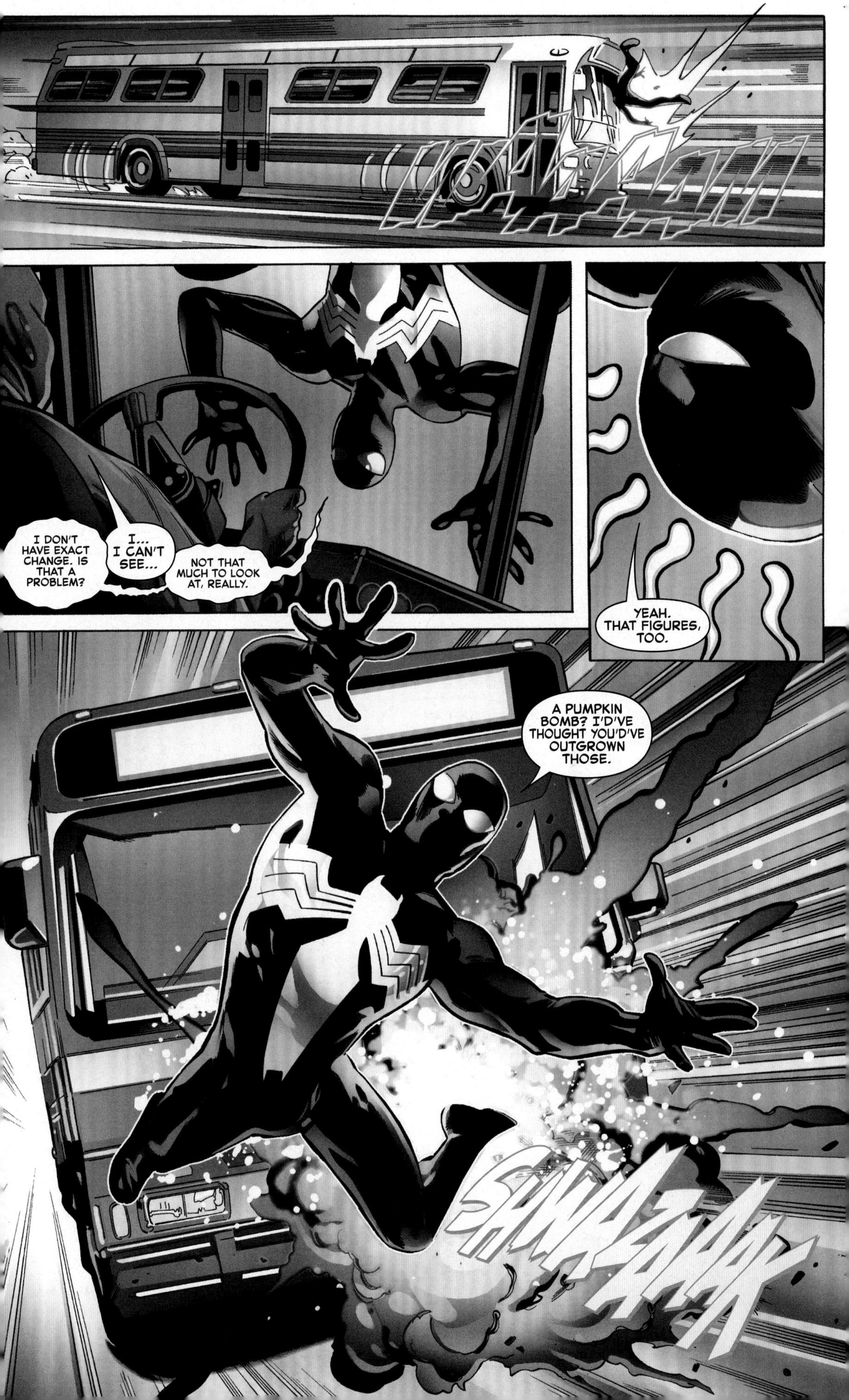

WHAAAAMM
I DON'T HAVE EXACT CHANGE. IS THAT A PROBLEM?
I... I CAN'T SEE...
NOT THAT MUCH TO LOOK AT, REALLY.
YEAH. THAT FIGURES, TOO.
A PUMPKIN BOMB? I'D'VE THOUGHT YOU'D'VE OUTGROWN THOSE.
SHWAAAAK

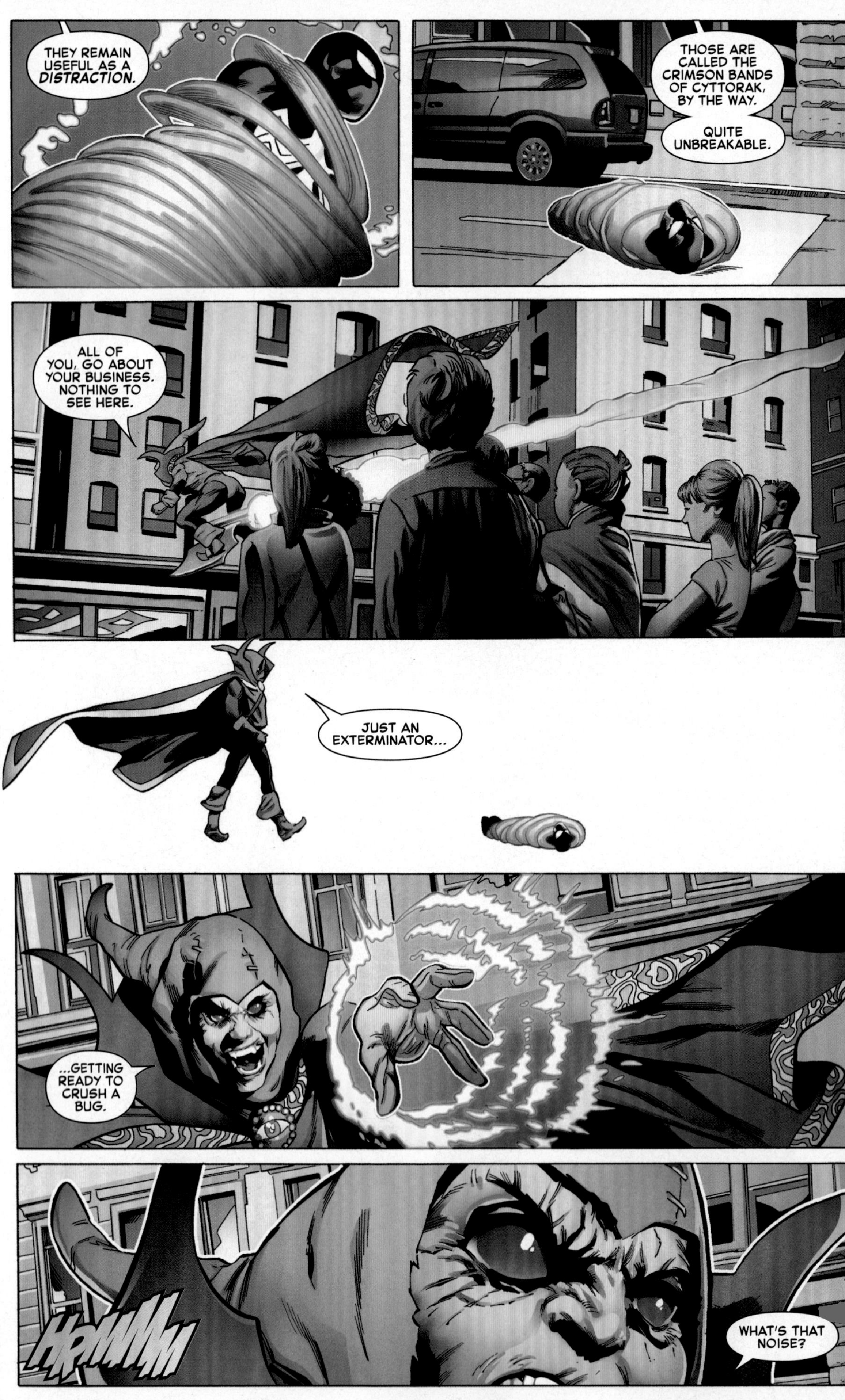
THEY REMAIN USEFUL AS A DISTRACTION.
THOSE ARE CALLED THE CRIMSON BANDS OF CYTTORAK, BY THE WAY.
QUITE UNBREAKABLE.
ALL OF YOU, GO ABOUT YOUR BUSINESS. NOTHING TO SEE HERE.
JUST AN EXTERMINATOR...
...GETTING READY TO CRUSH A BUG.
HMMMM
WHAT'S THAT NOISE?

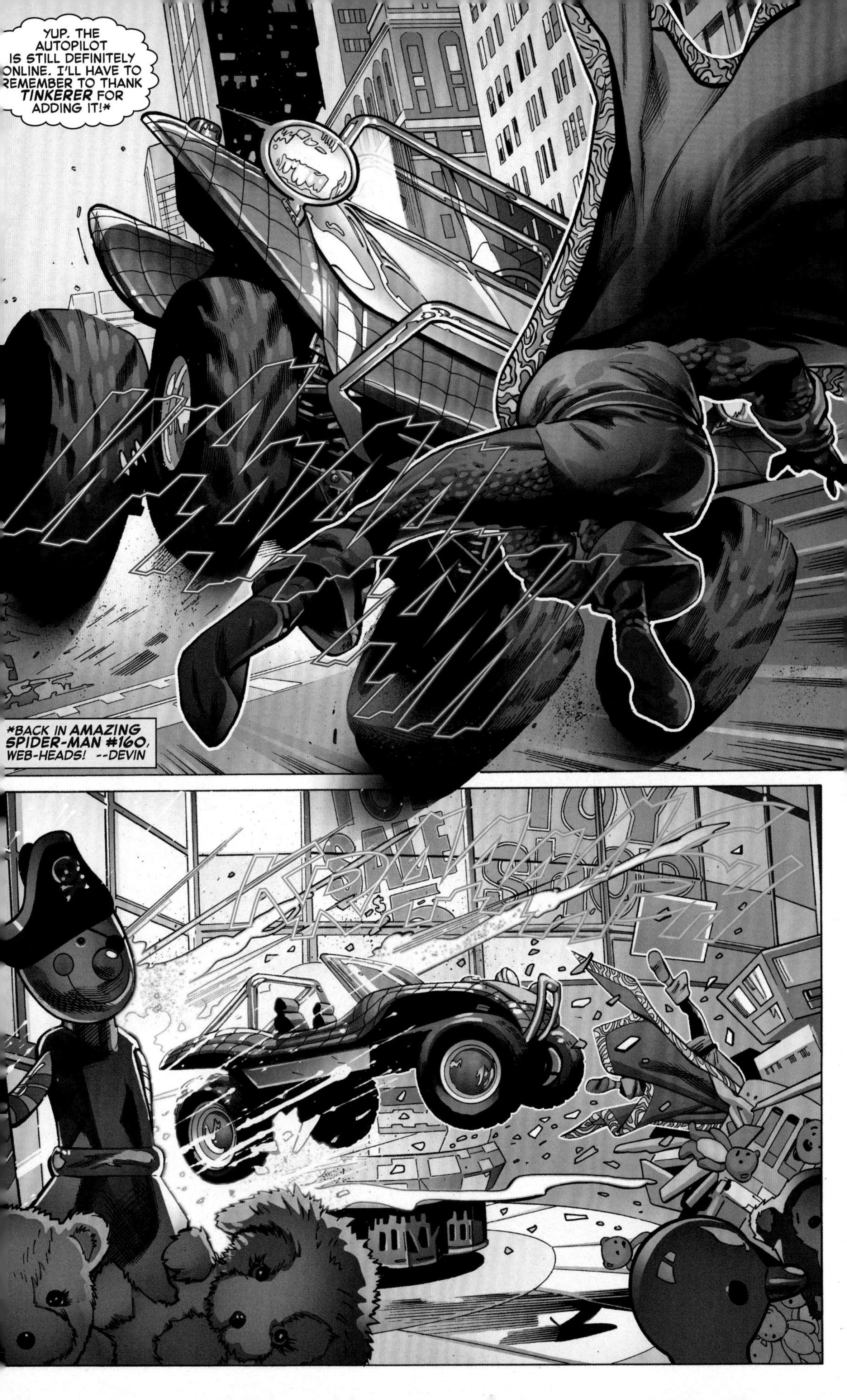
YUP. THE AUTOPILOT IS STILL DEFINITELY ONLINE. I'LL HAVE TO REMEMBER TO THANK TINKERER FOR ADDING IT!*
*BACK IN AMAZING SPIDER-MAN #160, WEB-HEADS! --DEVIN

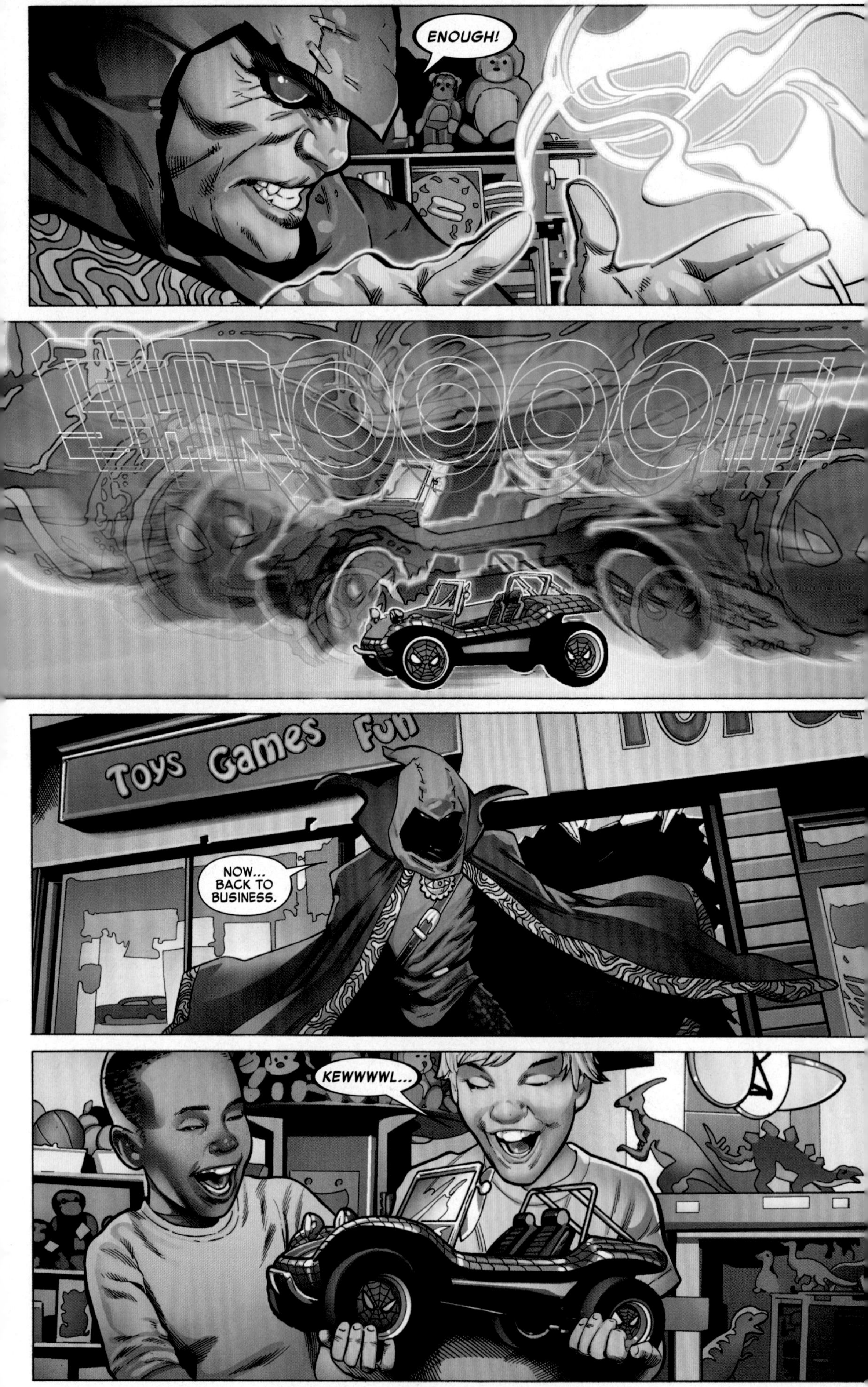

ENOUGH!
VVRROOOOOM
Toys Games Fun
NOW... BACK TO BUSINESS.
KEWWWWL...

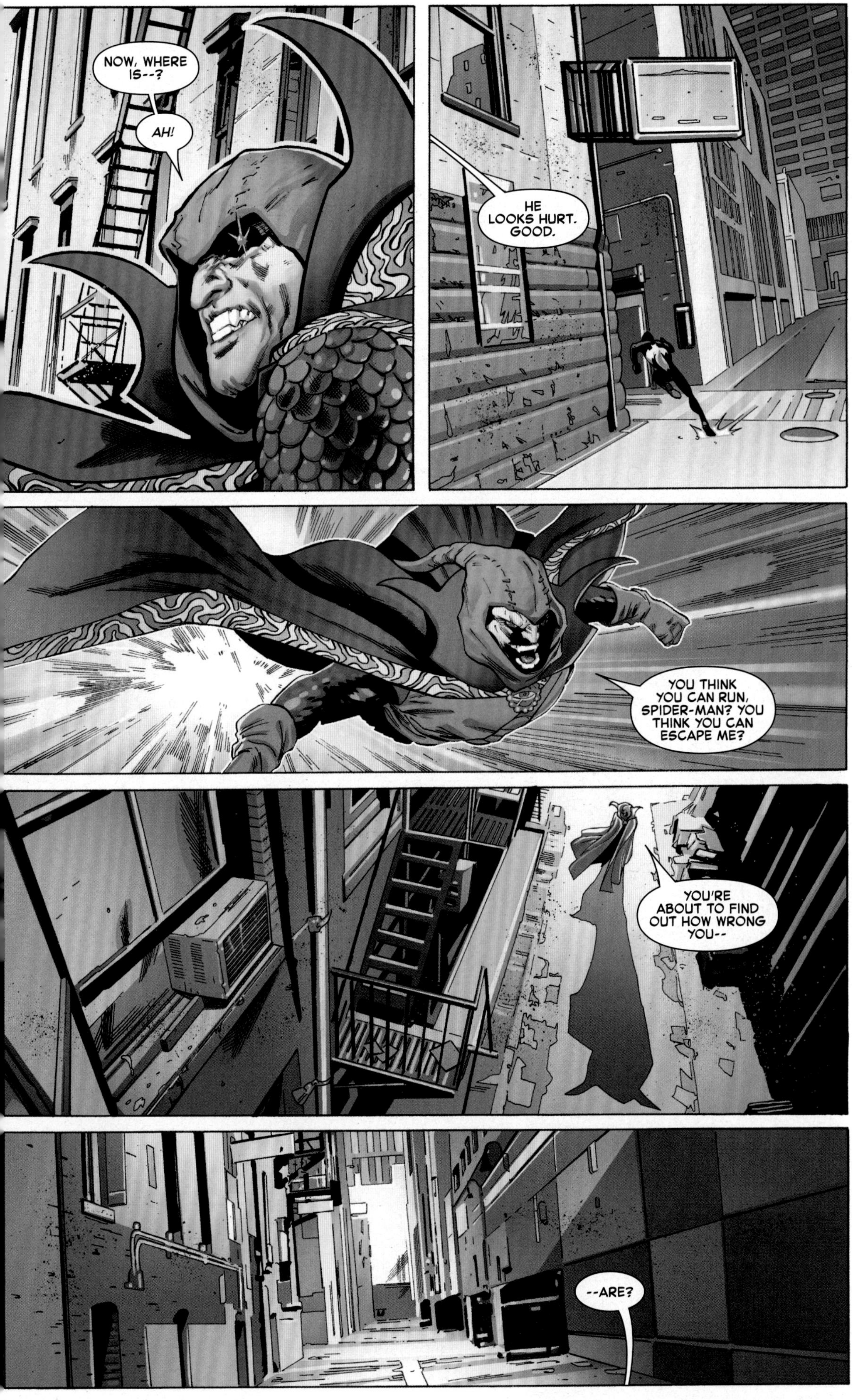
NOW, WHERE IS--?
AH!
HE LOOKS HURT. GOOD.
YOU THINK YOU CAN RUN, SPIDER-MAN? YOU THINK YOU CAN ESCAPE ME?
YOU'RE ABOUT TO FIND OUT HOW WRONG YOU--
--ARE?

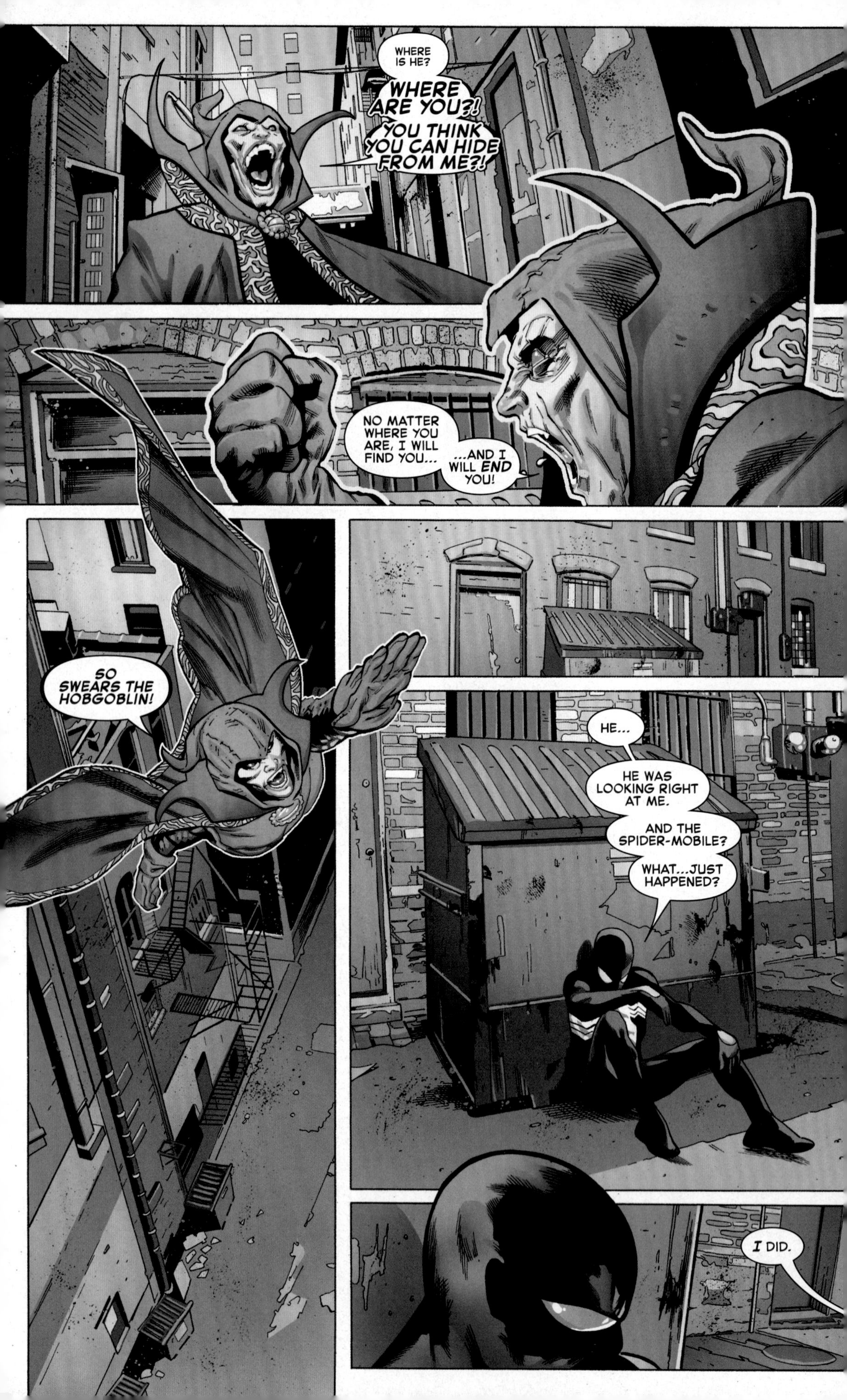
WHERE IS HE?
WHERE ARE YOU?!
YOU THINK YOU CAN HIDE FROM ME?!
NO MATTER WHERE YOU ARE, I WILL FIND YOU...
...AND I WILL END YOU!
SO SWEARS THE HOBGOBLIN!
HE...
HE WAS LOOKING RIGHT AT ME.
AND THE SPIDER-MOBILE?
WHAT...JUST HAPPENED?
I DID.

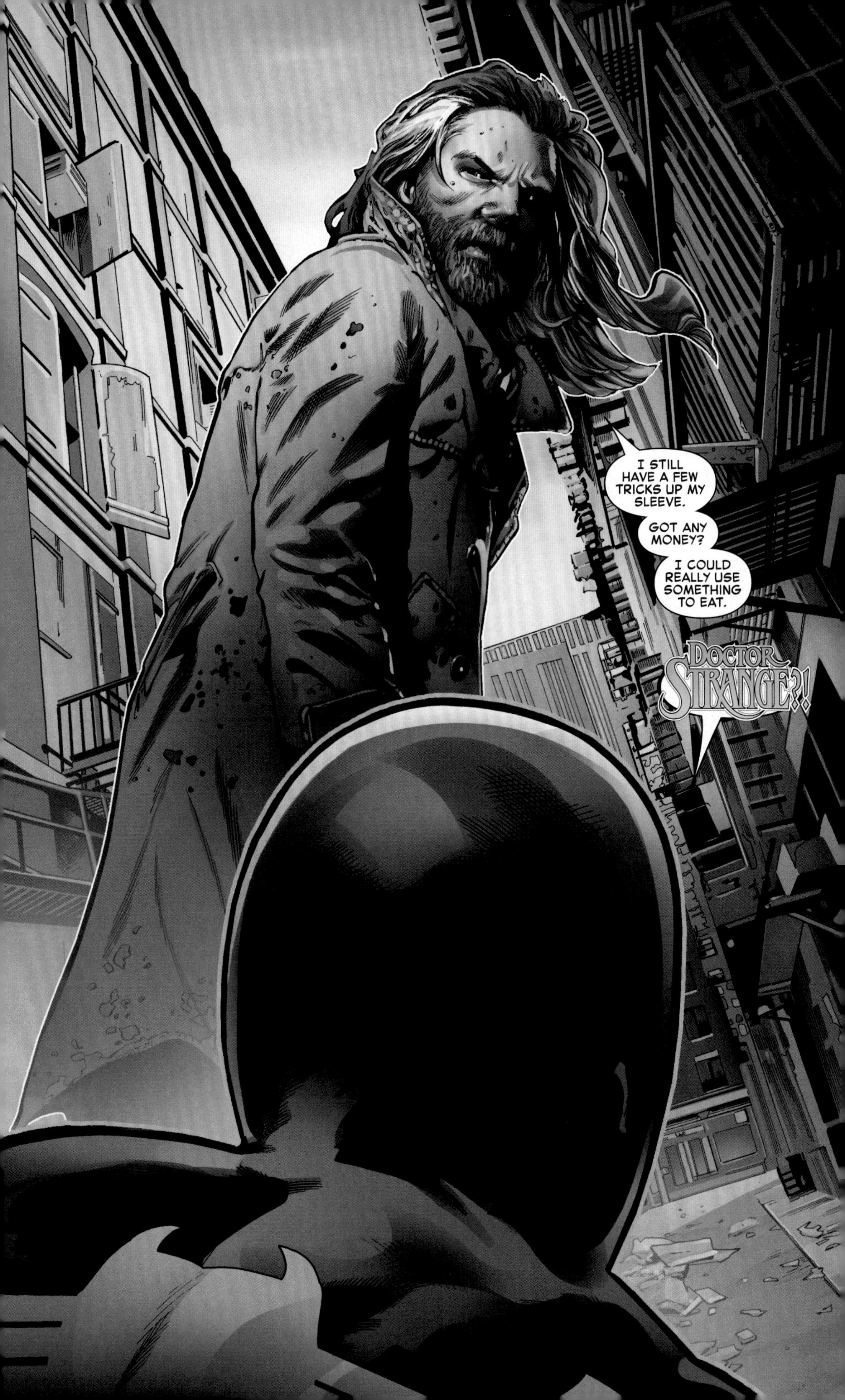
I STILL HAVE A FEW TRICKS UP MY SLEEVE.
GOT ANY MONEY?
I COULD REALLY USE SOMETHING TO EAT.
DOCTOR STRANGE?!

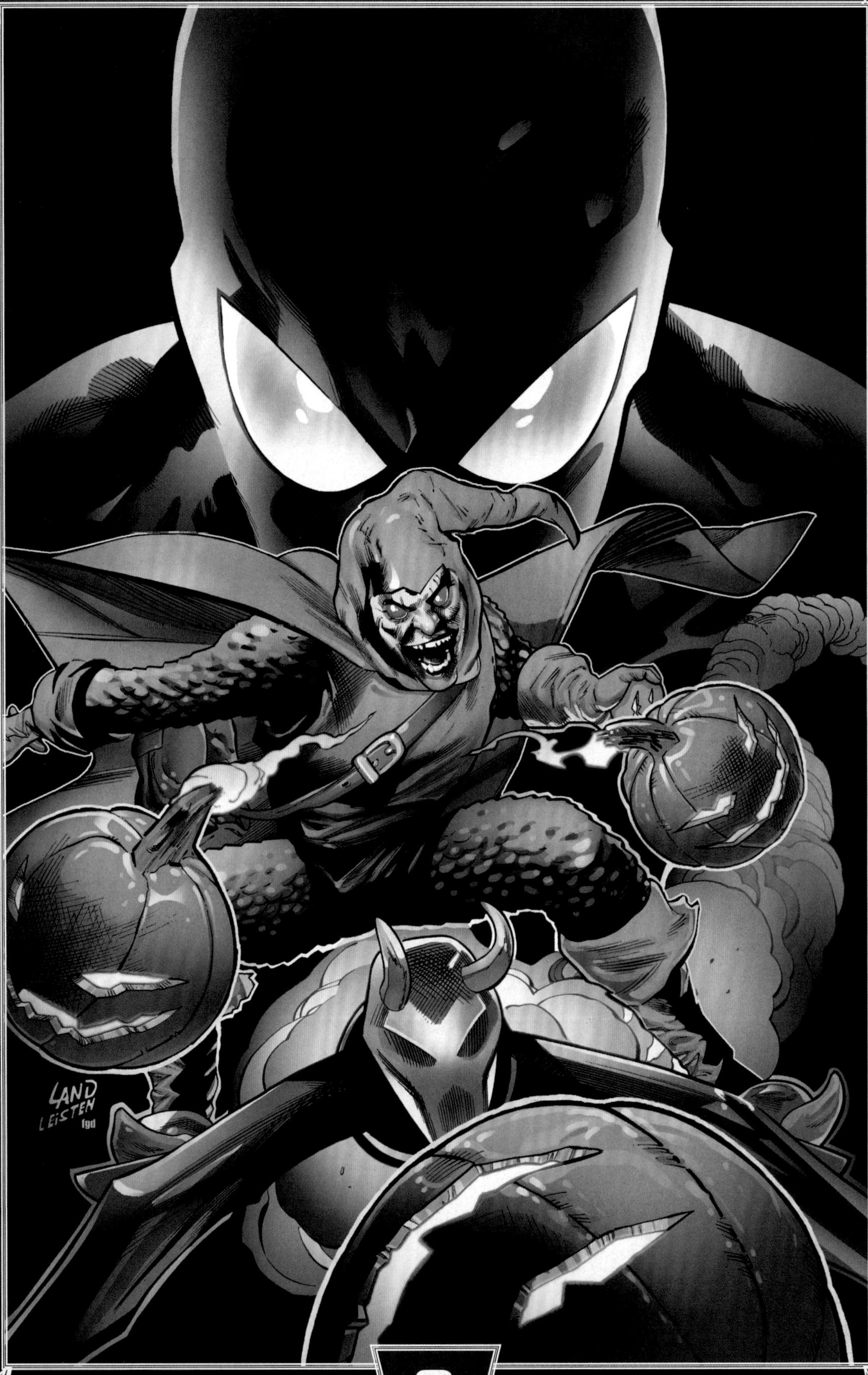
LAND
LEISTEN
fgd

2

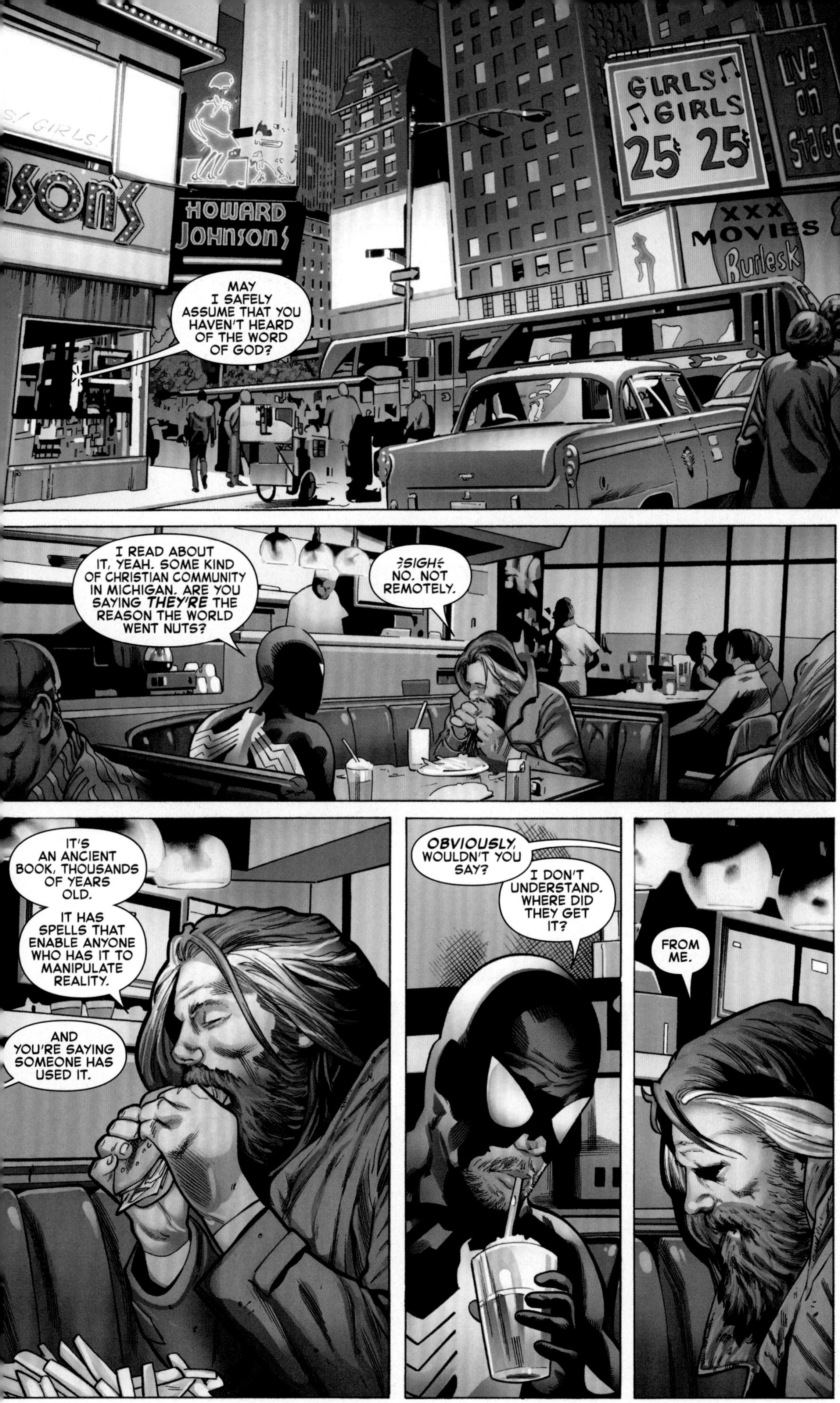
GIRLS GIRLS 25¢ 25¢
LIVE ON STAGE
HOWARD JOHNSONS
XXX MOVIES Burlesk
MAY I SAFELY ASSUME THAT YOU HAVEN'T HEARD OF THE WORD OF GOD?
I READ ABOUT IT, YEAH. SOME KIND OF CHRISTIAN COMMUNITY IN MICHIGAN. ARE YOU SAYING THEY'RE THE REASON THE WORLD WENT NUTS?
SIGH NO. NOT REMOTELY.
IT'S AN ANCIENT BOOK, THOUSANDS OF YEARS OLD.
IT HAS SPELLS THAT ENABLE ANYONE WHO HAS IT TO MANIPULATE REALITY.
AND YOU'RE SAYING SOMEONE HAS USED IT.
OBVIOUSLY, WOULDN'T YOU SAY?
I DON'T UNDERSTAND. WHERE DID THEY GET IT?
FROM ME.

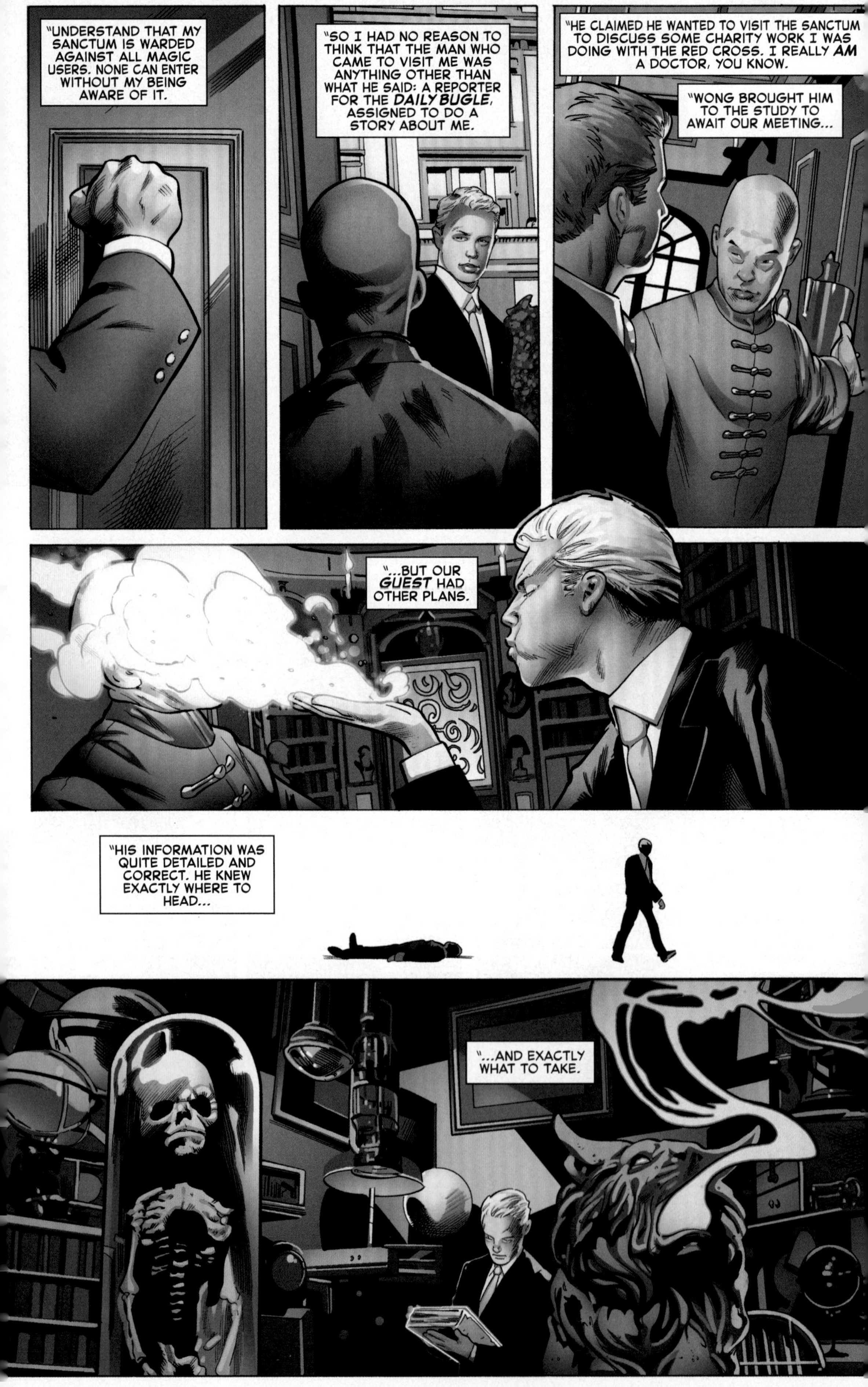
"UNDERSTAND THAT MY SANCTUM IS WARDED AGAINST ALL MAGIC USERS. NONE CAN ENTER WITHOUT MY BEING AWARE OF IT.
"SO I HAD NO REASON TO THINK THAT THE MAN WHO CAME TO VISIT ME WAS ANYTHING OTHER THAN WHAT HE SAID: A REPORTER FOR THE DAILY BUGLE, ASSIGNED TO DO A STORY ABOUT ME.
"HE CLAIMED HE WANTED TO VISIT THE SANCTUM TO DISCUSS SOME CHARITY WORK I WAS DOING WITH THE RED CROSS. I REALLY AM A DOCTOR, YOU KNOW.
"WONG BROUGHT HIM TO THE STUDY TO AWAIT OUR MEETING...
"...BUT OUR GUEST HAD OTHER PLANS.
"HIS INFORMATION WAS QUITE DETAILED AND CORRECT. HE KNEW EXACTLY WHERE TO HEAD...
"...AND EXACTLY WHAT TO TAKE.

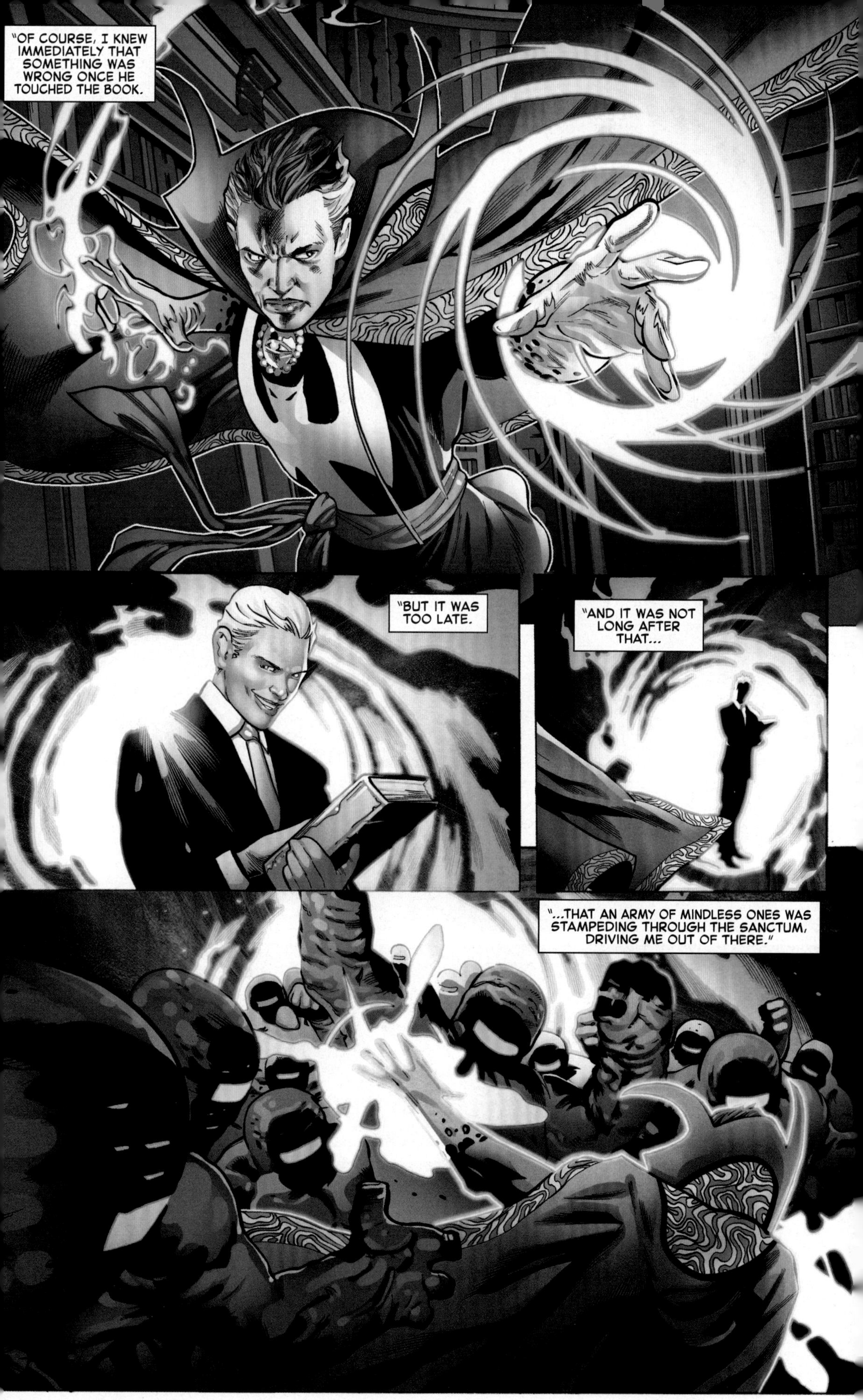
"OF COURSE, I KNEW IMMEDIATELY THAT SOMETHING WAS WRONG ONCE HE TOUCHED THE BOOK.
"BUT IT WAS TOO LATE.
"AND IT WAS NOT LONG AFTER THAT...
"...THAT AN ARMY OF MINDLESS ONES WAS STAMPEDING THROUGH THE SANCTUM, DRIVING ME OUT OF THERE."

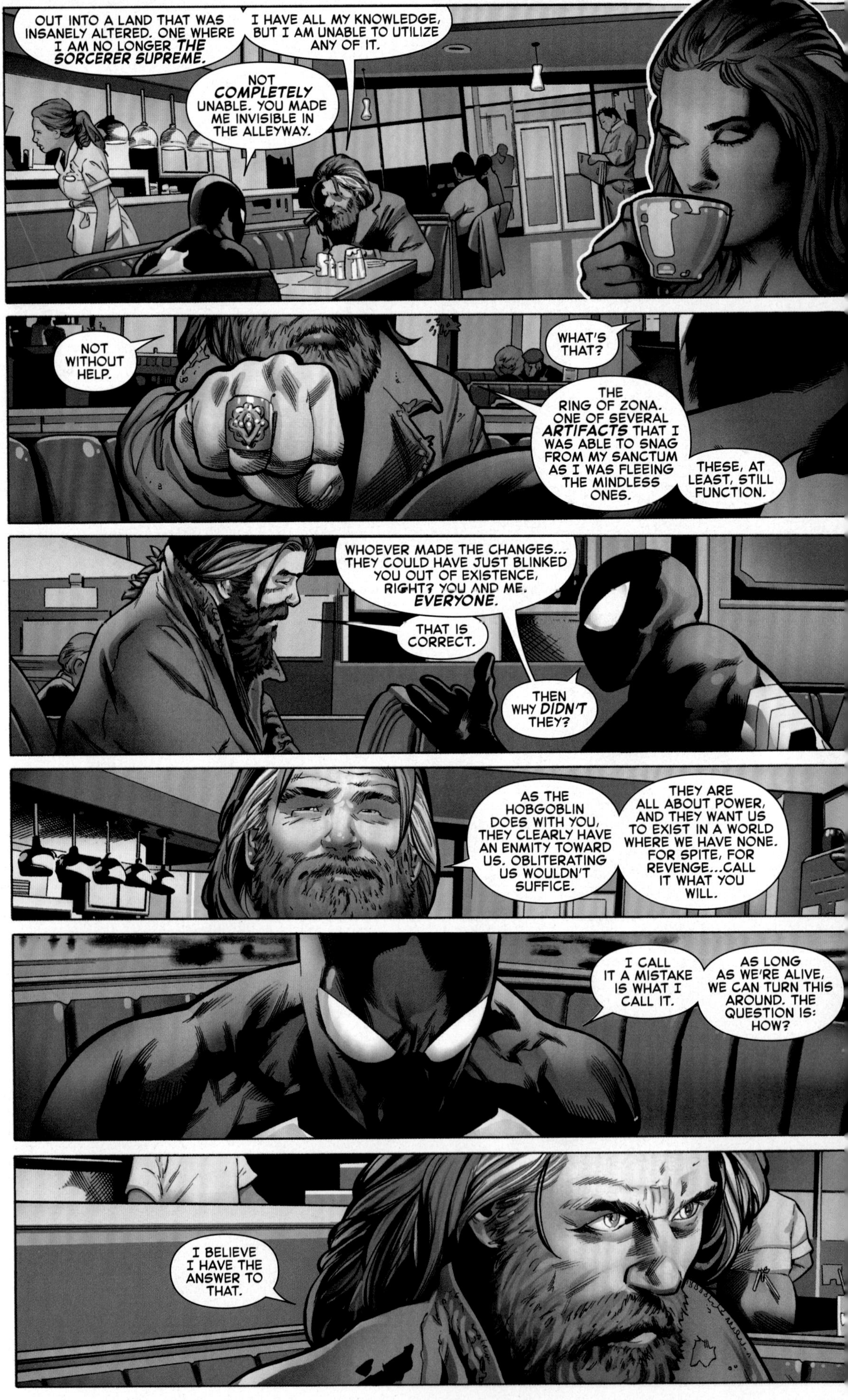
OUT INTO A LAND THAT WAS INSANELY ALTERED. ONE WHERE I AM NO LONGER THE SORCERER SUPREME.
I HAVE ALL MY KNOWLEDGE, BUT I AM UNABLE TO UTILIZE ANY OF IT.
NOT COMPLETELY UNABLE. YOU MADE ME INVISIBLE IN THE ALLEYWAY.
NOT WITHOUT HELP.
WHAT'S THAT?
THE RING OF ZONA. ONE OF SEVERAL ARTIFACTS THAT I WAS ABLE TO SNAG FROM MY SANCTUM AS I WAS FLEEING THE MINDLESS ONES.
THESE, AT LEAST, STILL FUNCTION.
WHOEVER MADE THE CHANGES... THEY COULD HAVE JUST BLINKED YOU OUT OF EXISTENCE, RIGHT? YOU AND ME. EVERYONE.
THAT IS CORRECT.
THEN WHY DIDN'T THEY?
AS THE HOBGOBLIN DOES WITH YOU, THEY CLEARLY HAVE AN ENMITY TOWARD US. OBLITERATING US WOULDN'T SUFFICE.
THEY ARE ALL ABOUT POWER, AND THEY WANT US TO EXIST IN A WORLD WHERE WE HAVE NONE. FOR SPITE, FOR REVENGE...CALL IT WHAT YOU WILL.
I CALL IT A MISTAKE IS WHAT I CALL IT.
AS LONG AS WE'RE ALIVE, WE CAN TURN THIS AROUND. THE QUESTION IS: HOW?
I BELIEVE I HAVE THE ANSWER TO THAT.

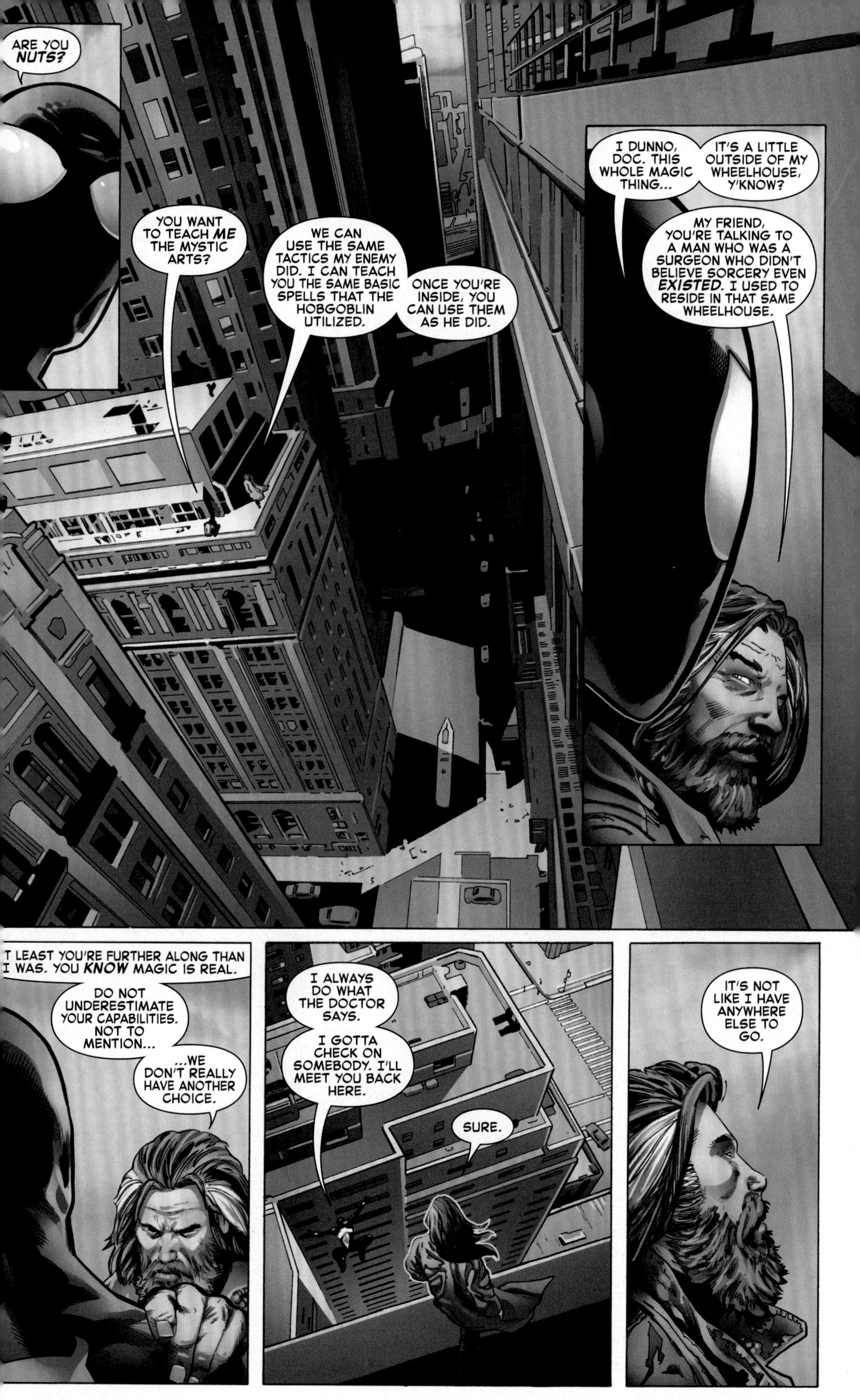

ARE YOU NUTS?
YOU WANT TO TEACH ME THE MYSTIC ARTS?
WE CAN USE THE SAME TACTICS MY ENEMY DID. I CAN TEACH YOU THE SAME BASIC SPELLS THAT THE HOBGOBLIN UTILIZED.
ONCE YOU'RE INSIDE, YOU CAN USE THEM AS HE DID.
I DUNNO, DOC. THIS WHOLE MAGIC THING...
IT'S A LITTLE OUTSIDE OF MY WHEELHOUSE, Y'KNOW?
MY FRIEND, YOU'RE TALKING TO A MAN WHO WAS A SURGEON WHO DIDN'T BELIEVE SORCERY EVEN EXISTED. I USED TO RESIDE IN THAT SAME WHEELHOUSE.
T LEAST YOU'RE FURTHER ALONG THAN I WAS. YOU KNOW MAGIC IS REAL.
DO NOT UNDERESTIMATE YOUR CAPABILITIES. NOT TO MENTION...
...WE DON'T REALLY HAVE ANOTHER CHOICE.
I ALWAYS DO WHAT THE DOCTOR SAYS.
I GOTTA CHECK ON SOMEBODY. I'LL MEET YOU BACK HERE.
SURE.
IT'S NOT LIKE I HAVE ANYWHERE ELSE TO GO.

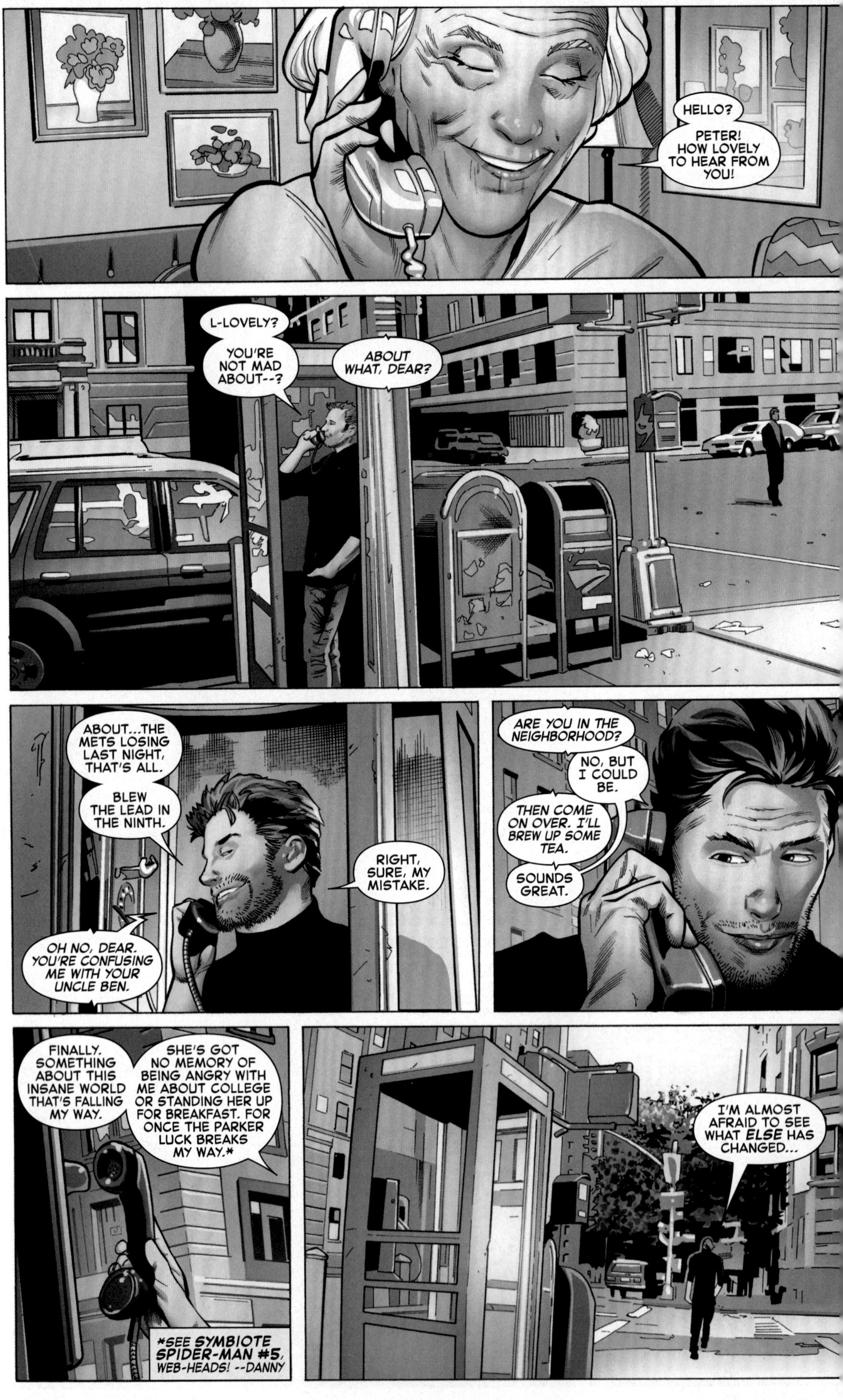
HELLO?
PETER! HOW LOVELY TO HEAR FROM YOU!
L-LOVELY?
YOU'RE NOT MAD ABOUT--?
ABOUT WHAT, DEAR?
ABOUT...THE METS LOSING LAST NIGHT, THAT'S ALL.
BLEW THE LEAD IN THE NINTH.
OH NO, DEAR. YOU'RE CONFUSING ME WITH YOUR UNCLE BEN.
RIGHT, SURE, MY MISTAKE.
ARE YOU IN THE NEIGHBORHOOD?
NO, BUT I COULD BE.
THEN COME ON OVER. I'LL BREW UP SOME TEA.
SOUNDS GREAT.
FINALLY. SOMETHING ABOUT THIS INSANE WORLD THAT'S FALLING MY WAY.
SHE'S GOT NO MEMORY OF BEING ANGRY WITH ME ABOUT COLLEGE OR STANDING HER UP FOR BREAKFAST. FOR ONCE THE PARKER LUCK BREAKS MY WAY.*
*SEE SYMBIOTE SPIDER-MAN #5, WEB-HEADS! --DANNY
I'M ALMOST AFRAID TO SEE WHAT ELSE HAS CHANGED...

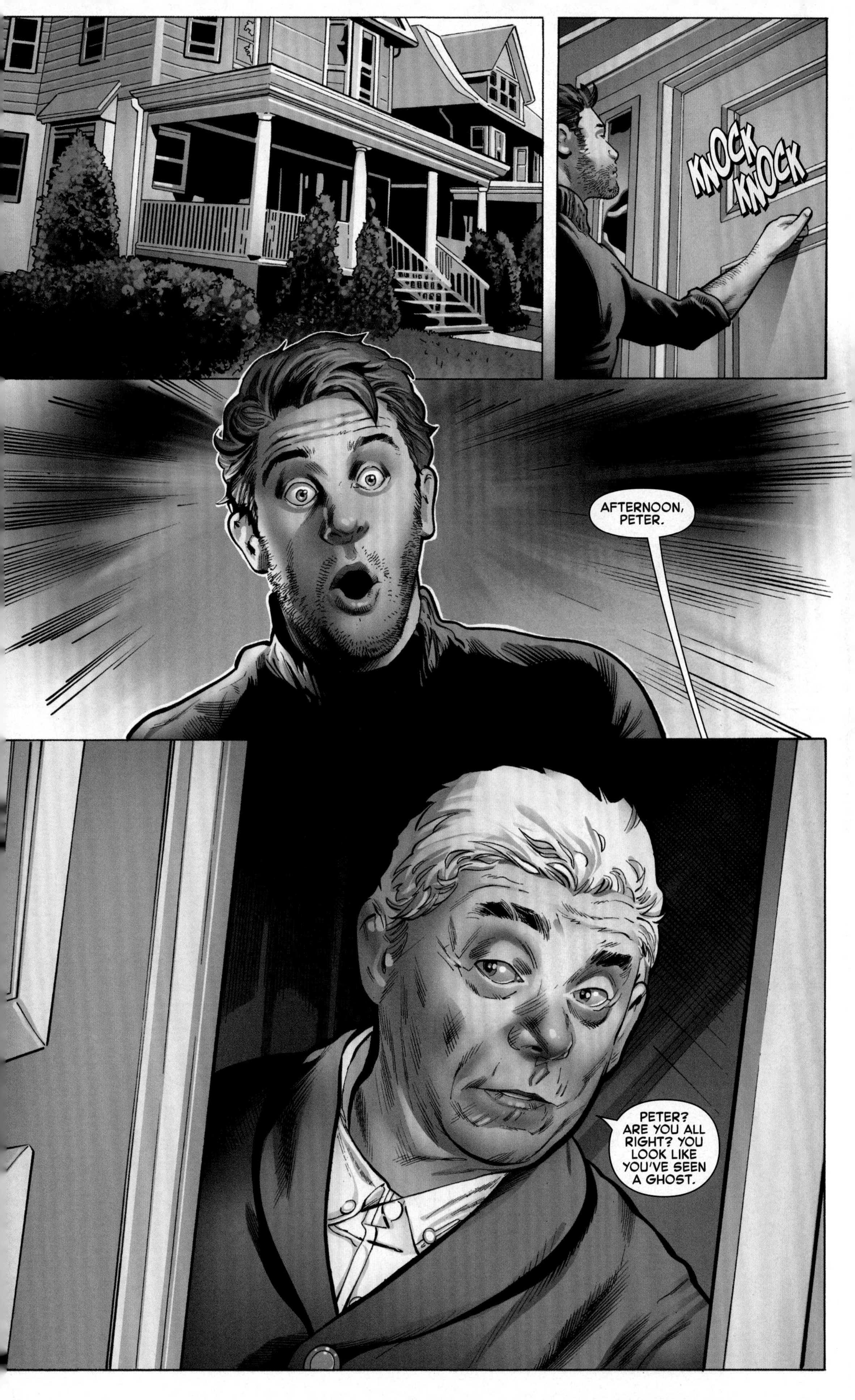
KNOCK KNOCK
AFTERNOON, PETER.
PETER? ARE YOU ALL RIGHT? YOU LOOK LIKE YOU'VE SEEN A GHOST.

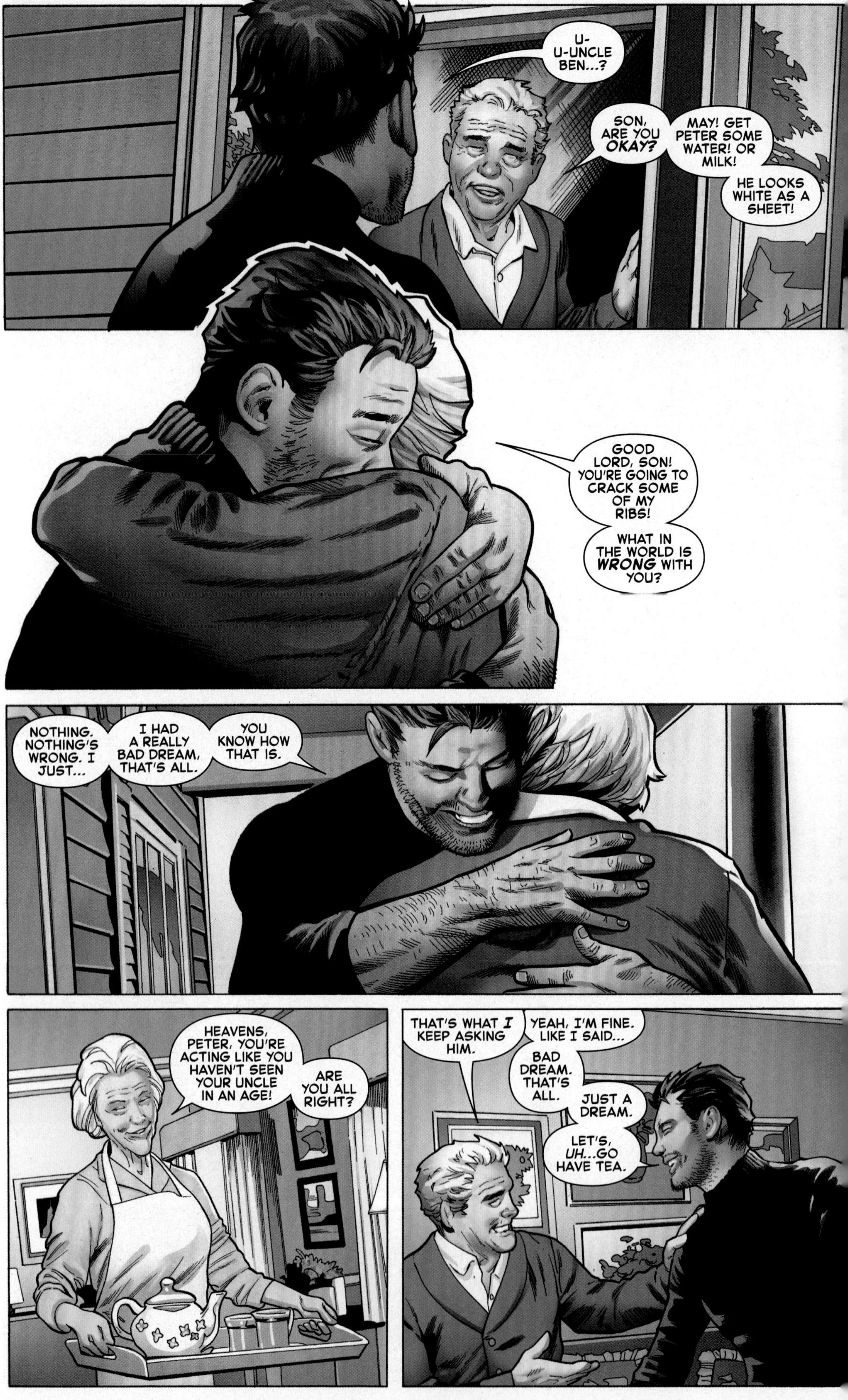
U- U-UNCLE BEN...?
SON, ARE YOU OKAY?
MAY! GET PETER SOME WATER! OR MILK!
HE LOOKS WHITE AS A SHEET!
GOOD LORD, SON! YOU'RE GOING TO CRACK SOME OF MY RIBS!
WHAT IN THE WORLD IS WRONG WITH YOU?
NOTHING. NOTHING'S WRONG. I JUST...
I HAD A REALLY BAD DREAM, THAT'S ALL.
YOU KNOW HOW THAT IS.
HEAVENS, PETER, YOU'RE ACTING LIKE YOU HAVEN'T SEEN YOUR UNCLE IN AN AGE!
ARE YOU ALL RIGHT?
THAT'S WHAT I KEEP ASKING HIM.
YEAH, I'M FINE. LIKE I SAID...
BAD DREAM. THAT'S ALL.
JUST A DREAM.
LET'S, UH...GO HAVE TEA.

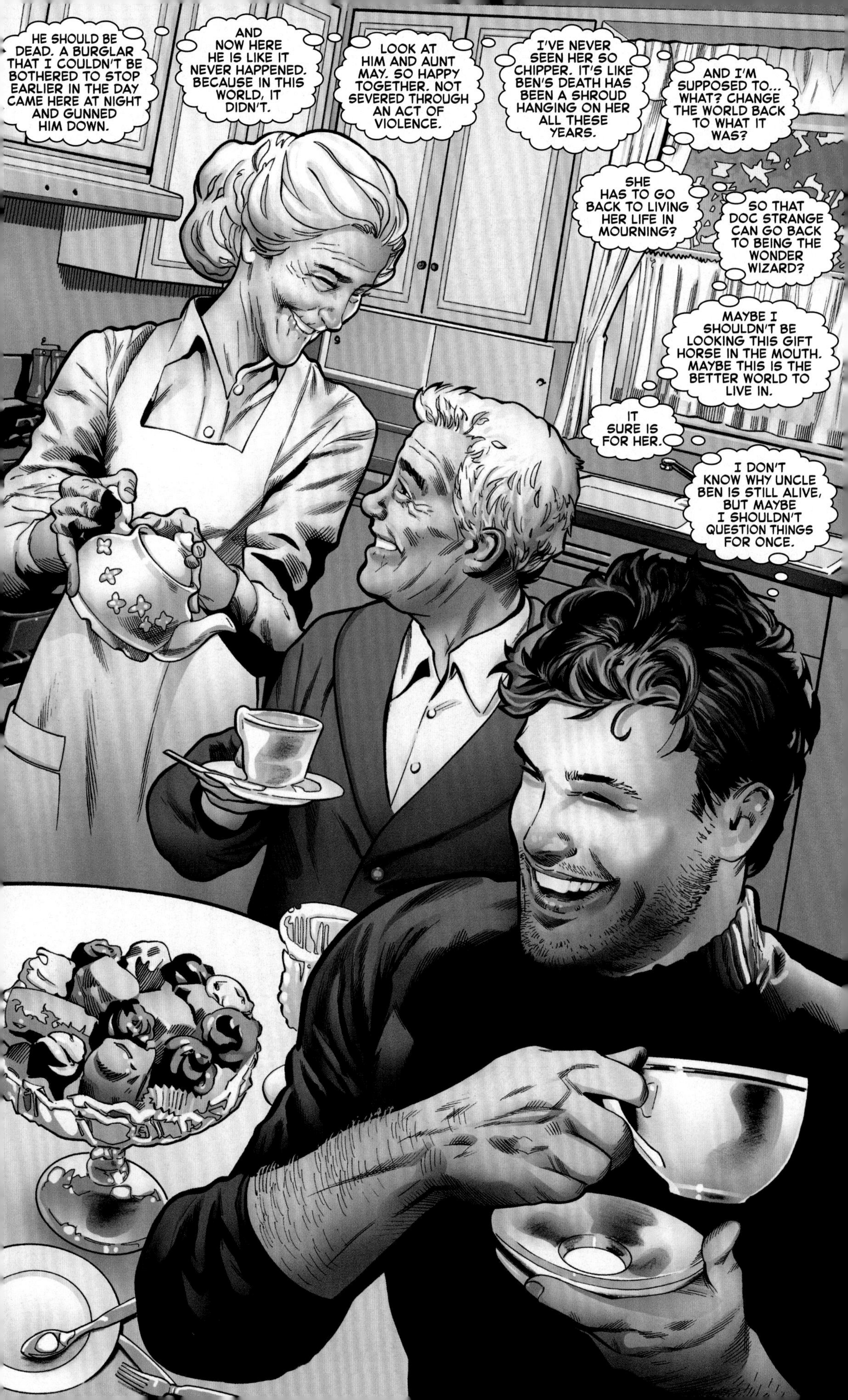
HE SHOULD BE DEAD. A BURGLAR THAT I COULDN'T BE BOTHERED TO STOP EARLIER IN THE DAY CAME HERE AT NIGHT AND GUNNED HIM DOWN.
AND NOW HERE HE IS LIKE IT NEVER HAPPENED. BECAUSE IN THIS WORLD, IT DIDN'T.
LOOK AT HIM AND AUNT MAY. SO HAPPY TOGETHER. NOT SEVERED THROUGH AN ACT OF VIOLENCE.
I'VE NEVER SEEN HER SO CHIPPER. IT'S LIKE BEN'S DEATH HAS BEEN A SHROUD HANGING ON HER ALL THESE YEARS.
AND I'M SUPPOSED TO... WHAT? CHANGE THE WORLD BACK TO WHAT IT WAS?
SHE HAS TO GO BACK TO LIVING HER LIFE IN MOURNING?
SO THAT DOC STRANGE CAN GO BACK TO BEING THE WONDER WIZARD?
MAYBE I SHOULDN'T BE LOOKING THIS GIFT HORSE IN THE MOUTH. MAYBE THIS IS THE BETTER WORLD TO LIVE IN.
IT SURE IS FOR HER.
I DON'T KNOW WHY UNCLE BEN IS STILL ALIVE, BUT MAYBE I SHOULDN'T QUESTION THINGS FOR ONCE.

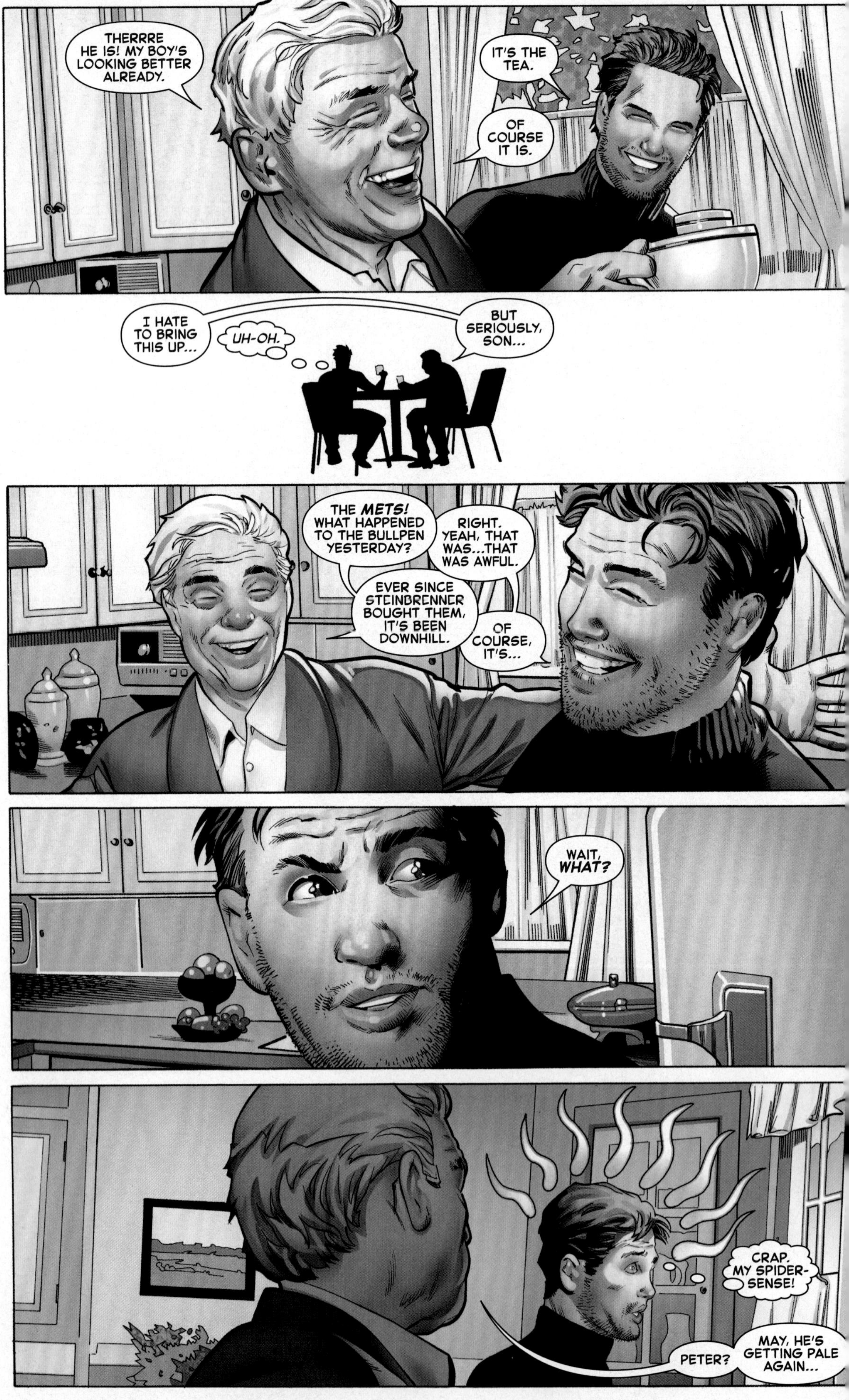
THERRRE HE IS! MY BOY'S LOOKING BETTER ALREADY.
IT'S THE TEA.
OF COURSE IT IS.
I HATE TO BRING THIS UP...
UH-OH.
BUT SERIOUSLY, SON...
THE METS! WHAT HAPPENED TO THE BULLPEN YESTERDAY?
RIGHT. YEAH, THAT WAS...THAT WAS AWFUL.
EVER SINCE STEINBRENNER BOUGHT THEM, IT'S BEEN DOWNHILL.
OF COURSE, IT'S...
WAIT, WHAT?
CRAP. MY SPIDER-SENSE!
PETER?
MAY, HE'S GETTING PALE AGAIN...

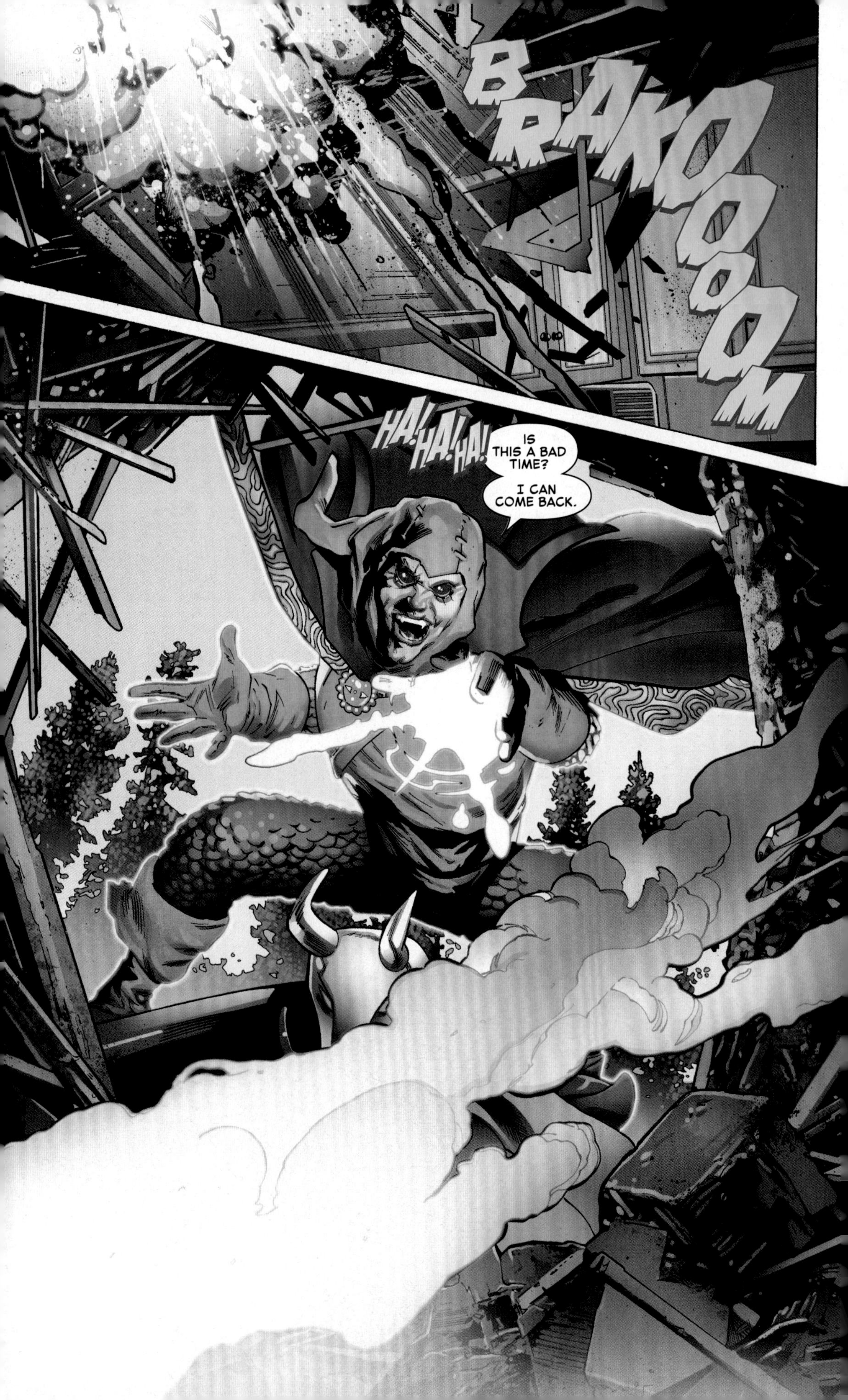
BRAKOOOOM
HA! HA! HA!
IS THIS A BAD TIME?
I CAN COME BACK.

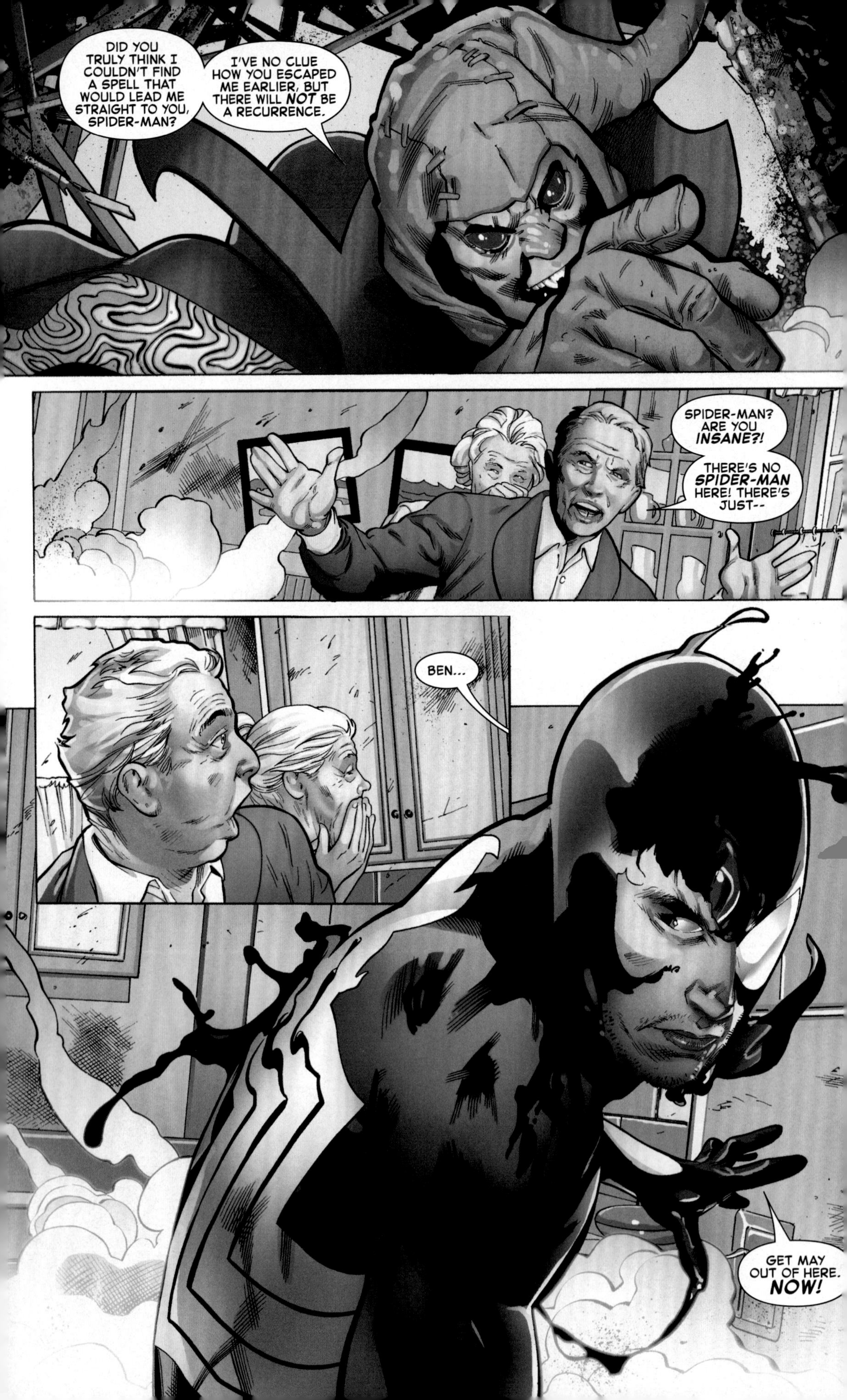
DID YOU TRULY THINK I COULDN'T FIND A SPELL THAT WOULD LEAD ME STRAIGHT TO YOU, SPIDER-MAN?
I'VE NO CLUE HOW YOU ESCAPED ME EARLIER, BUT THERE WILL NOT BE A RECURRENCE.
SPIDER-MAN? ARE YOU INSANE?!
THERE'S NO SPIDER-MAN HERE! THERE'S JUST--
BEN...
GET MAY OUT OF HERE. NOW!

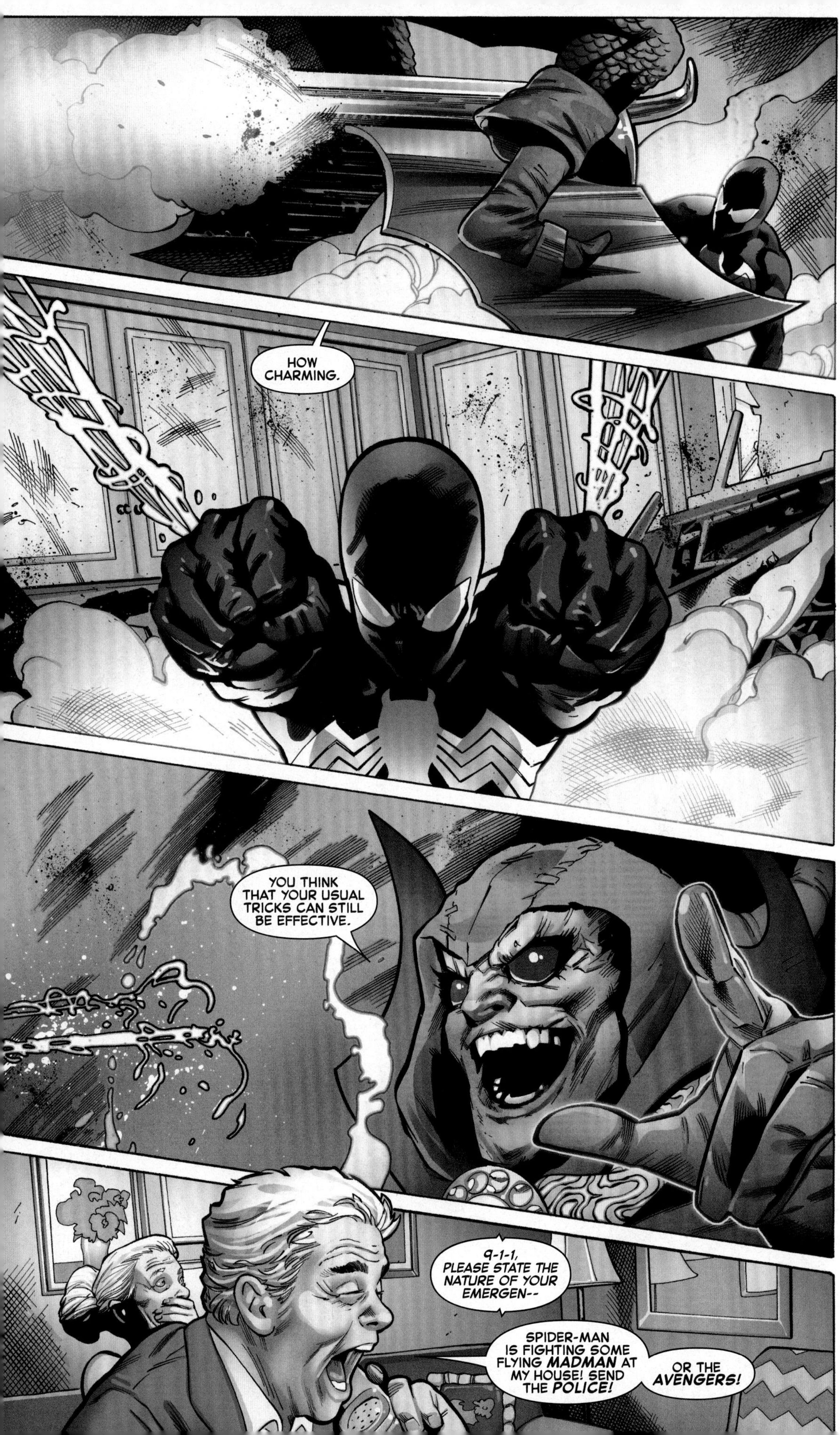
HOW CHARMING.
YOU THINK THAT YOUR USUAL TRICKS CAN STILL BE EFFECTIVE.
9-1-1, PLEASE STATE THE NATURE OF YOUR EMERGEN--
SPIDER-MAN IS FIGHTING SOME FLYING MADMAN AT MY HOUSE! SEND THE POLICE!
OR THE AVENGERS!

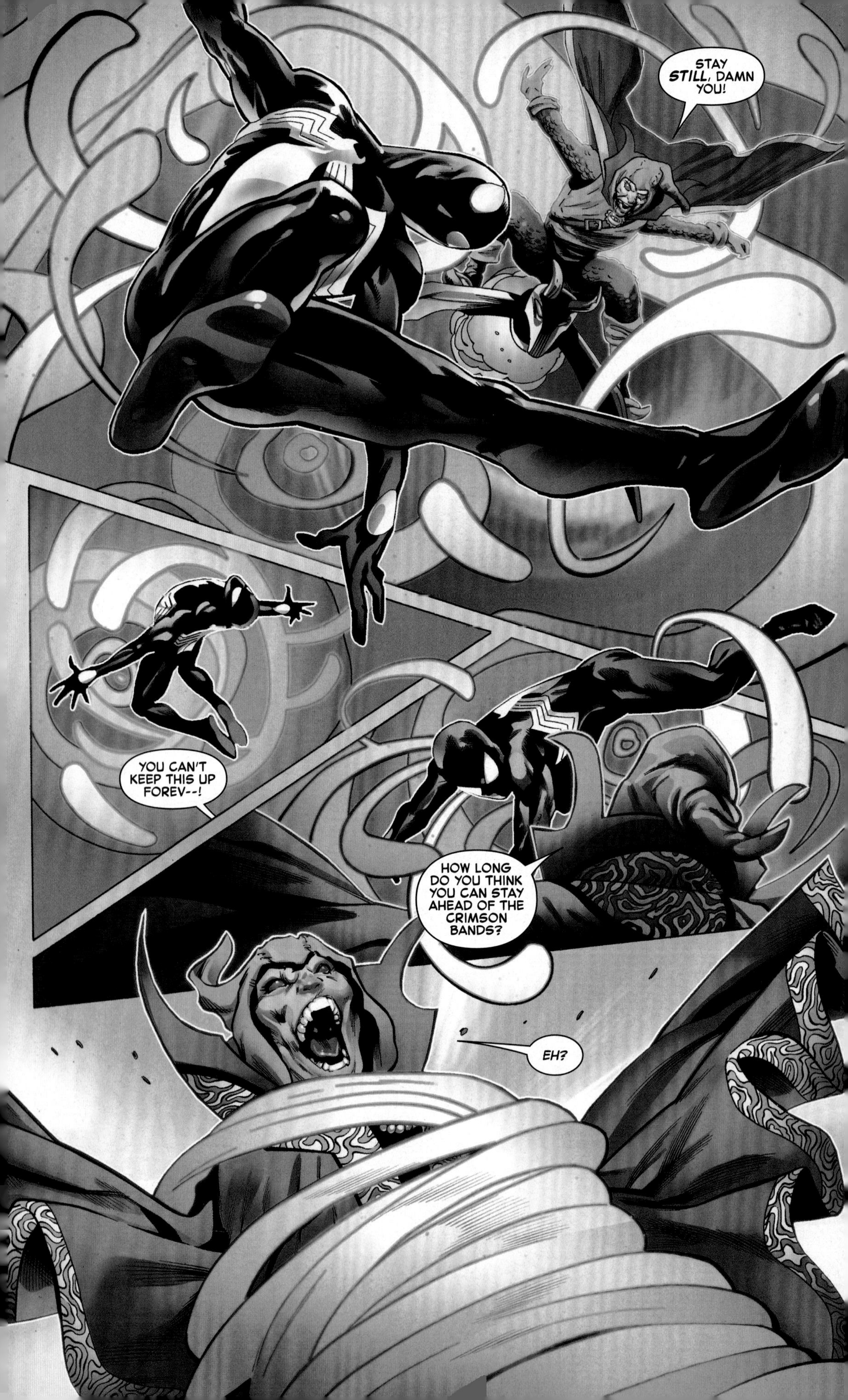
STAY STILL, DAMN YOU!
YOU CAN'T KEEP THIS UP FOREV--!
HOW LONG DO YOU THINK YOU CAN STAY AHEAD OF THE CRIMSON BANDS?
EH?

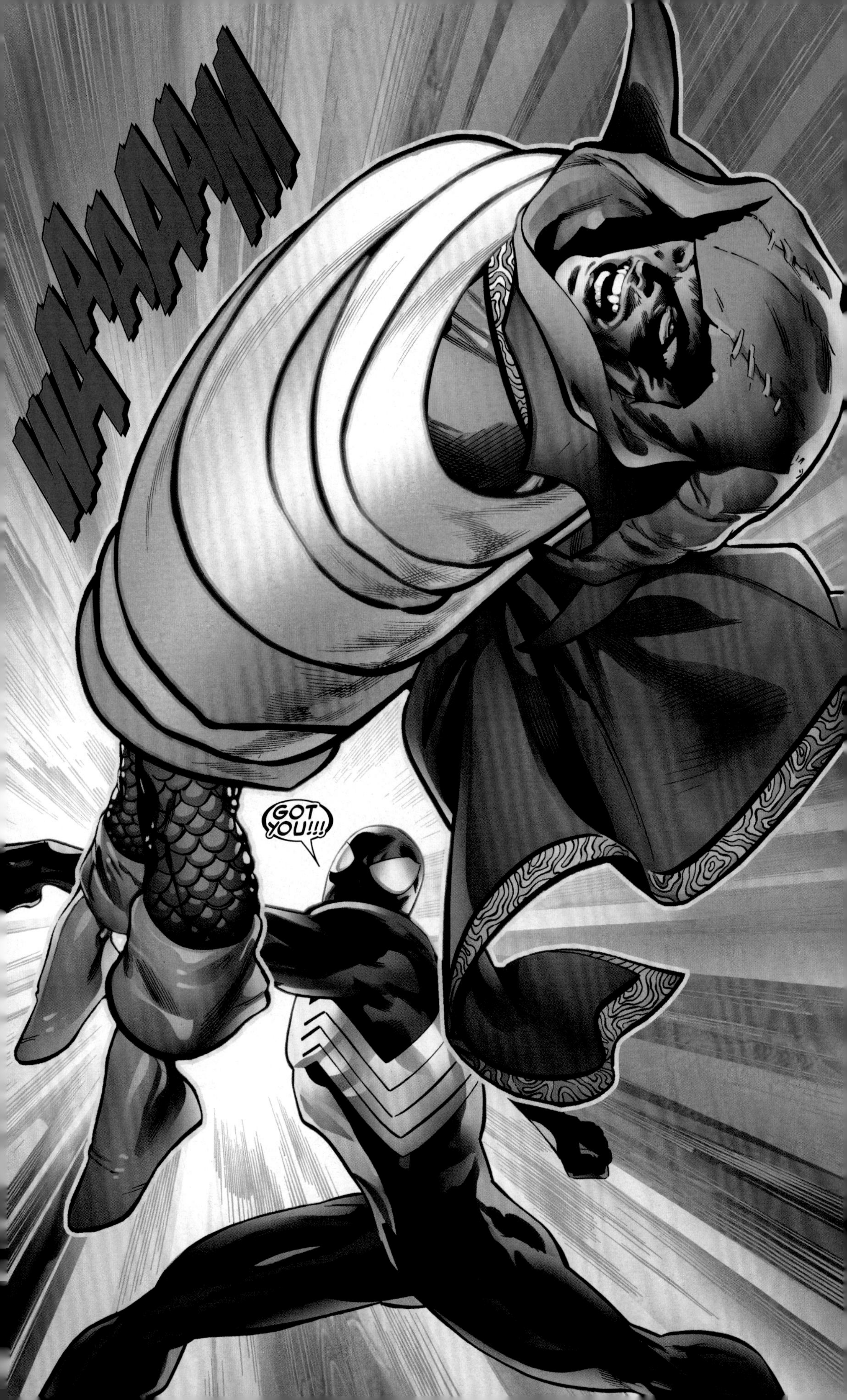
WAAAM
GOT YOU!!!

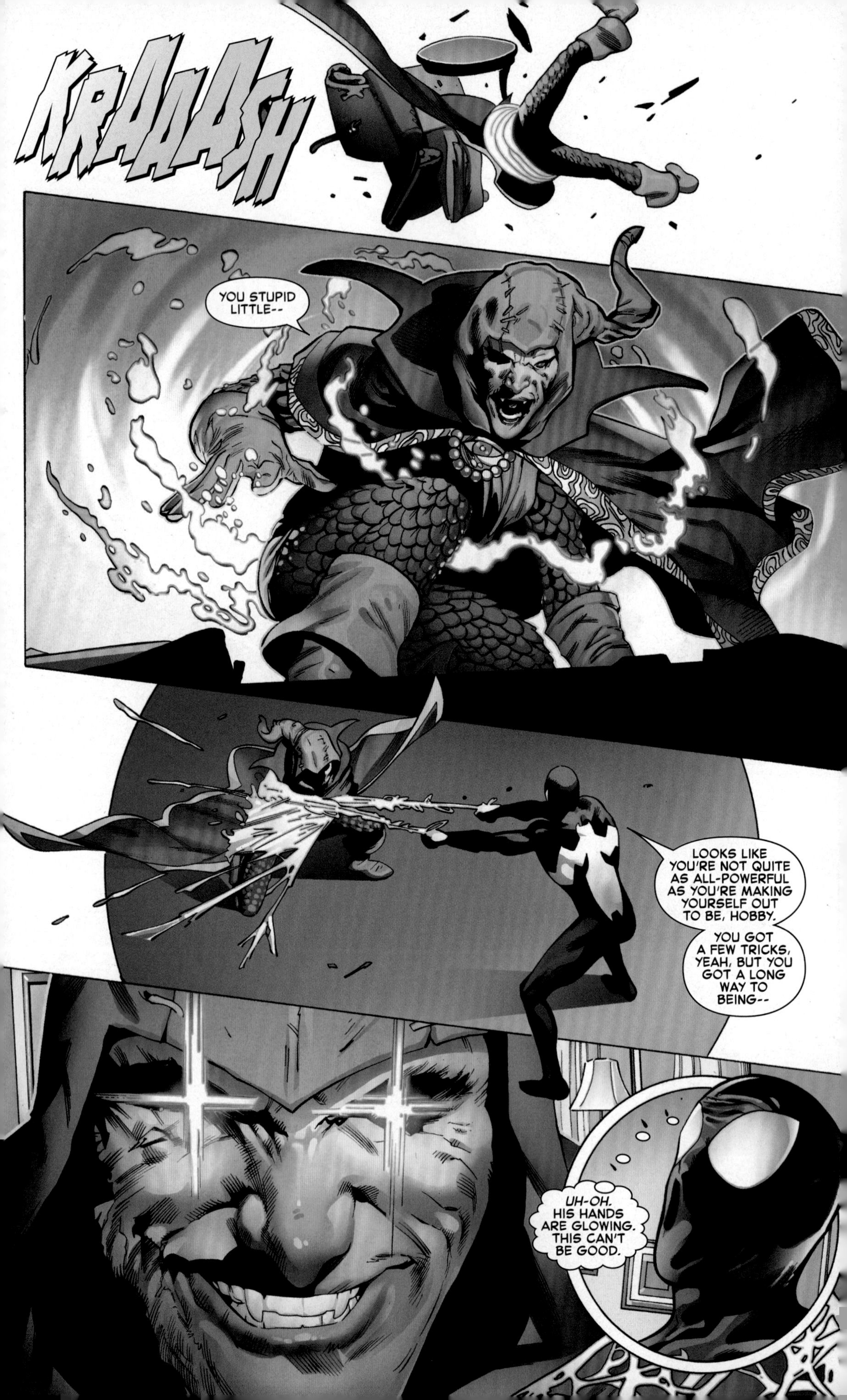
KRAAASH
YOU STUPID LITTLE--
LOOKS LIKE YOU'RE NOT QUITE AS ALL-POWERFUL AS YOU'RE MAKING YOURSELF OUT TO BE, HOBBY.
YOU GOT A FEW TRICKS, YEAH, BUT YOU GOT A LONG WAY TO BEING--
UH-OH. HIS HANDS ARE GLOWING. THIS CAN'T BE GOOD.

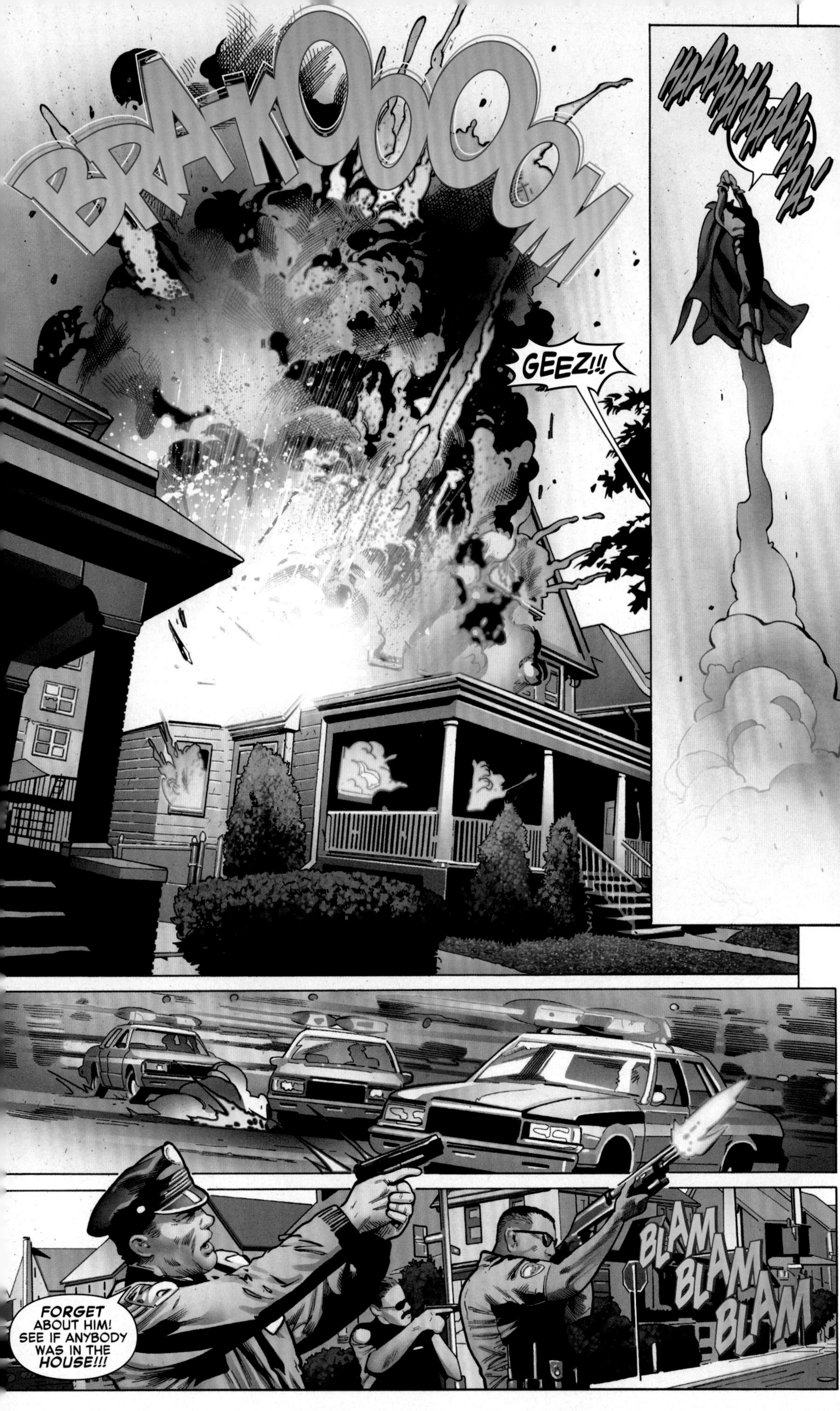
BRAKOOOOOM
HAAAHAHAHAAAHAA!
GEEZ!!!
FORGET ABOUT HIM! SEE IF ANYBODY WAS IN THE HOUSE!!!
BLAM BLAM BLAM

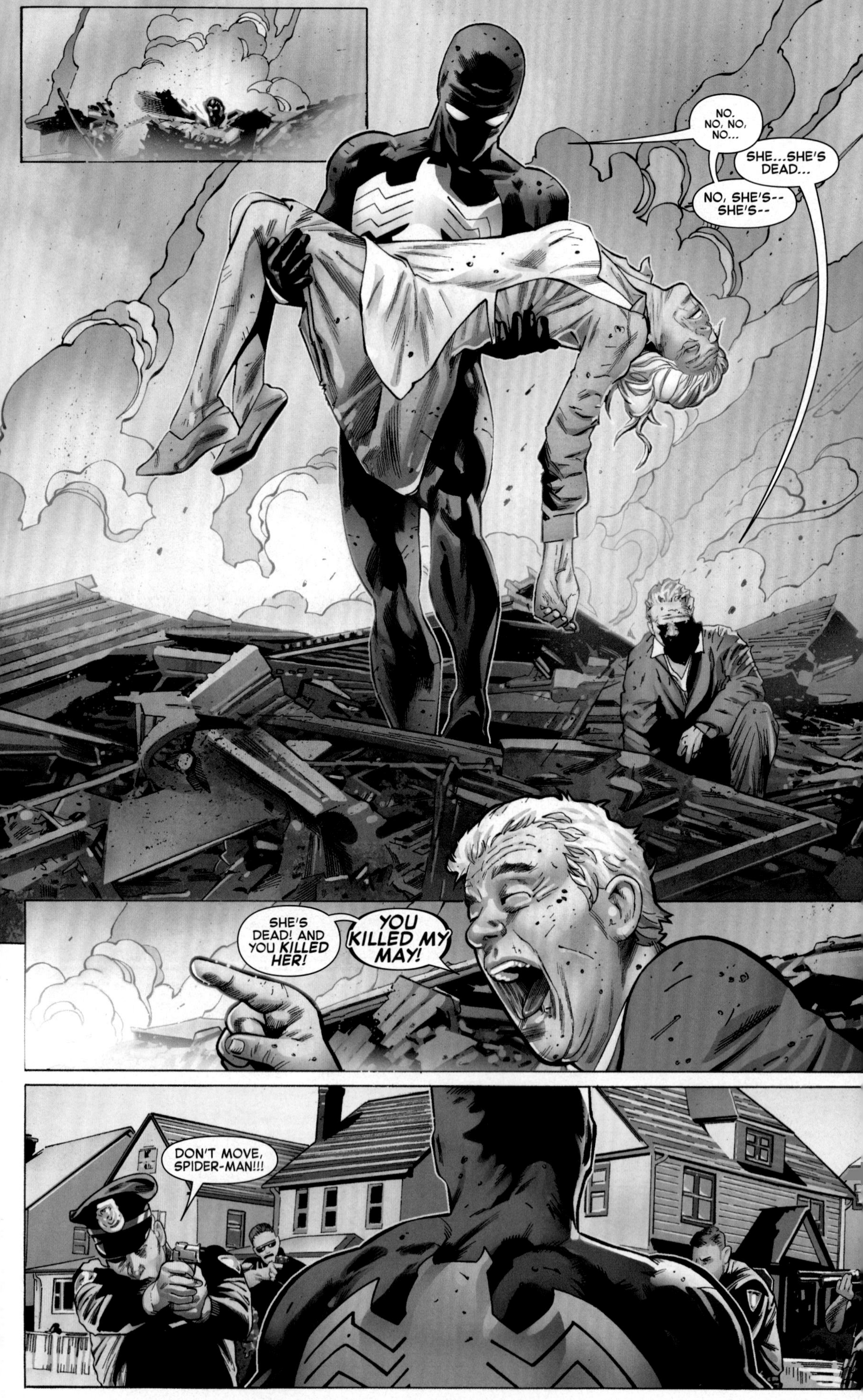
NO. NO, NO, NO...
SHE...SHE'S DEAD...
NO, SHE'S-- SHE'S--
SHE'S DEAD! AND YOU KILLED HER!
YOU KILLED MY MAY!
DON'T MOVE, SPIDER-MAN!!!

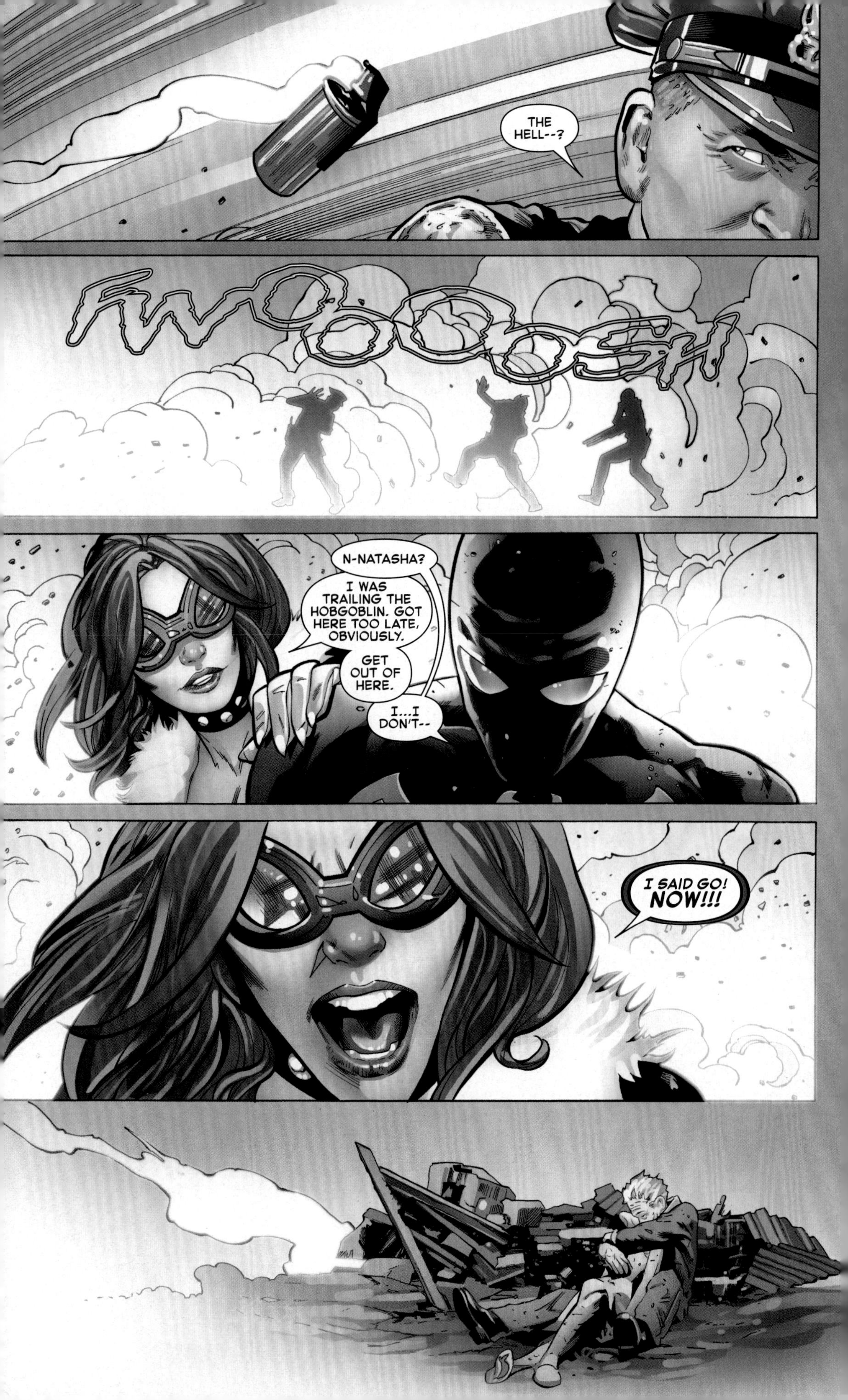
THE HELL--?
FWOOOOOSH!
N-NATASHA?
I WAS TRAILING THE HOBGOBLIN. GOT HERE TOO LATE, OBVIOUSLY.
GET OUT OF HERE.
I...I DON'T--
I SAID GO! NOW!!!

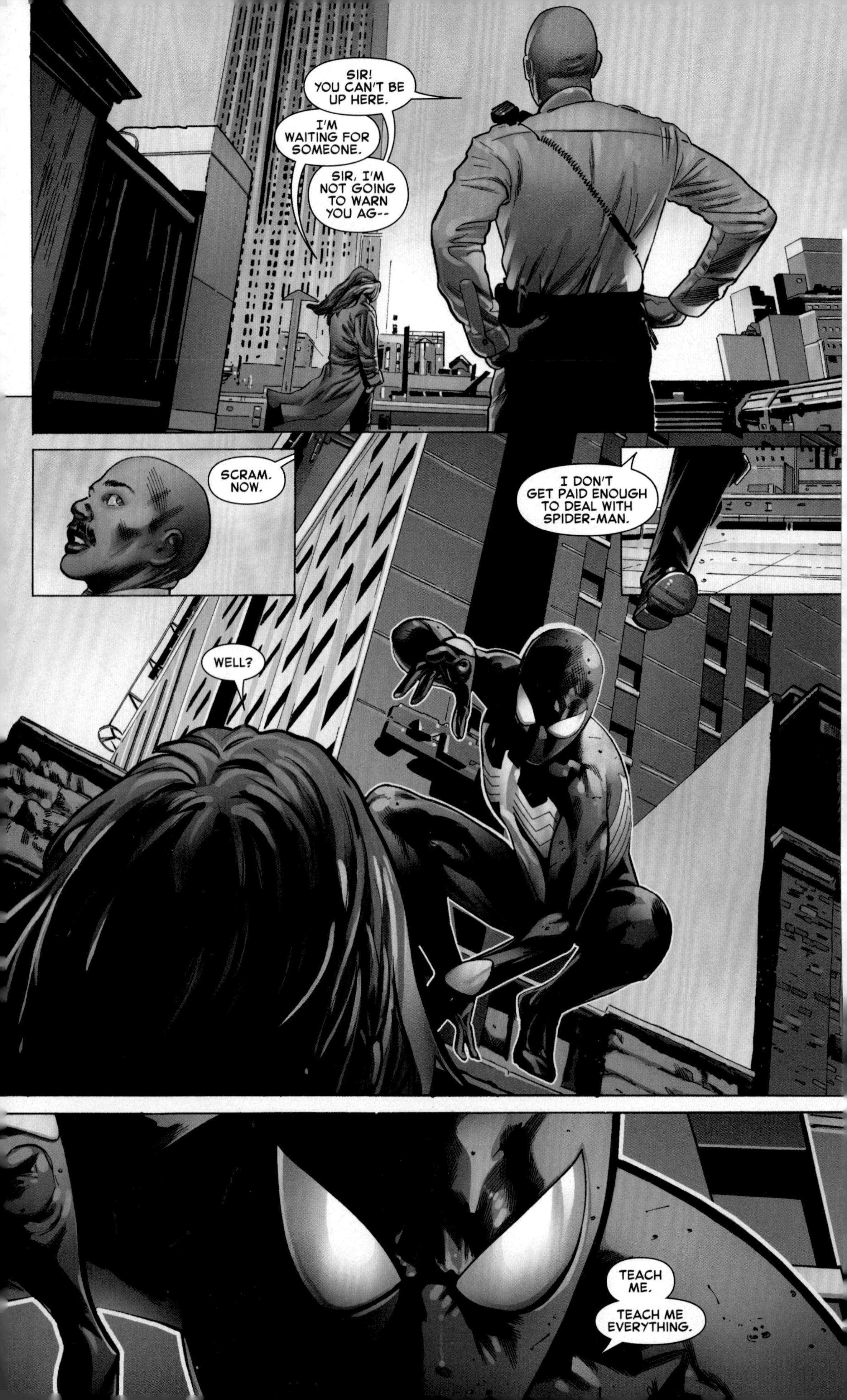
SIR! YOU CAN'T BE UP HERE.
I'M WAITING FOR SOMEONE.
SIR, I'M NOT GOING TO WARN YOU AG--
SCRAM. NOW.
I DON'T GET PAID ENOUGH TO DEAL WITH SPIDER-MAN.
WELL?
TEACH ME.
TEACH ME EVERYTHING.

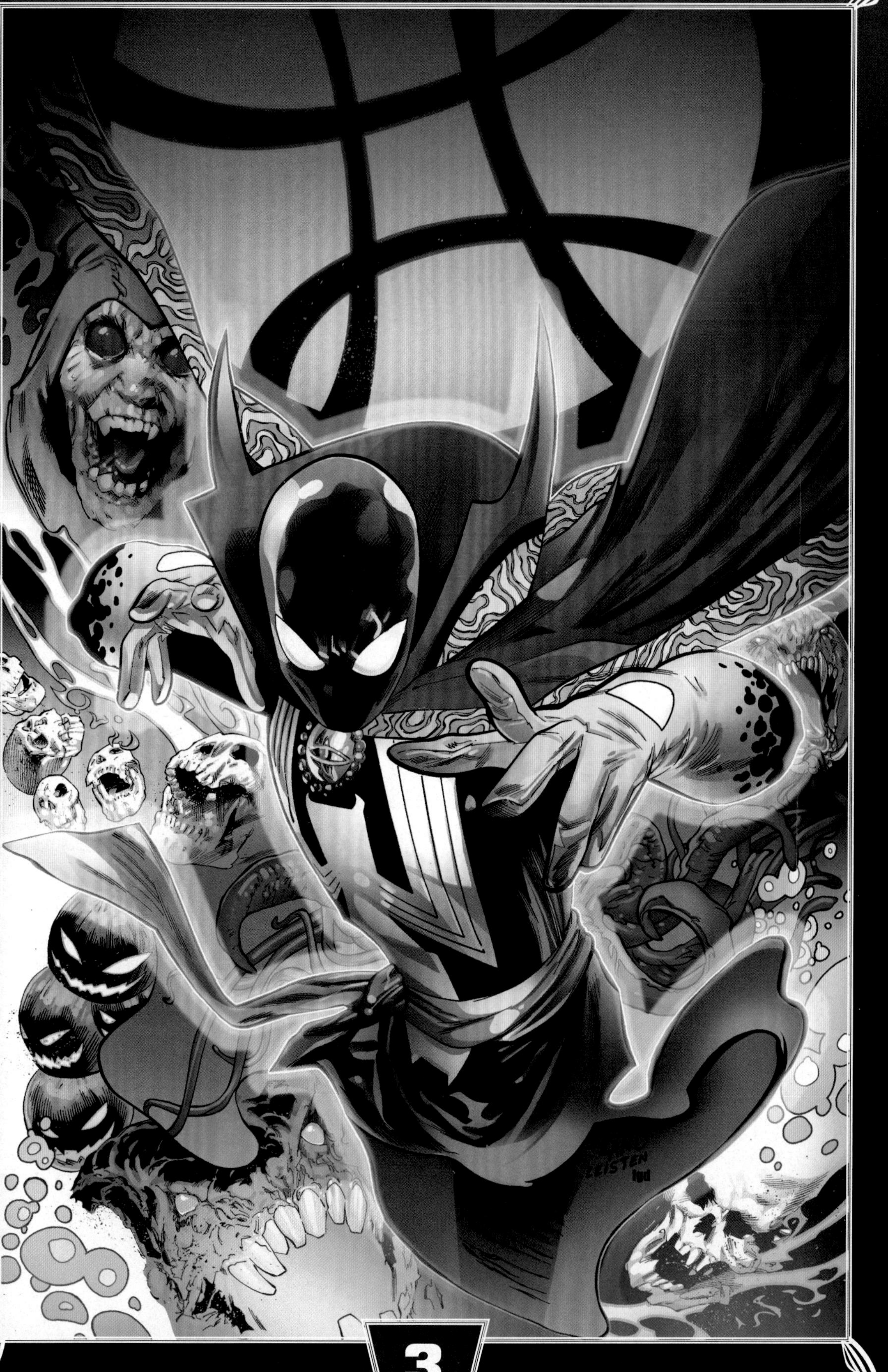

3

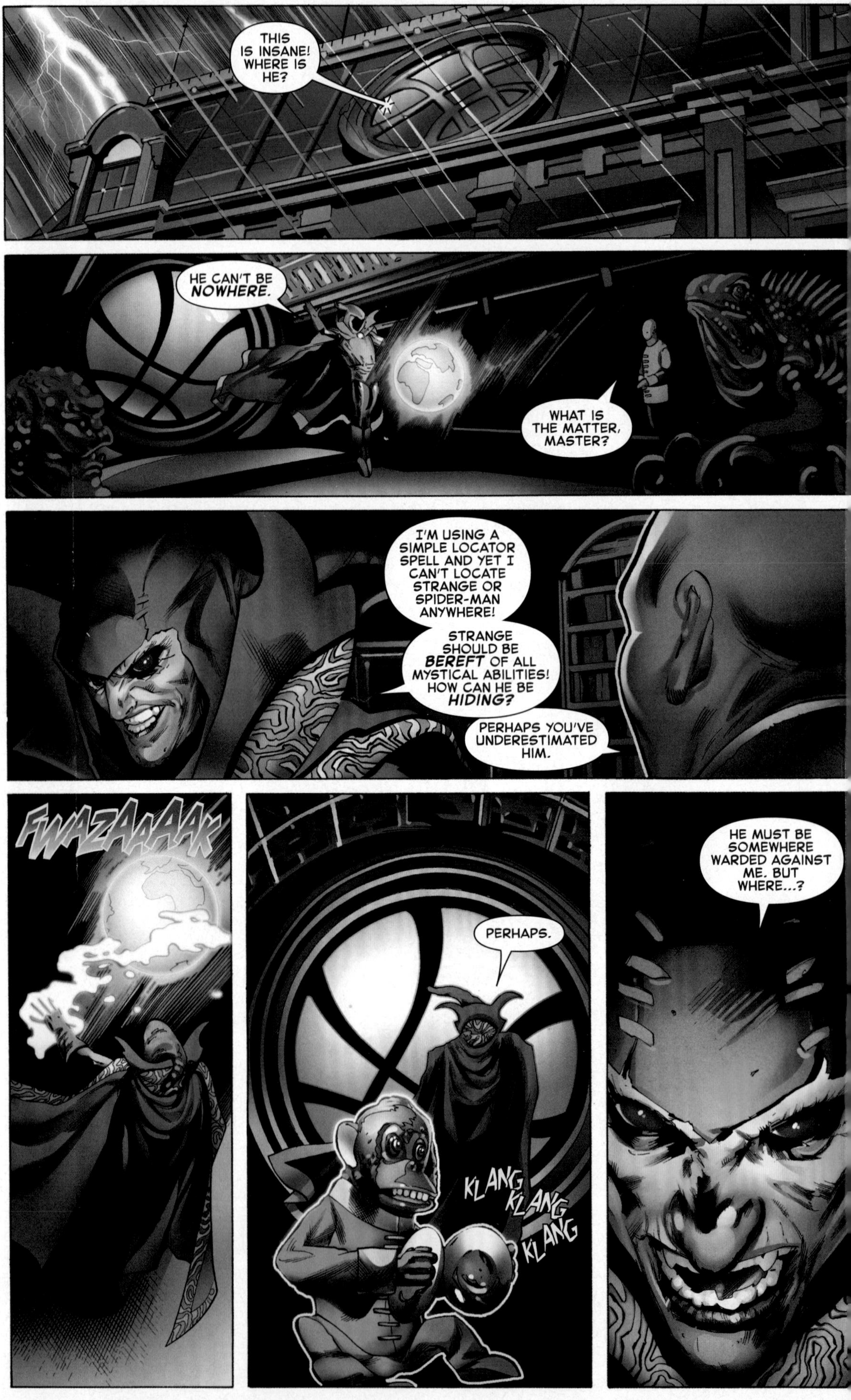
THIS IS INSANE! WHERE IS HE?
HE CAN'T BE *NOWHERE.*
WHAT IS THE MATTER, MASTER?
I'M USING A SIMPLE LOCATOR SPELL AND YET I CAN'T LOCATE STRANGE OR SPIDER-MAN ANYWHERE!
STRANGE SHOULD BE *BEREFT* OF ALL MYSTICAL ABILITIES! HOW CAN HE BE *HIDING?*
PERHAPS YOU'VE UNDERESTIMATED HIM.
FWAZAAAAAK
PERHAPS.
KLANG KLANG KLANG
HE MUST BE SOMEWHERE WARDED AGAINST ME. BUT WHERE...?

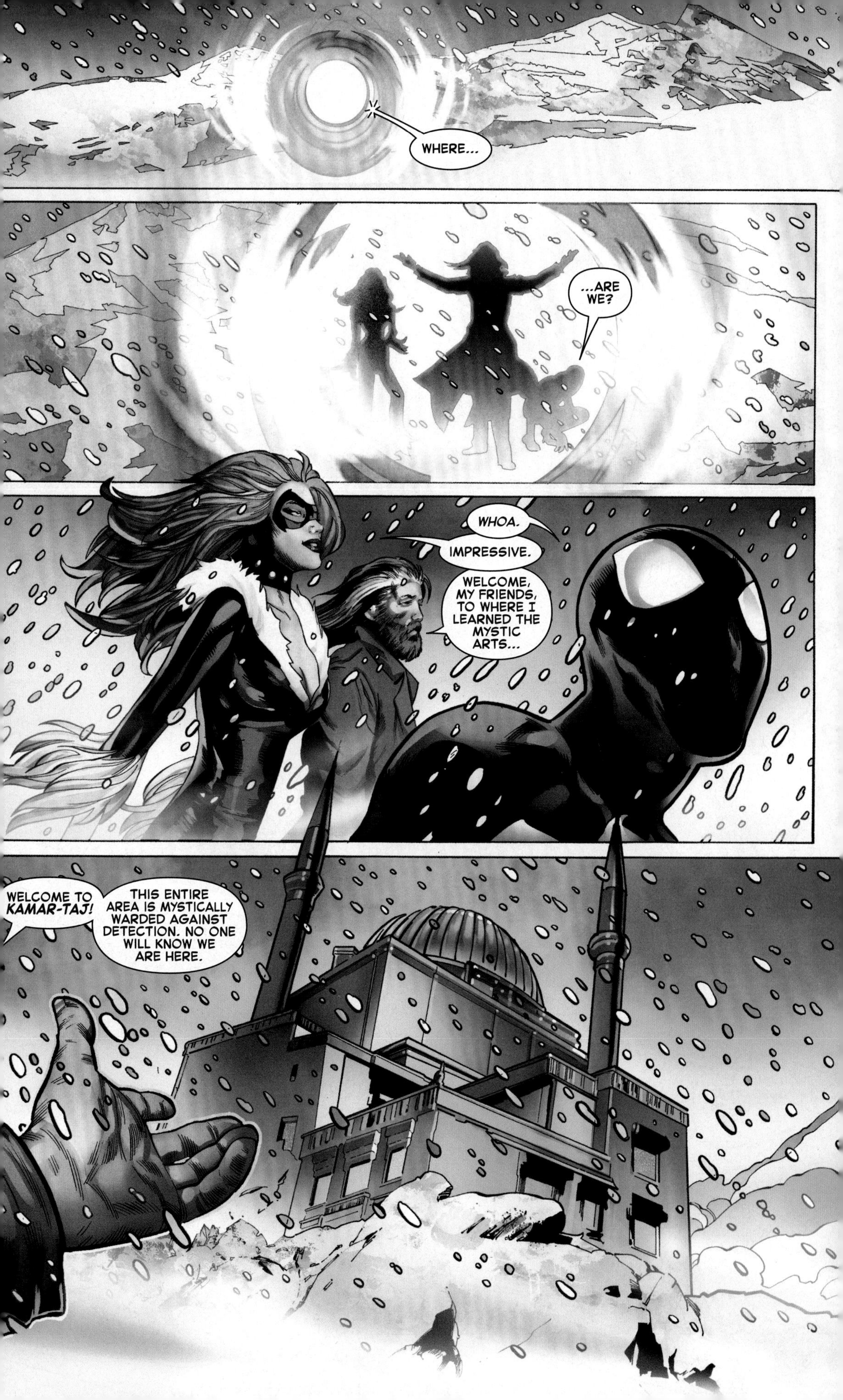
WHERE...
...ARE WE?
WHOA.
IMPRESSIVE.
WELCOME, MY FRIENDS, TO WHERE I LEARNED THE MYSTIC ARTS...
WELCOME TO KAMAR-TAJ!
THIS ENTIRE AREA IS MYSTICALLY WARDED AGAINST DETECTION. NO ONE WILL KNOW WE ARE HERE.

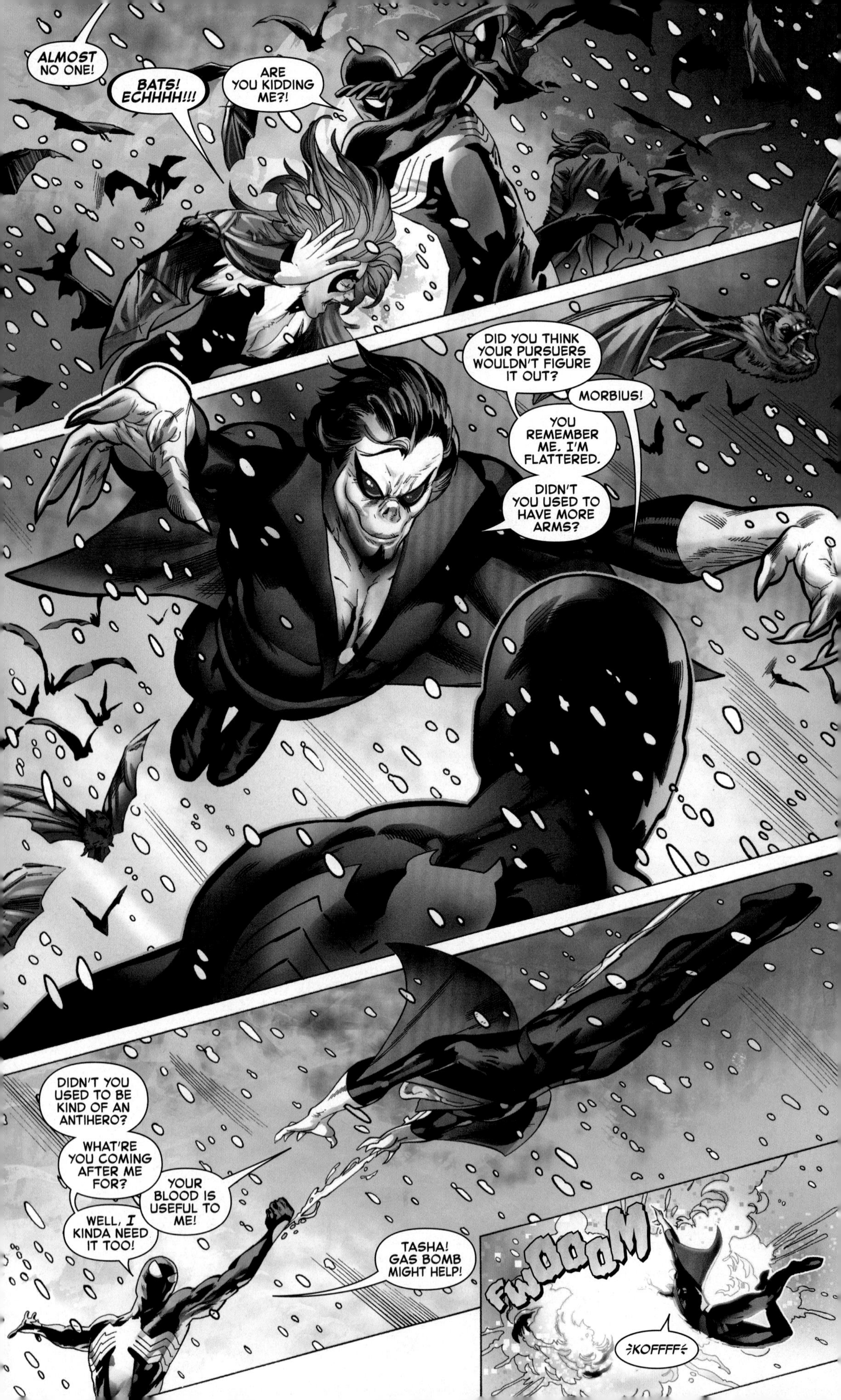
ALMOST NO ONE!
BATS! ECHHHH!!!
ARE YOU KIDDING ME?!
DID YOU THINK YOUR PURSUERS WOULDN'T FIGURE IT OUT?
MORBIUS!
YOU REMEMBER ME. I'M FLATTERED.
DIDN'T YOU USED TO HAVE MORE ARMS?
DIDN'T YOU USED TO BE KIND OF AN ANTIHERO?
WHAT'RE YOU COMING AFTER ME FOR?
YOUR BLOOD IS USEFUL TO ME!
WELL, I KINDA NEED IT TOO!
TASHA! GAS BOMB MIGHT HELP!
FWOOOOM
KOFFFF

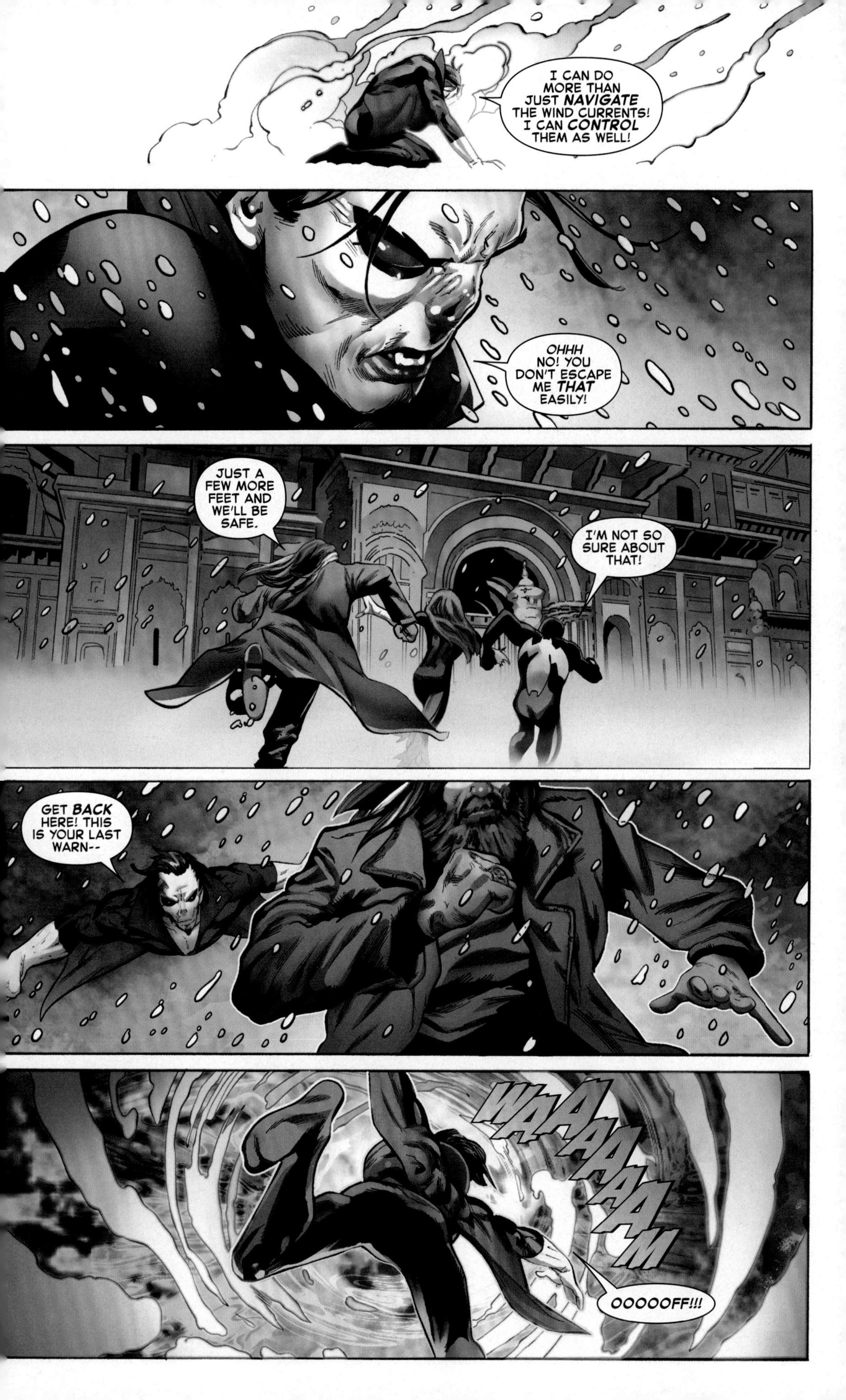
I CAN DO MORE THAN JUST NAVIGATE THE WIND CURRENTS! I CAN CONTROL THEM AS WELL!
OHHH NO! YOU DON'T ESCAPE ME THAT EASILY!
JUST A FEW MORE FEET AND WE'LL BE SAFE.
I'M NOT SO SURE ABOUT THAT!
GET BACK HERE! THIS IS YOUR LAST WARN--
WAAAAAAAM
OOOOOFF!!!

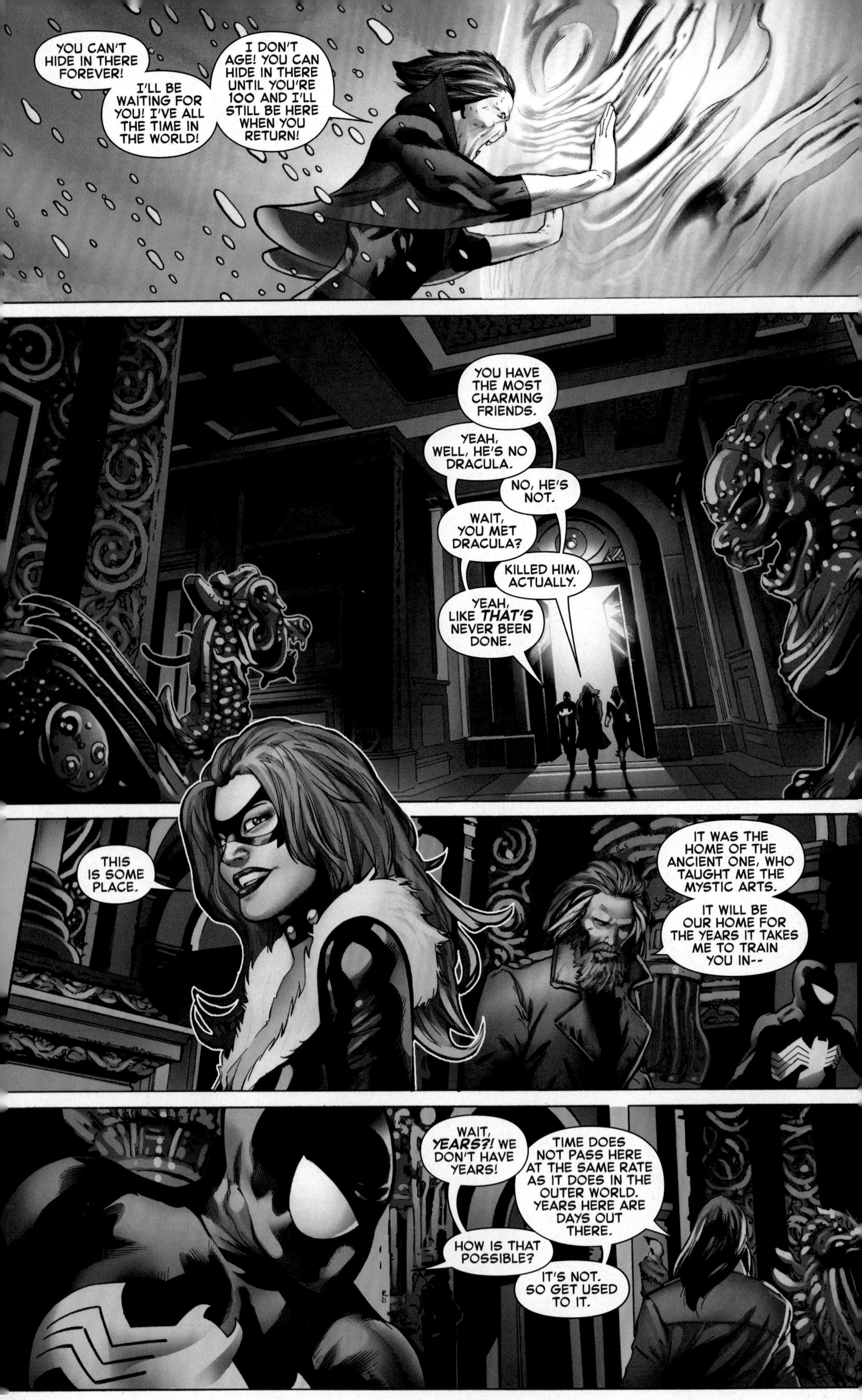

YOU CAN'T HIDE IN THERE FOREVER!
I'LL BE WAITING FOR YOU! I'VE ALL THE TIME IN THE WORLD!
I DON'T AGE! YOU CAN HIDE IN THERE UNTIL YOU'RE 100 AND I'LL STILL BE HERE WHEN YOU RETURN!
YOU HAVE THE MOST CHARMING FRIENDS.
YEAH, WELL, HE'S NO DRACULA.
NO, HE'S NOT.
WAIT, YOU MET DRACULA?
KILLED HIM, ACTUALLY.
YEAH, LIKE *THAT'S* NEVER BEEN DONE.
THIS IS SOME PLACE.
IT WAS THE HOME OF THE ANCIENT ONE, WHO TAUGHT ME THE MYSTIC ARTS.
IT WILL BE OUR HOME FOR THE YEARS IT TAKES ME TO TRAIN YOU IN--
WAIT, *YEARS?!* WE DON'T HAVE YEARS!
TIME DOES NOT PASS HERE AT THE SAME RATE AS IT DOES IN THE OUTER WORLD. YEARS HERE ARE DAYS OUT THERE.
HOW IS THAT POSSIBLE?
IT'S NOT. SO GET USED TO IT.

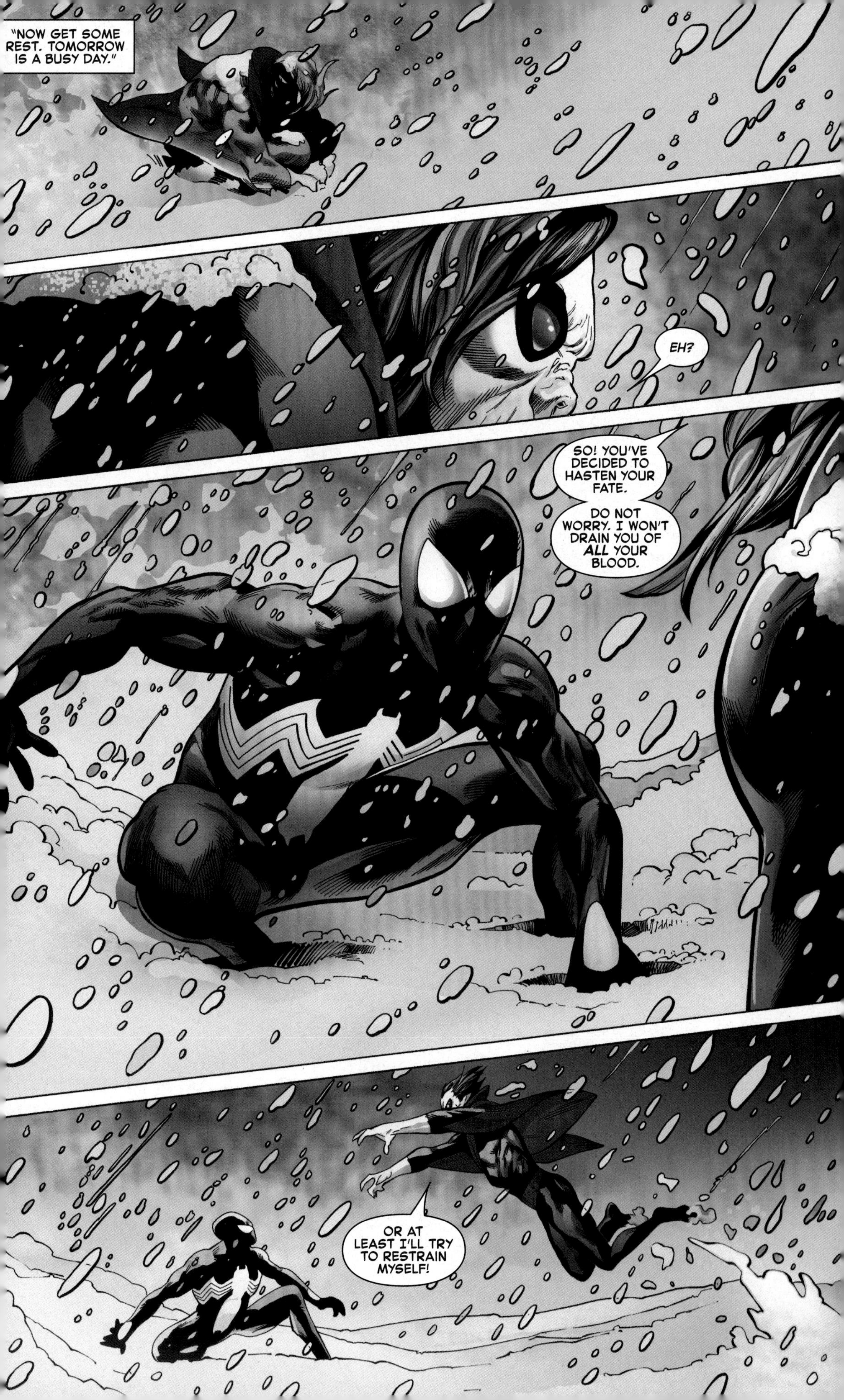
"NOW GET SOME REST. TOMORROW IS A BUSY DAY."
EH?
SO! YOU'VE DECIDED TO HASTEN YOUR FATE.
DO NOT WORRY. I WON'T DRAIN YOU OF ALL YOUR BLOOD.
OR AT LEAST I'LL TRY TO RESTRAIN MYSELF!

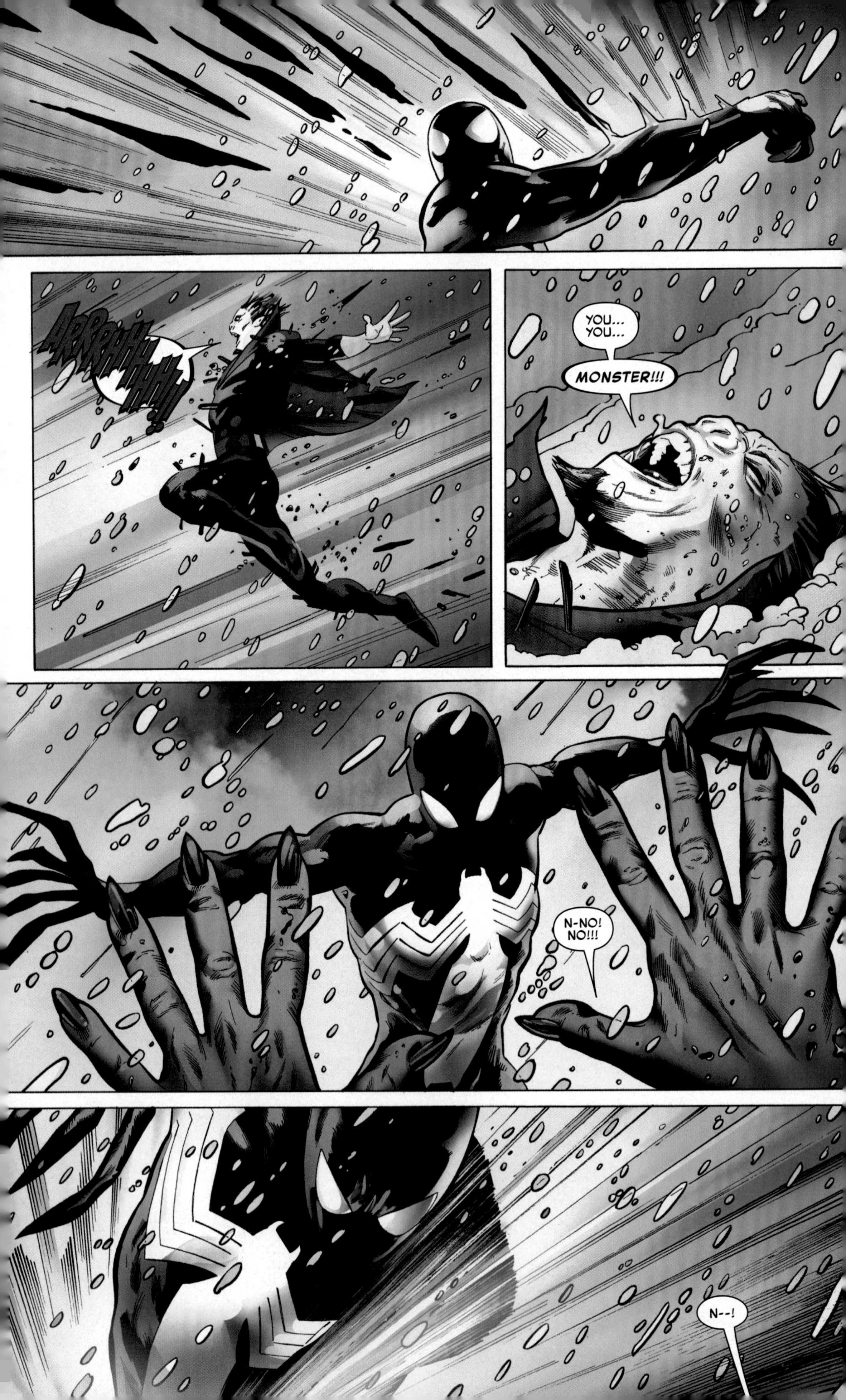
ARRRAHHHHH!!
YOU... YOU...
MONSTER!!!
N-NO! NO!!!
N--!

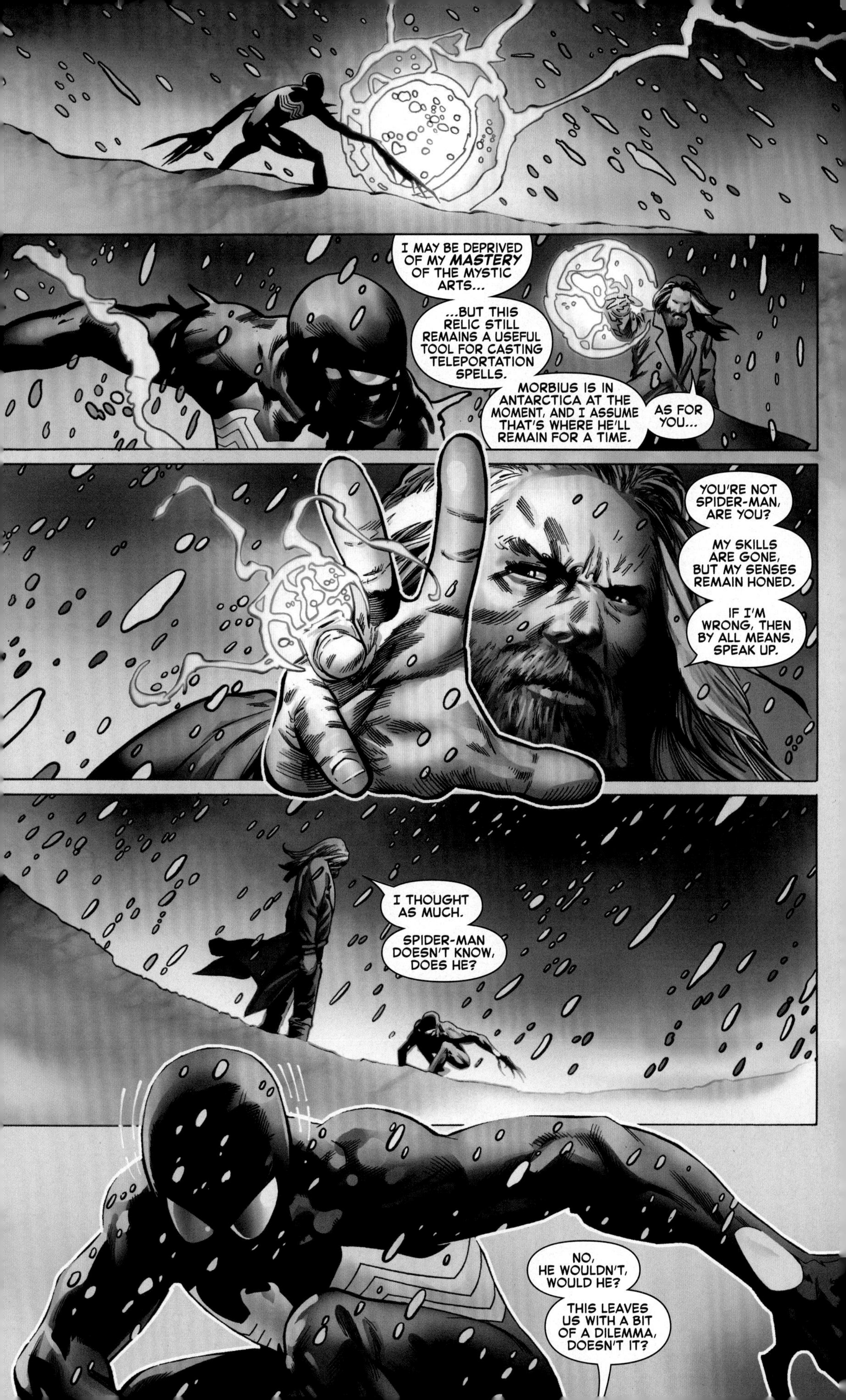
I MAY BE DEPRIVED OF MY *MASTERY* OF THE MYSTIC ARTS...
...BUT THIS RELIC STILL REMAINS A USEFUL TOOL FOR CASTING TELEPORTATION SPELLS.
MORBIUS IS IN ANTARCTICA AT THE MOMENT, AND I ASSUME THAT'S WHERE HE'LL REMAIN FOR A TIME.
AS FOR YOU...
YOU'RE NOT SPIDER-MAN, ARE YOU?
MY SKILLS ARE GONE, BUT MY SENSES REMAIN HONED.
IF I'M WRONG, THEN BY ALL MEANS, SPEAK UP.
I THOUGHT AS MUCH.
SPIDER-MAN DOESN'T KNOW, DOES HE?
NO, HE WOULDN'T, WOULD HE?
THIS LEAVES US WITH A BIT OF A DILEMMA, DOESN'T IT?

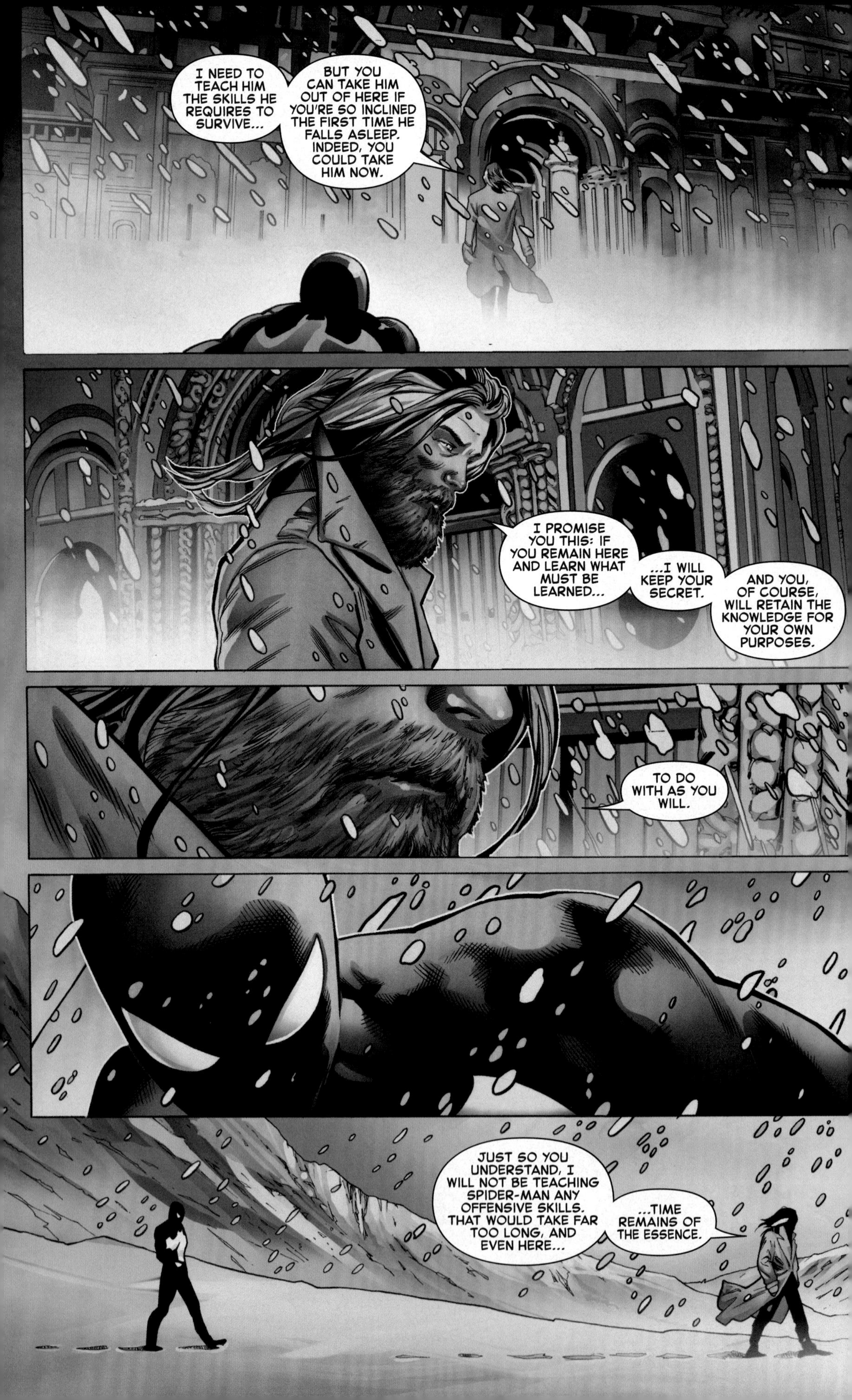
I NEED TO TEACH HIM THE SKILLS HE REQUIRES TO SURVIVE...
BUT YOU CAN TAKE HIM OUT OF HERE IF YOU'RE SO INCLINED THE FIRST TIME HE FALLS ASLEEP. INDEED, YOU COULD TAKE HIM NOW.
I PROMISE YOU THIS: IF YOU REMAIN HERE AND LEARN WHAT MUST BE LEARNED...
...I WILL KEEP YOUR SECRET.
AND YOU, OF COURSE, WILL RETAIN THE KNOWLEDGE FOR YOUR OWN PURPOSES.
TO DO WITH AS YOU WILL.
JUST SO YOU UNDERSTAND, I WILL NOT BE TEACHING SPIDER-MAN ANY OFFENSIVE SKILLS. THAT WOULD TAKE FAR TOO LONG, AND EVEN HERE...
...TIME REMAINS OF THE ESSENCE.

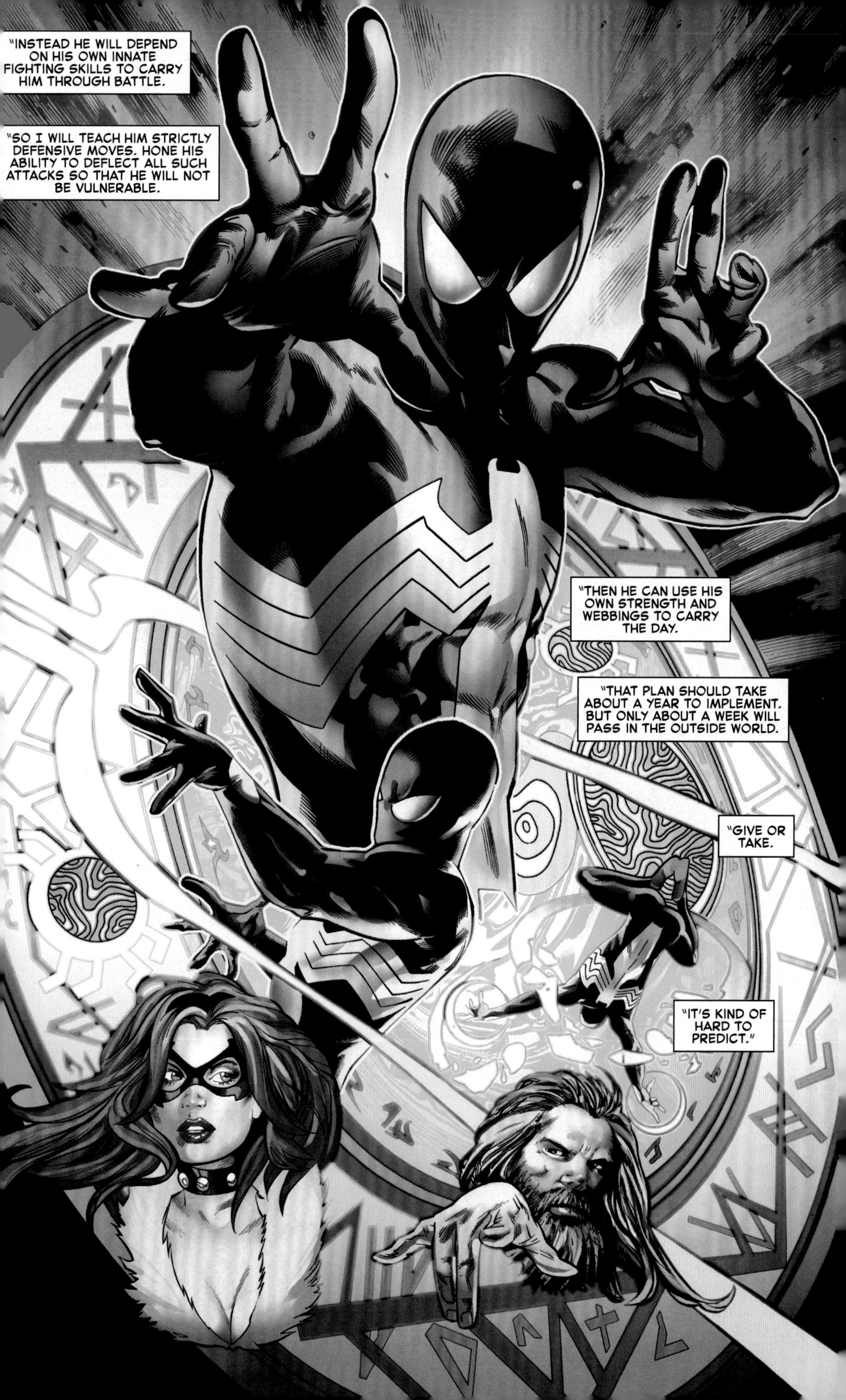
"INSTEAD HE WILL DEPEND ON HIS OWN INNATE FIGHTING SKILLS TO CARRY HIM THROUGH BATTLE.
"SO I WILL TEACH HIM STRICTLY DEFENSIVE MOVES. HONE HIS ABILITY TO DEFLECT ALL SUCH ATTACKS SO THAT HE WILL NOT BE VULNERABLE.
"THEN HE CAN USE HIS OWN STRENGTH AND WEBBINGS TO CARRY THE DAY.
"THAT PLAN SHOULD TAKE ABOUT A YEAR TO IMPLEMENT. BUT ONLY ABOUT A WEEK WILL PASS IN THE OUTSIDE WORLD.
"GIVE OR TAKE.
"IT'S KIND OF HARD TO PREDICT."

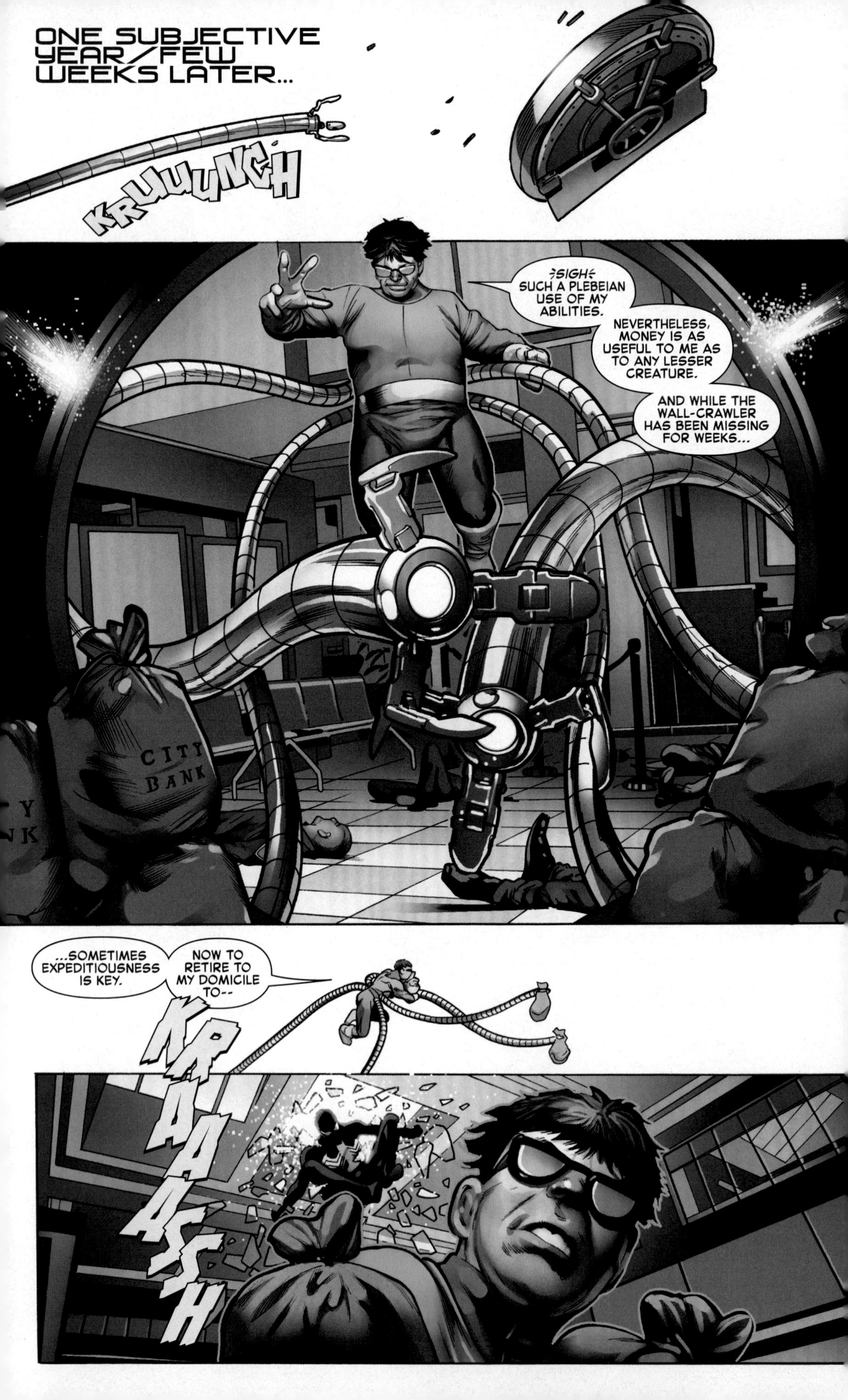
ONE SUBJECTIVE YEAR/FEW WEEKS LATER...
KRUUUUNCH
⚡SIGH⚡ SUCH A PLEBEIAN USE OF MY ABILITIES.
NEVERTHELESS, MONEY IS AS USEFUL TO ME AS TO ANY LESSER CREATURE.
AND WHILE THE WALL-CRAWLER HAS BEEN MISSING FOR WEEKS...
CITY BANK
...SOMETIMES EXPEDITIOUSNESS IS KEY.
NOW TO RETIRE TO MY DOMICILE TO--
KRAAAASH

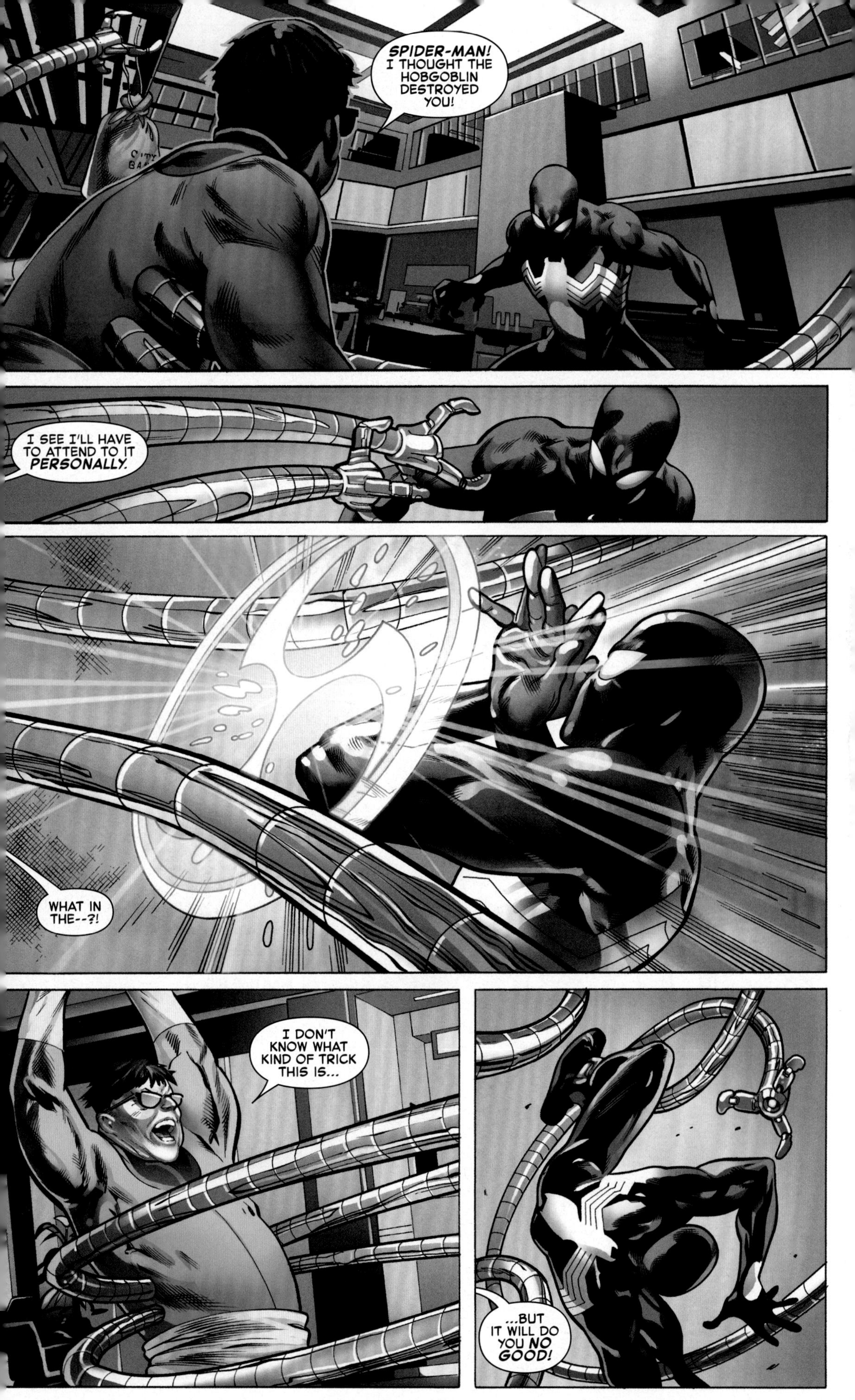
CITY BANK
SPIDER-MAN! I THOUGHT THE HOBGOBLIN DESTROYED YOU!
I SEE I'LL HAVE TO ATTEND TO IT *PERSONALLY.*
WHAT IN THE--?!
I DON'T KNOW WHAT KIND OF TRICK THIS IS...
...BUT IT WILL DO YOU *NO GOOD!*

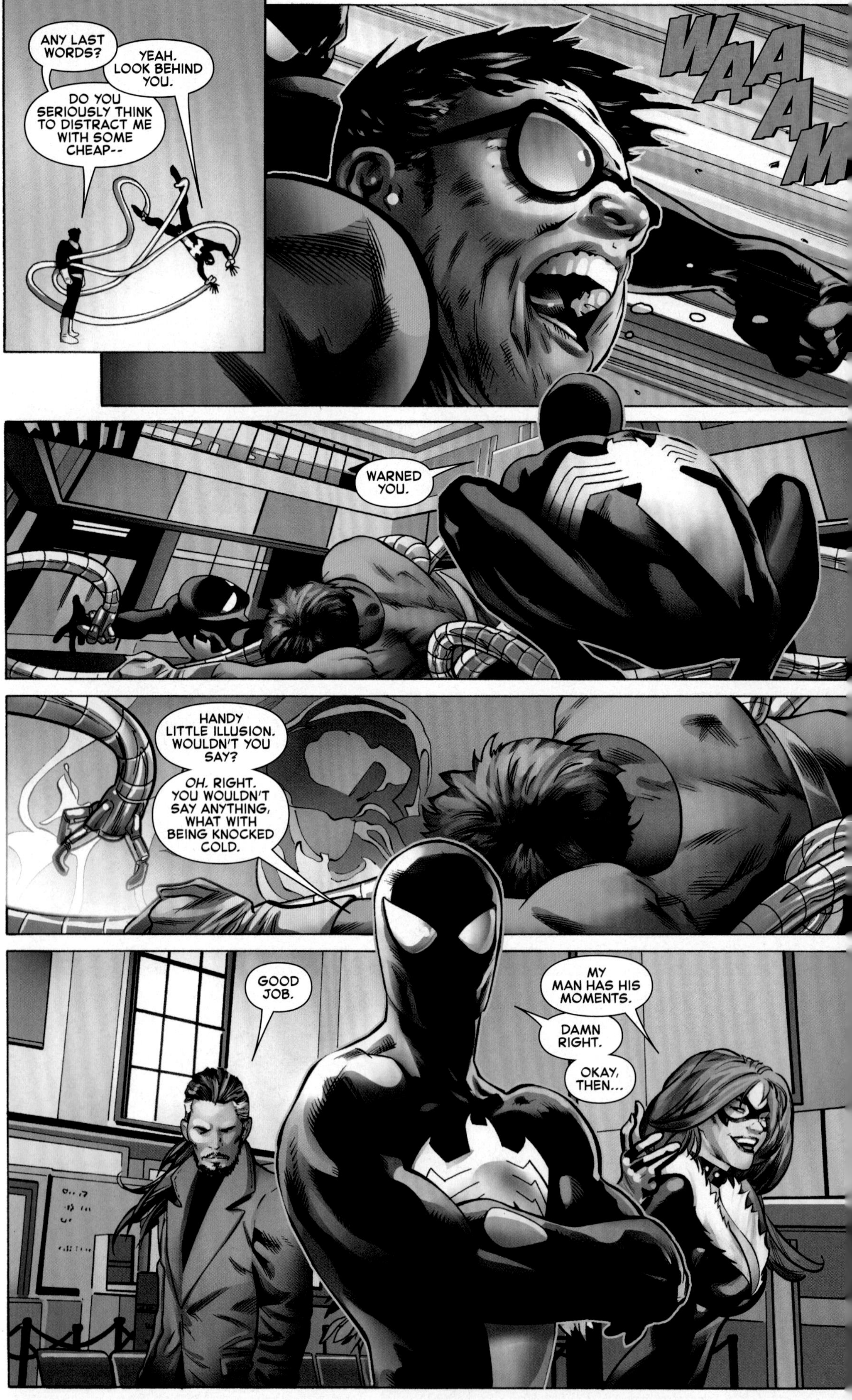
ANY LAST WORDS?
YEAH. LOOK BEHIND YOU.
DO YOU SERIOUSLY THINK TO DISTRACT ME WITH SOME CHEAP--
WAAAAM
WARNED YOU.
HANDY LITTLE ILLUSION. WOULDN'T YOU SAY?
OH. RIGHT. YOU WOULDN'T SAY ANYTHING, WHAT WITH BEING KNOCKED COLD.
GOOD JOB.
MY MAN HAS HIS MOMENTS.
DAMN RIGHT.
OKAY, THEN...

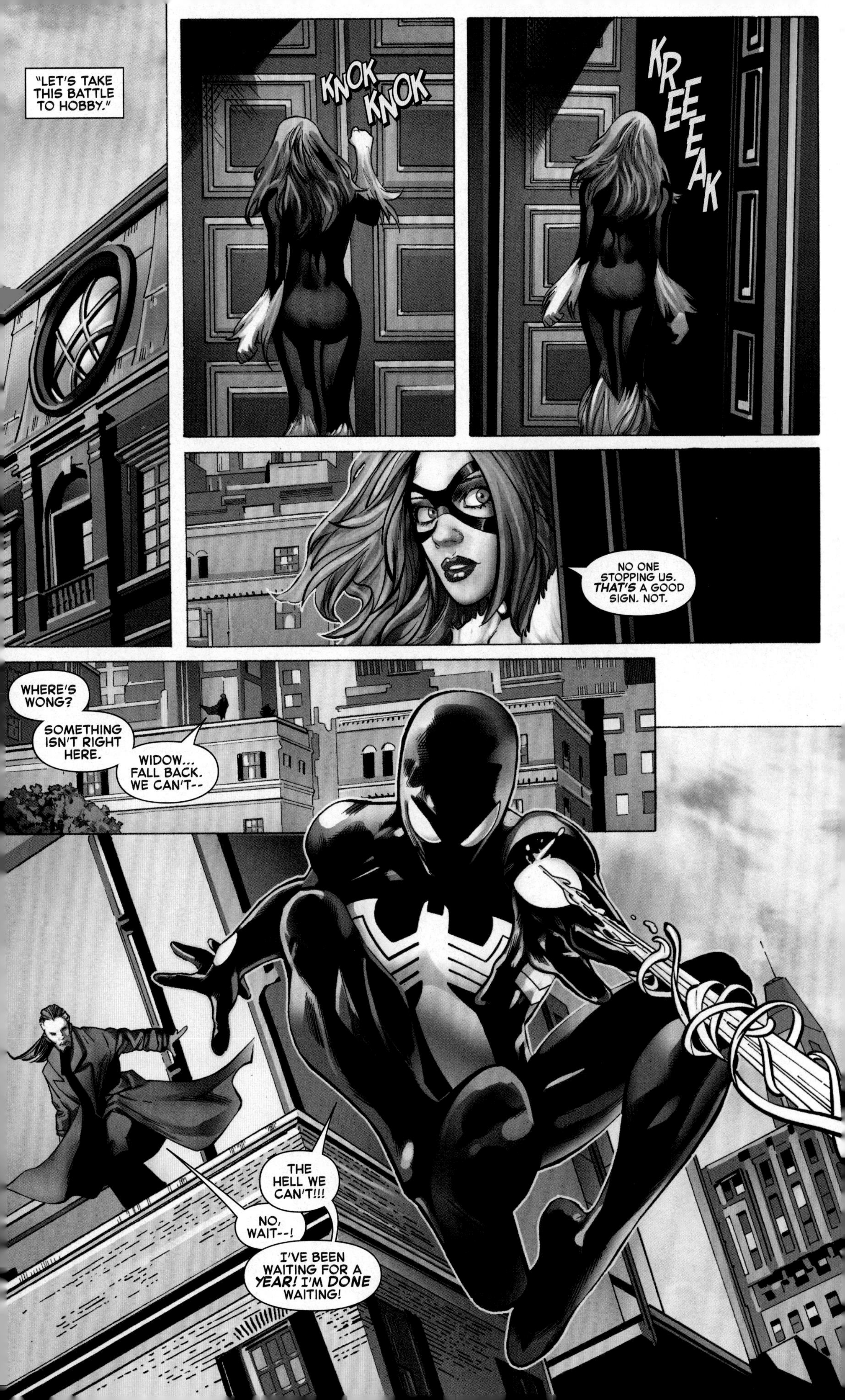
"LET'S TAKE THIS BATTLE TO HOBBY."
KNOK KNOK
KREEEAK
NO ONE STOPPING US. THAT'S A GOOD SIGN. NOT.
WHERE'S WONG?
SOMETHING ISN'T RIGHT HERE.
WIDOW... FALL BACK. WE CAN'T--
THE HELL WE CAN'T!!!
NO, WAIT--!
I'VE BEEN WAITING FOR A YEAR! I'M DONE WAITING!

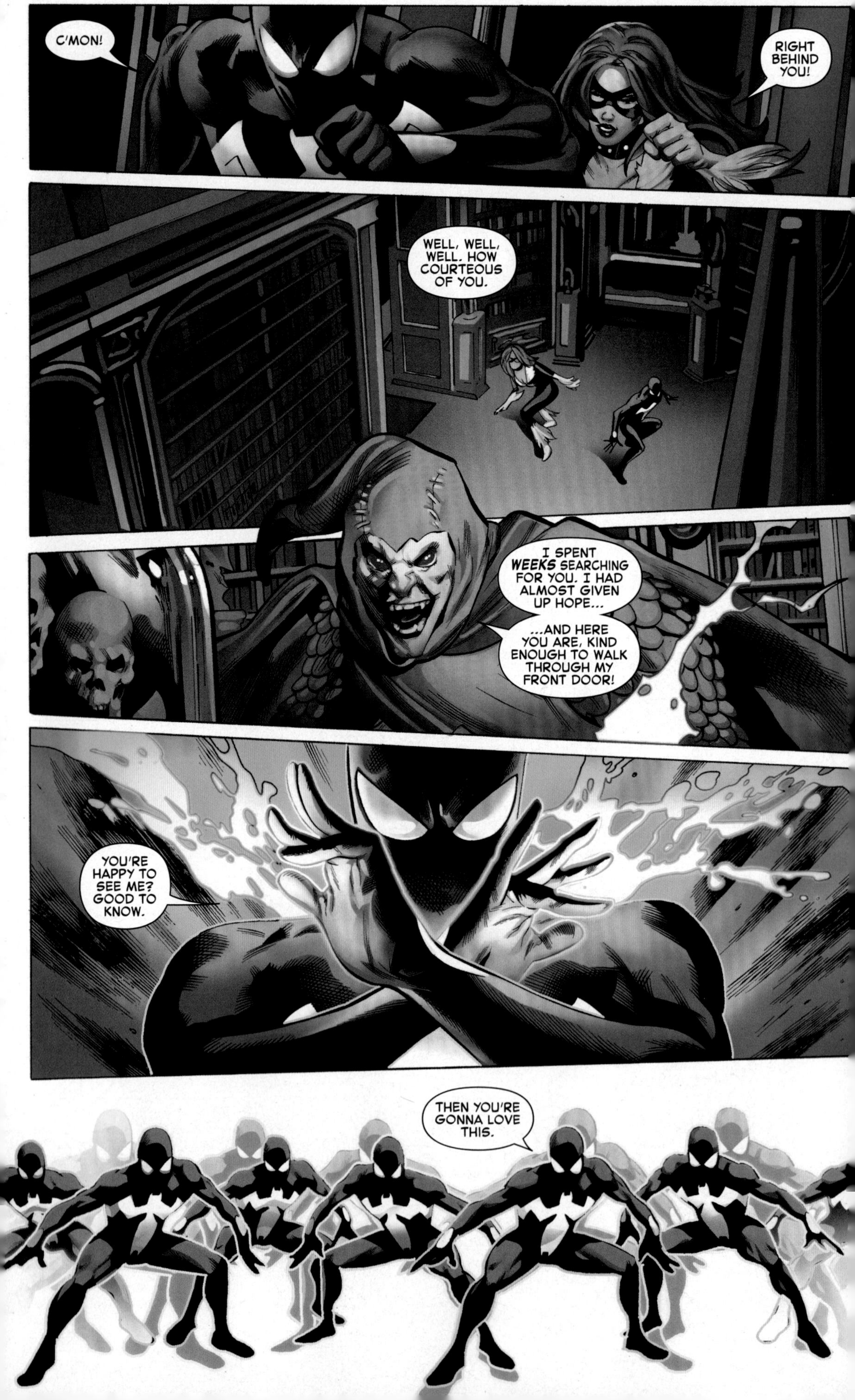
C'MON!
RIGHT BEHIND YOU!
WELL, WELL, WELL. HOW COURTEOUS OF YOU.
I SPENT WEEKS SEARCHING FOR YOU. I HAD ALMOST GIVEN UP HOPE...
...AND HERE YOU ARE, KIND ENOUGH TO WALK THROUGH MY FRONT DOOR!
YOU'RE HAPPY TO SEE ME? GOOD TO KNOW.
THEN YOU'RE GONNA LOVE THIS.

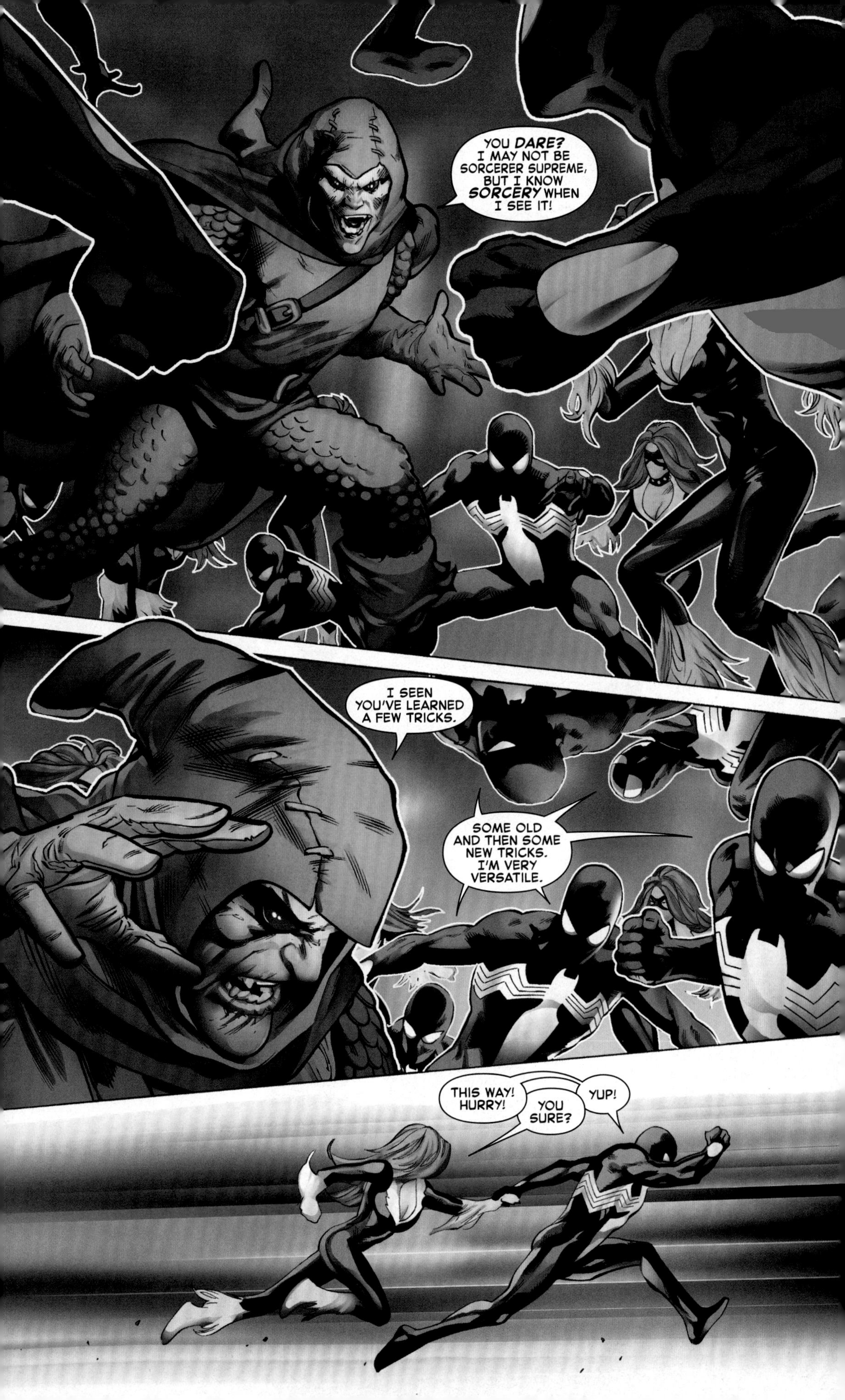

YOU DARE? I MAY NOT BE SORCERER SUPREME, BUT I KNOW SORCERY WHEN I SEE IT!
I SEEN YOU'VE LEARNED A FEW TRICKS.
SOME OLD AND THEN SOME NEW TRICKS. I'M VERY VERSATILE.
THIS WAY! HURRY!
YOU SURE?
YUP!

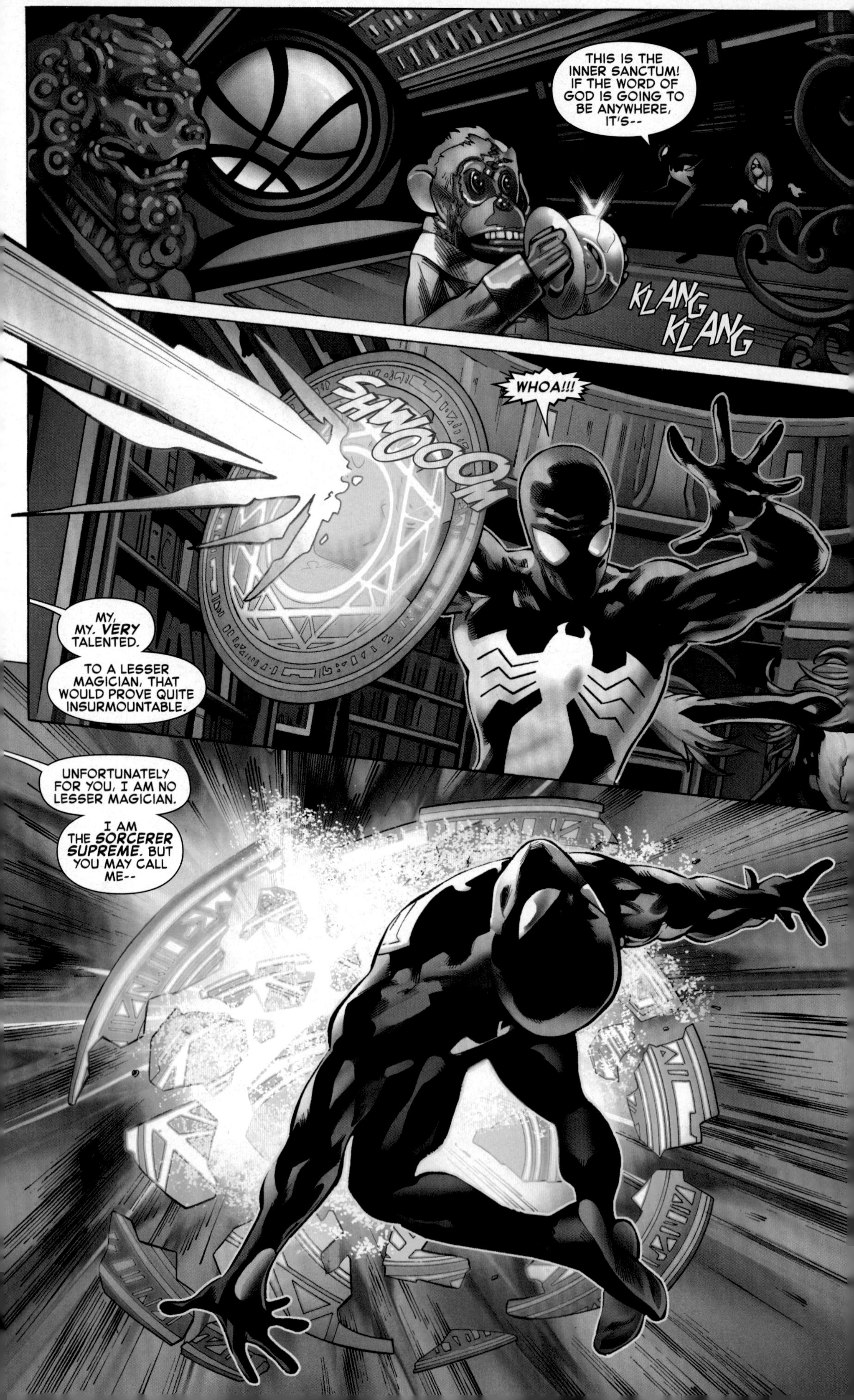
THIS IS THE INNER SANCTUM! IF THE WORD OF GOD IS GOING TO BE ANYWHERE, IT'S--
KLANG KLANG
SHWOOOOM
WHOA!!!
MY, MY. VERY TALENTED.
TO A LESSER MAGICIAN, THAT WOULD PROVE QUITE INSURMOUNTABLE.
UNFORTUNATELY FOR YOU, I AM NO LESSER MAGICIAN.
I AM THE SORCERER SUPREME. BUT YOU MAY CALL ME--

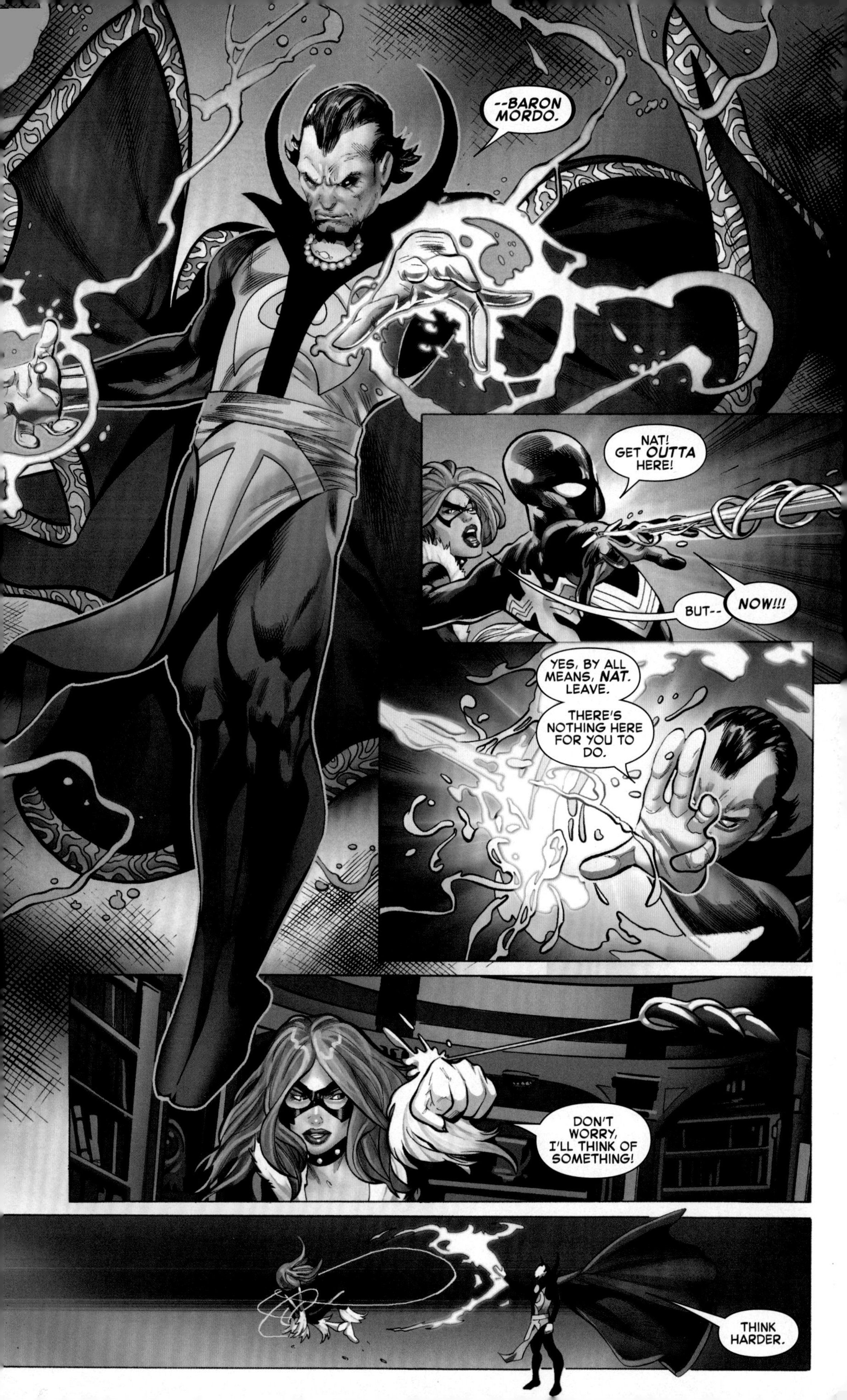
--BARON MORDO.
NAT! GET OUTTA HERE!
BUT--
NOW!!!
YES, BY ALL MEANS, NAT. LEAVE.
THERE'S NOTHING HERE FOR YOU TO DO.
DON'T WORRY, I'LL THINK OF SOMETHING!
THINK HARDER.

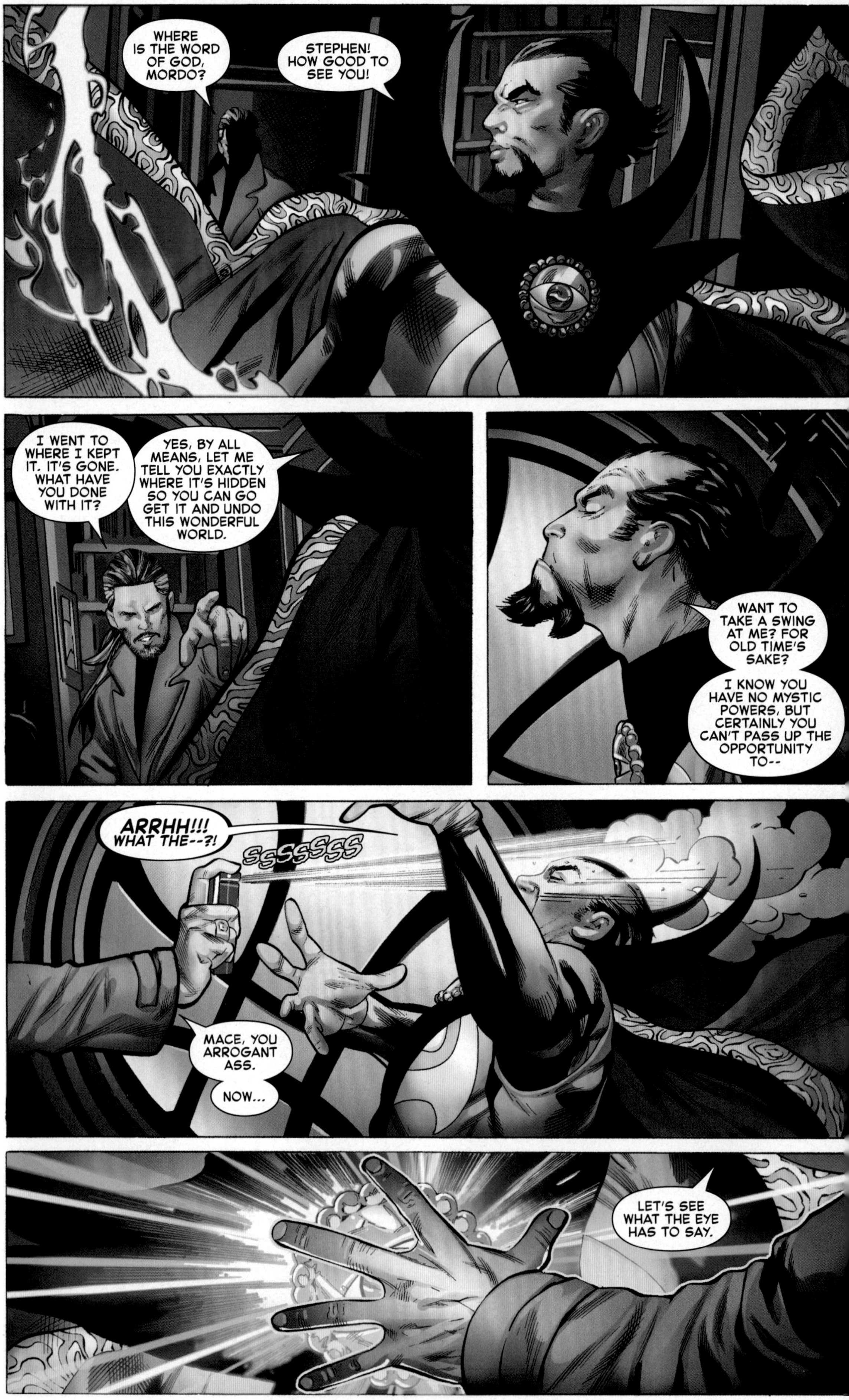
WHERE IS THE WORD OF GOD, MORDO?
STEPHEN! HOW GOOD TO SEE YOU!
I WENT TO WHERE I KEPT IT. IT'S GONE. WHAT HAVE YOU DONE WITH IT?
YES, BY ALL MEANS, LET ME TELL YOU EXACTLY WHERE IT'S HIDDEN SO YOU CAN GO GET IT AND UNDO THIS WONDERFUL WORLD.
WANT TO TAKE A SWING AT ME? FOR OLD TIME'S SAKE?
I KNOW YOU HAVE NO MYSTIC POWERS, BUT CERTAINLY YOU CAN'T PASS UP THE OPPORTUNITY TO--
ARRHH!!! WHAT THE--?!
SSSSSSS
MACE, YOU ARROGANT ASS.
NOW...
LET'S SEE WHAT THE EYE HAS TO SAY.

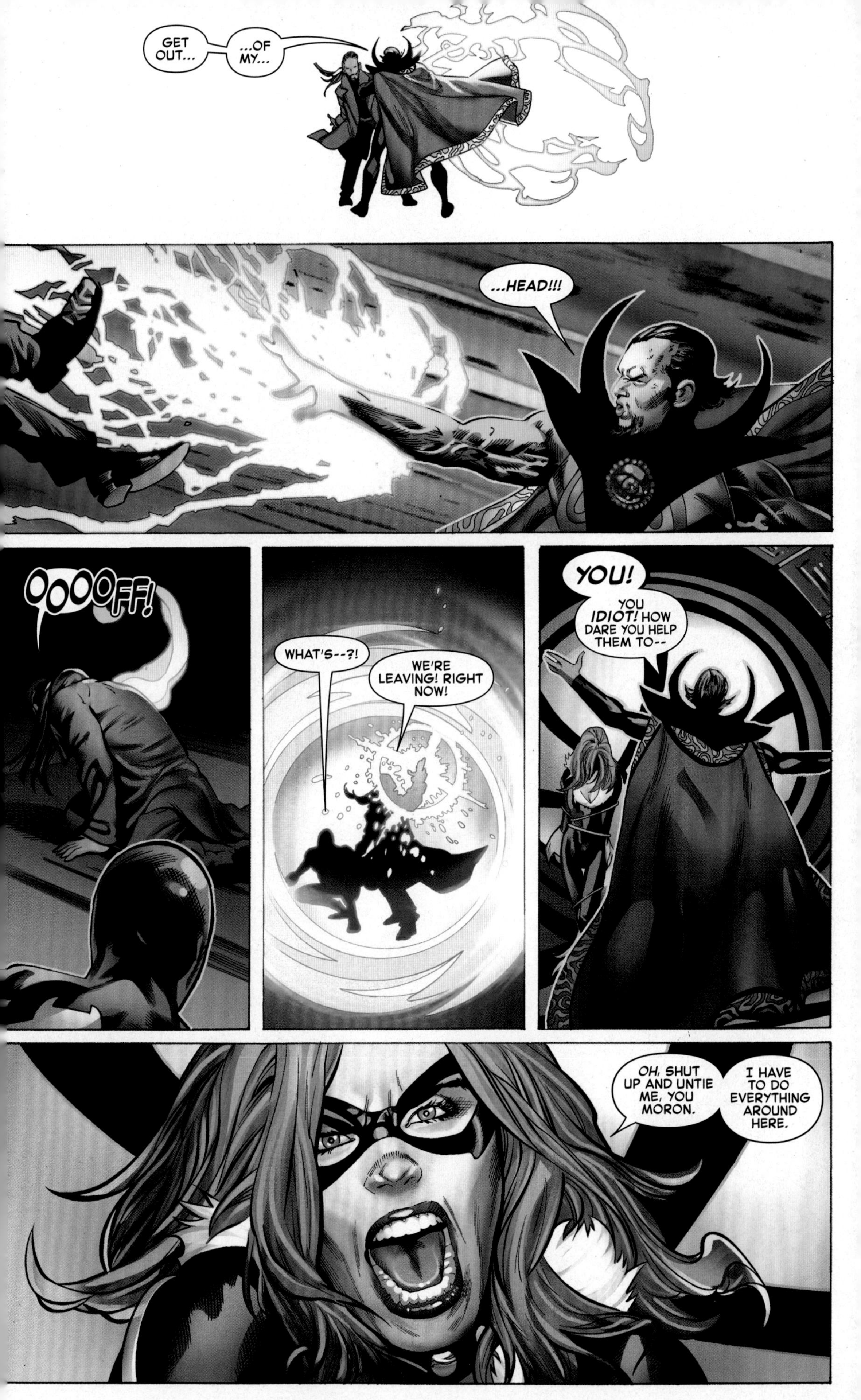
GET OUT...
...OF MY...
...HEAD!!!
OOOOFF!
WHAT'S--?!
WE'RE LEAVING! RIGHT NOW!
YOU!
YOU IDIOT! HOW DARE YOU HELP THEM TO--
OH, SHUT UP AND UNTIE ME, YOU MORON.
I HAVE TO DO EVERYTHING AROUND HERE.

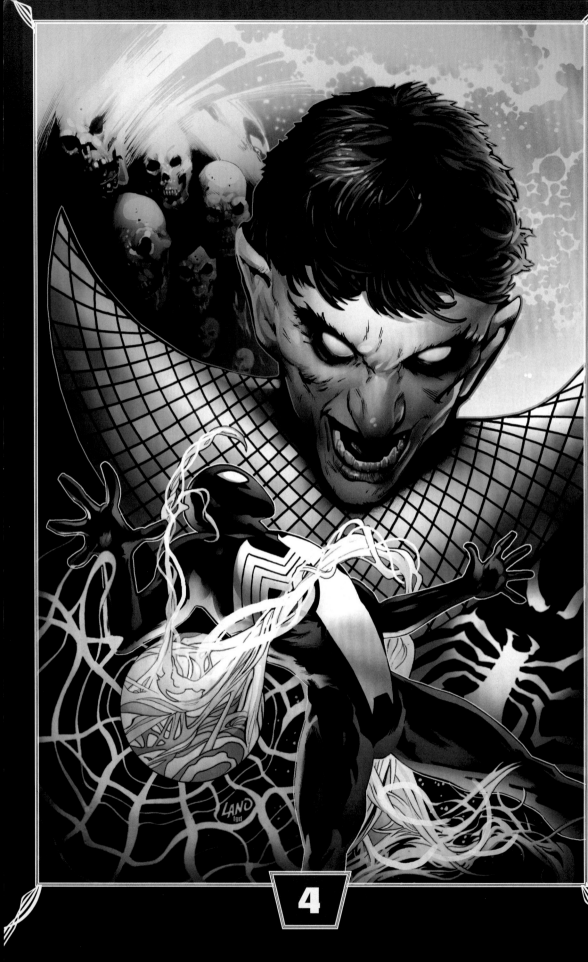

4

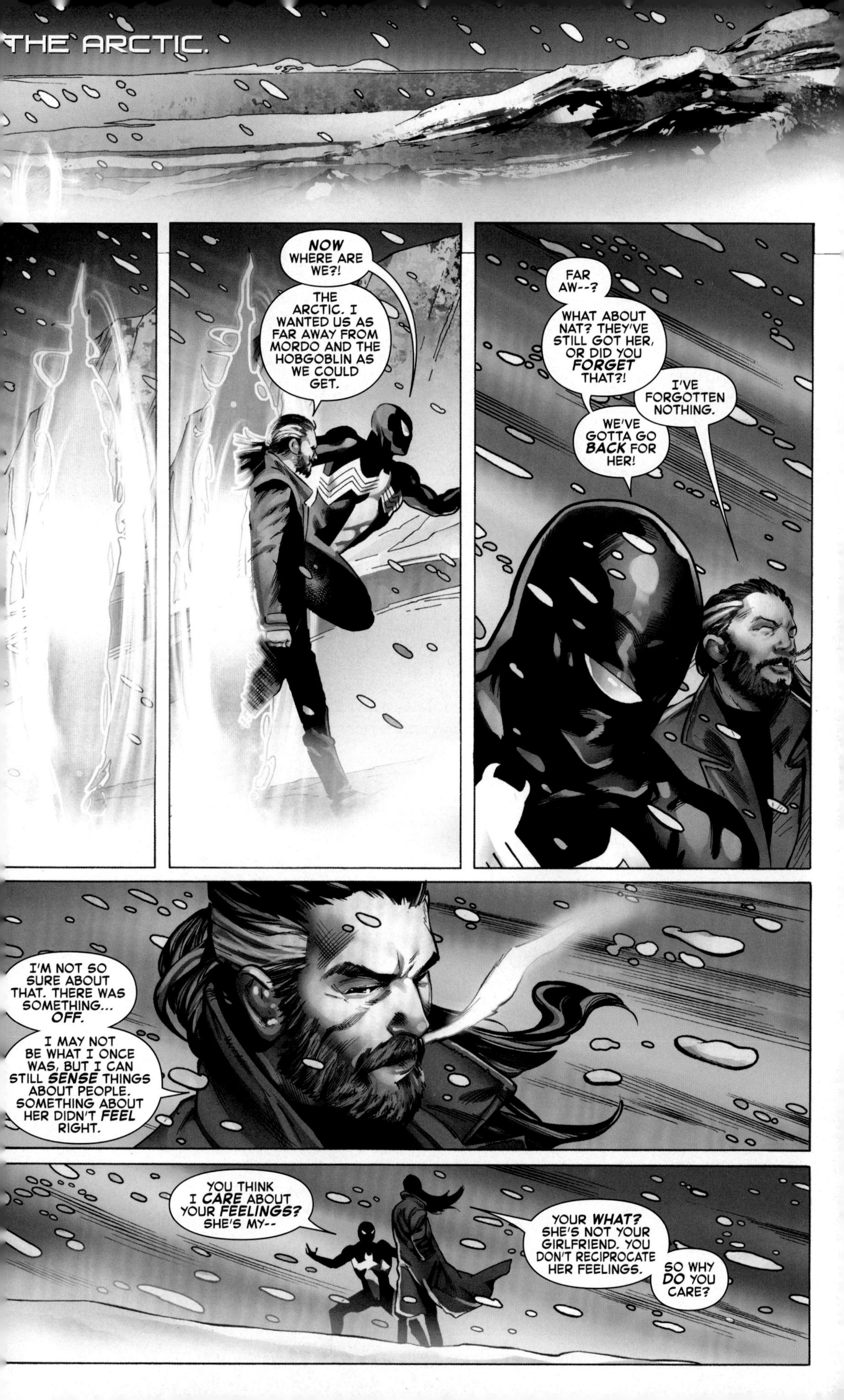
THE ARCTIC.
NOW WHERE ARE WE?!
THE ARCTIC. I WANTED US AS FAR AWAY FROM MORDO AND THE HOBGOBLIN AS WE COULD GET.
FAR AW--?
WHAT ABOUT NAT? THEY'VE STILL GOT HER, OR DID YOU FORGET THAT?!
I'VE FORGOTTEN NOTHING.
WE'VE GOTTA GO BACK FOR HER!
I'M NOT SO SURE ABOUT THAT. THERE WAS SOMETHING... OFF.
I MAY NOT BE WHAT I ONCE WAS, BUT I CAN STILL SENSE THINGS ABOUT PEOPLE. SOMETHING ABOUT HER DIDN'T FEEL RIGHT.
YOU THINK I CARE ABOUT YOUR FEELINGS? SHE'S MY--
YOUR WHAT? SHE'S NOT YOUR GIRLFRIEND. YOU DON'T RECIPROCATE HER FEELINGS.
SO WHY DO YOU CARE?

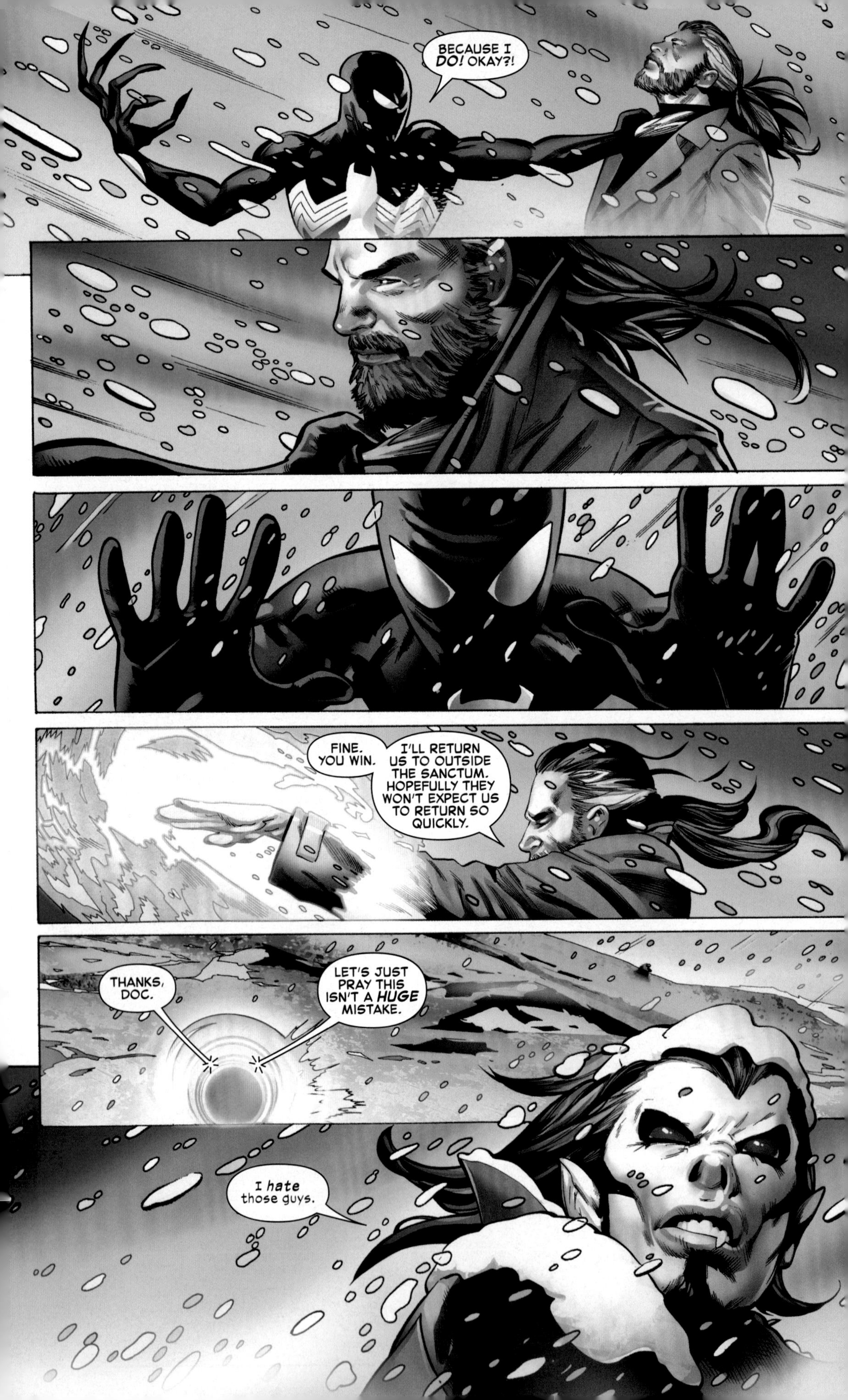
BECAUSE I *DO!* OKAY?!
FINE. YOU WIN.
I'LL RETURN US TO OUTSIDE THE SANCTUM. HOPEFULLY THEY WON'T EXPECT US TO RETURN SO QUICKLY.
THANKS, DOC.
LET'S JUST PRAY THIS ISN'T A *HUGE* MISTAKE.
I *hate* those guys.

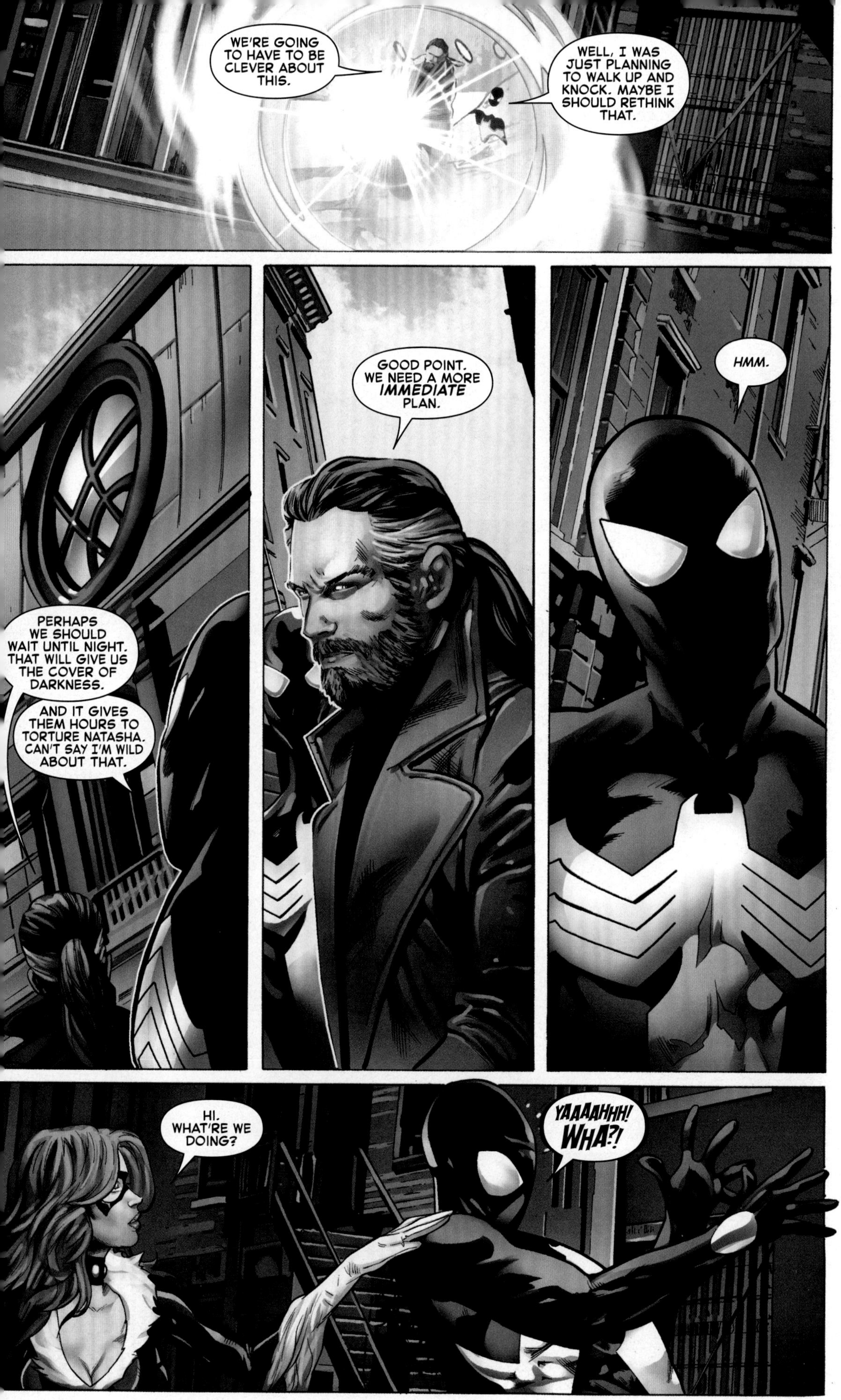
WE'RE GOING TO HAVE TO BE CLEVER ABOUT THIS.
WELL, I WAS JUST PLANNING TO WALK UP AND KNOCK. MAYBE I SHOULD RETHINK THAT.
PERHAPS WE SHOULD WAIT UNTIL NIGHT. THAT WILL GIVE US THE COVER OF DARKNESS.
AND IT GIVES THEM HOURS TO TORTURE NATASHA. CAN'T SAY I'M WILD ABOUT THAT.
GOOD POINT. WE NEED A MORE *IMMEDIATE* PLAN.
HMM.
HI. WHAT'RE WE DOING?
YAAAAHHH! WHA?!

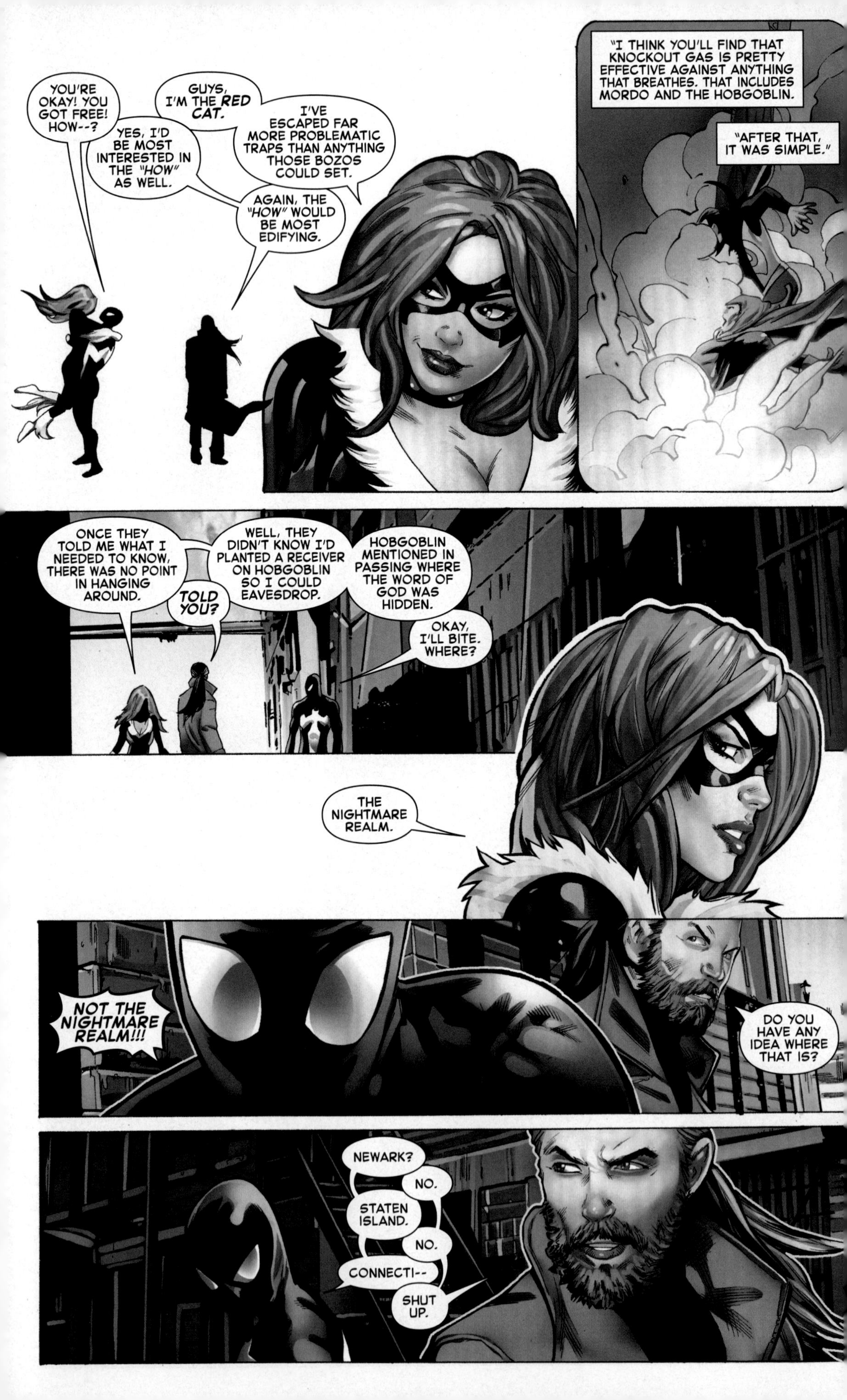
YOU'RE OKAY! YOU GOT FREE! HOW--?
YES, I'D BE MOST INTERESTED IN THE "HOW" AS WELL.
GUYS, I'M THE RED CAT.
I'VE ESCAPED FAR MORE PROBLEMATIC TRAPS THAN ANYTHING THOSE BOZOS COULD SET.
AGAIN, THE "HOW" WOULD BE MOST EDIFYING.
"I THINK YOU'LL FIND THAT KNOCKOUT GAS IS PRETTY EFFECTIVE AGAINST ANYTHING THAT BREATHES. THAT INCLUDES MORDO AND THE HOBGOBLIN.
"AFTER THAT, IT WAS SIMPLE."
ONCE THEY TOLD ME WHAT I NEEDED TO KNOW, THERE WAS NO POINT IN HANGING AROUND.
TOLD YOU?
WELL, THEY DIDN'T KNOW I'D PLANTED A RECEIVER ON HOBGOBLIN SO I COULD EAVESDROP.
HOBGOBLIN MENTIONED IN PASSING WHERE THE WORD OF GOD WAS HIDDEN.
OKAY, I'LL BITE. WHERE?
THE NIGHTMARE REALM.
NOT THE NIGHTMARE REALM!!!
DO YOU HAVE ANY IDEA WHERE THAT IS?
NEWARK?
NO.
STATEN ISLAND.
NO.
CONNECTI--
SHUT UP.

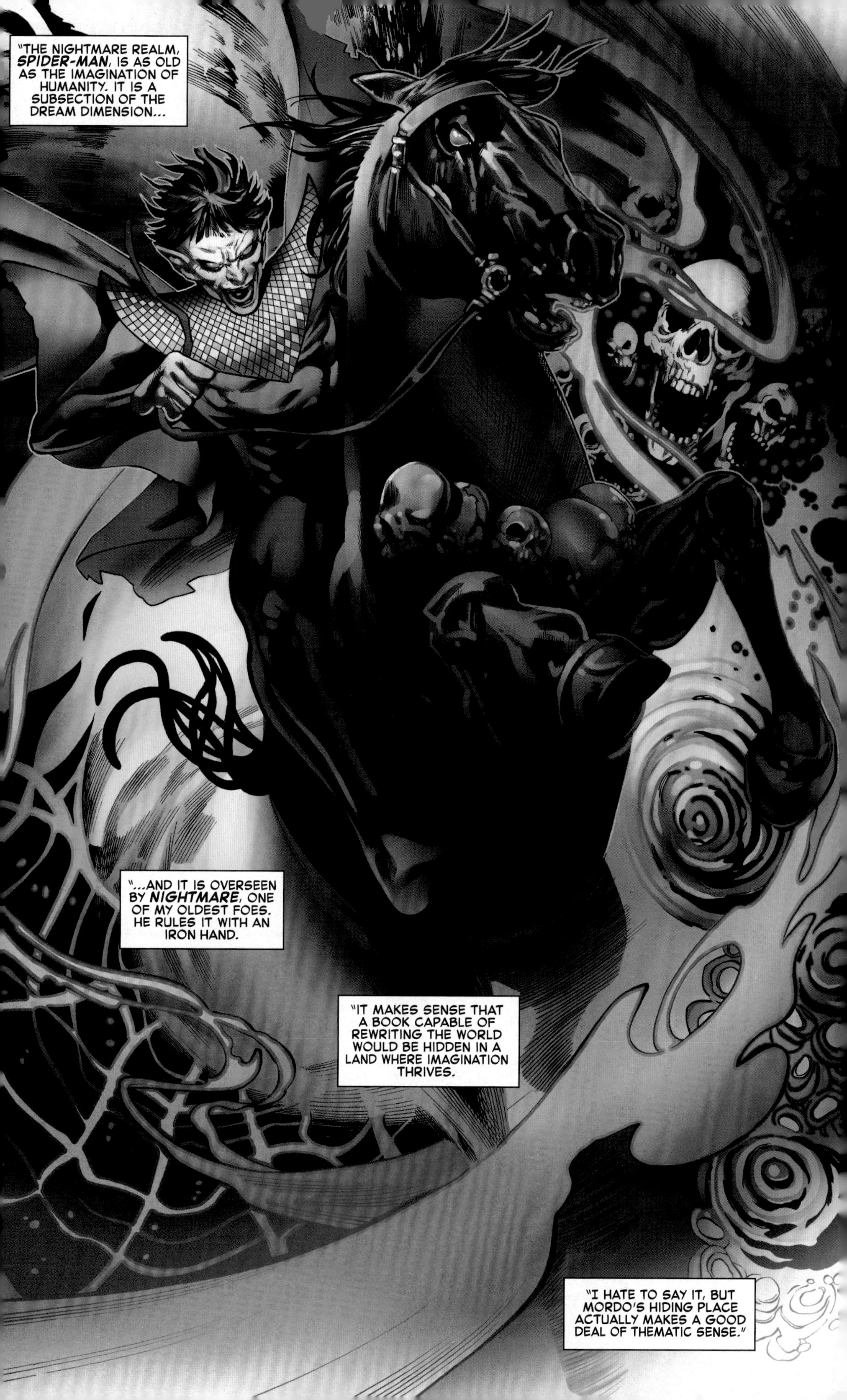
"THE NIGHTMARE REALM, SPIDER-MAN, IS AS OLD AS THE IMAGINATION OF HUMANITY. IT IS A SUBSECTION OF THE DREAM DIMENSION...
"...AND IT IS OVERSEEN BY NIGHTMARE, ONE OF MY OLDEST FOES. HE RULES IT WITH AN IRON HAND.
"IT MAKES SENSE THAT A BOOK CAPABLE OF REWRITING THE WORLD WOULD BE HIDDEN IN A LAND WHERE IMAGINATION THRIVES.
"I HATE TO SAY IT, BUT MORDO'S HIDING PLACE ACTUALLY MAKES A GOOD DEAL OF THEMATIC SENSE."

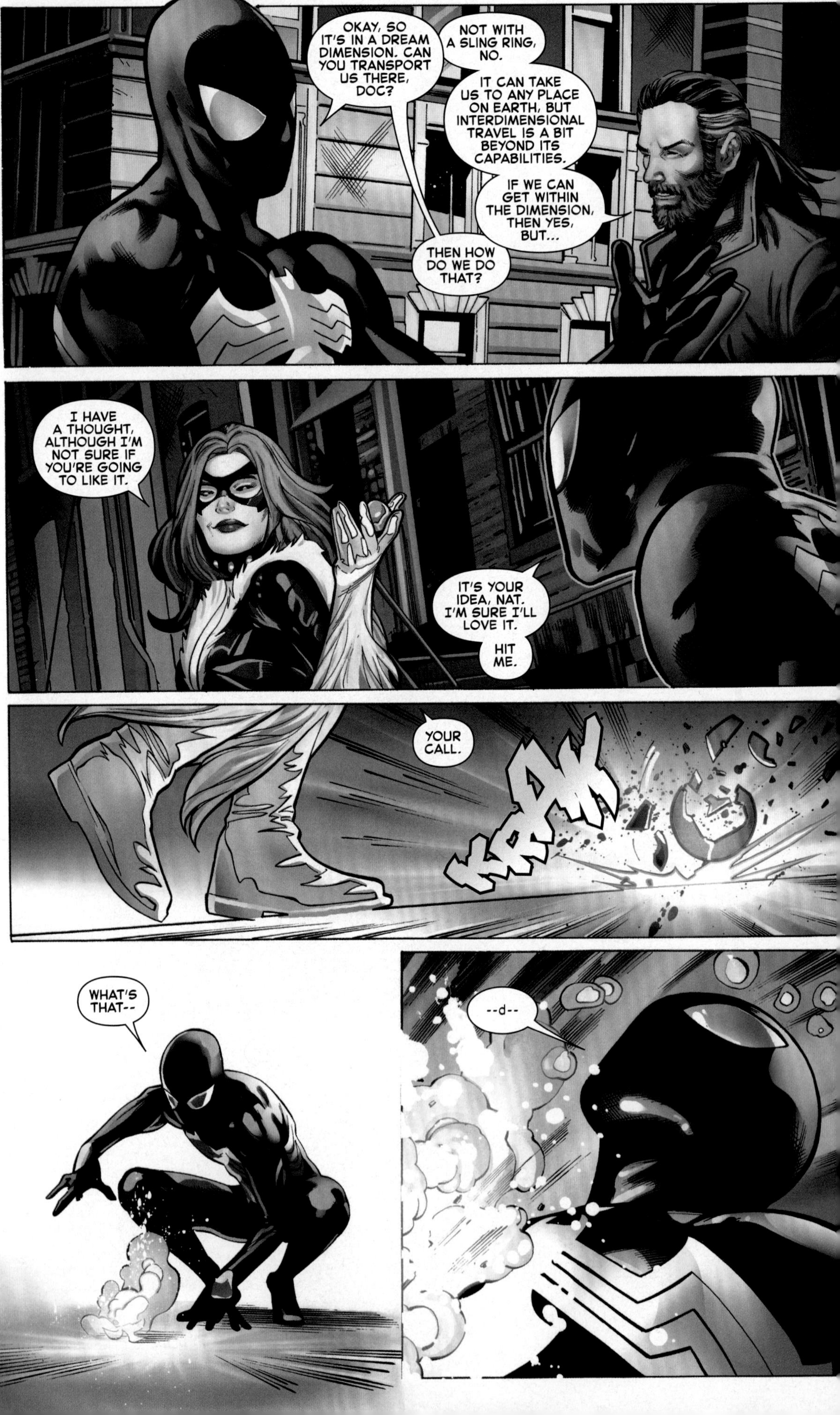

OKAY, SO IT'S IN A DREAM DIMENSION. CAN YOU TRANSPORT US THERE, DOC?
NOT WITH A SLING RING, NO.
IT CAN TAKE US TO ANY PLACE ON EARTH, BUT INTERDIMENSIONAL TRAVEL IS A BIT BEYOND ITS CAPABILITIES.
IF WE CAN GET WITHIN THE DIMENSION, THEN YES, BUT...
THEN HOW DO WE DO THAT?
I HAVE A THOUGHT, ALTHOUGH I'M NOT SURE IF YOU'RE GOING TO LIKE IT.
IT'S YOUR IDEA, NAT. I'M SURE I'LL LOVE IT.
HIT ME.
YOUR CALL.
KRAK
WHAT'S THAT--
--d--

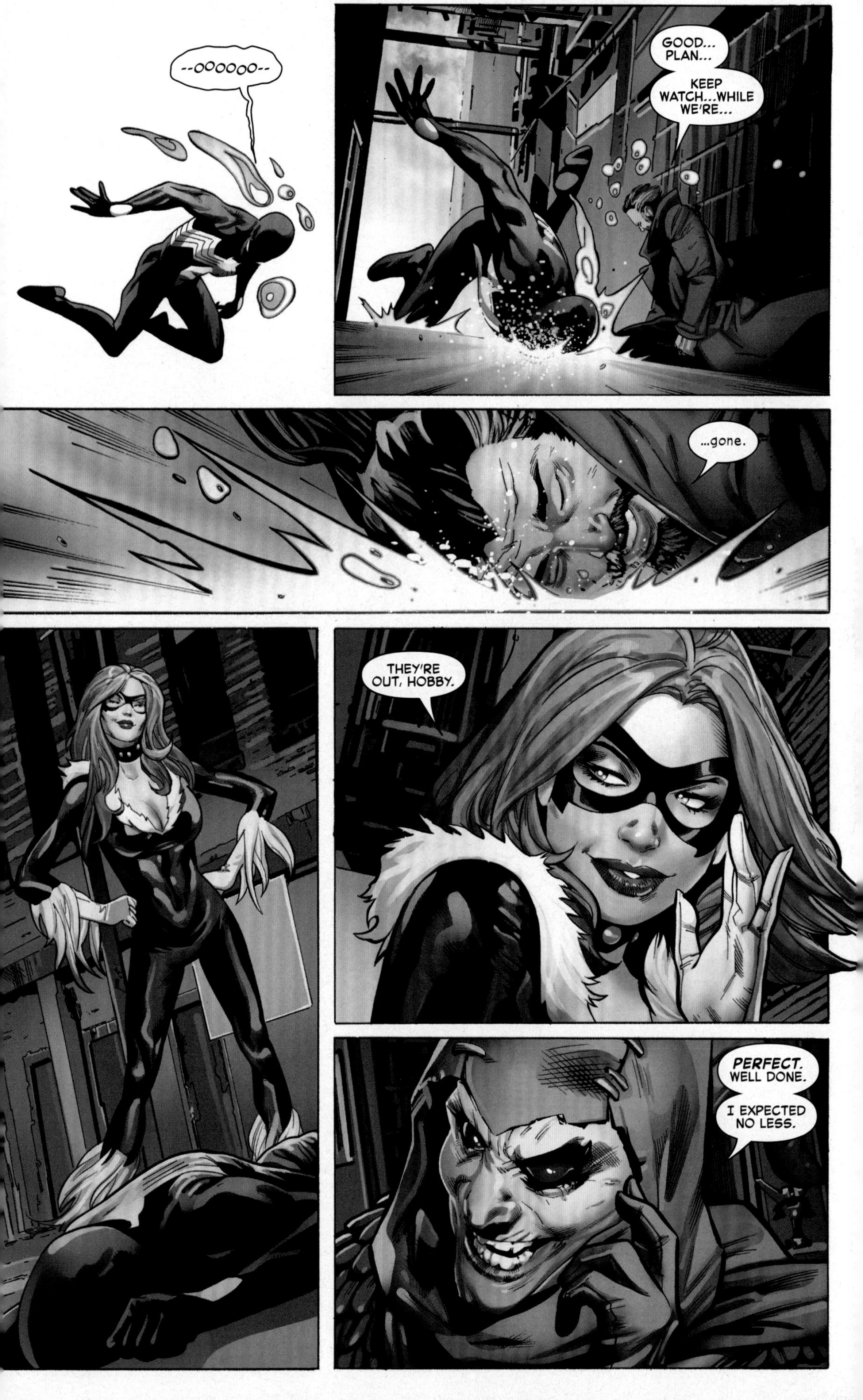
--OOOOOO--
GOOD... PLAN...
KEEP WATCH...WHILE WE'RE...
...gone.
THEY'RE OUT, HOBBY.
PERFECT. WELL DONE.
I EXPECTED NO LESS.

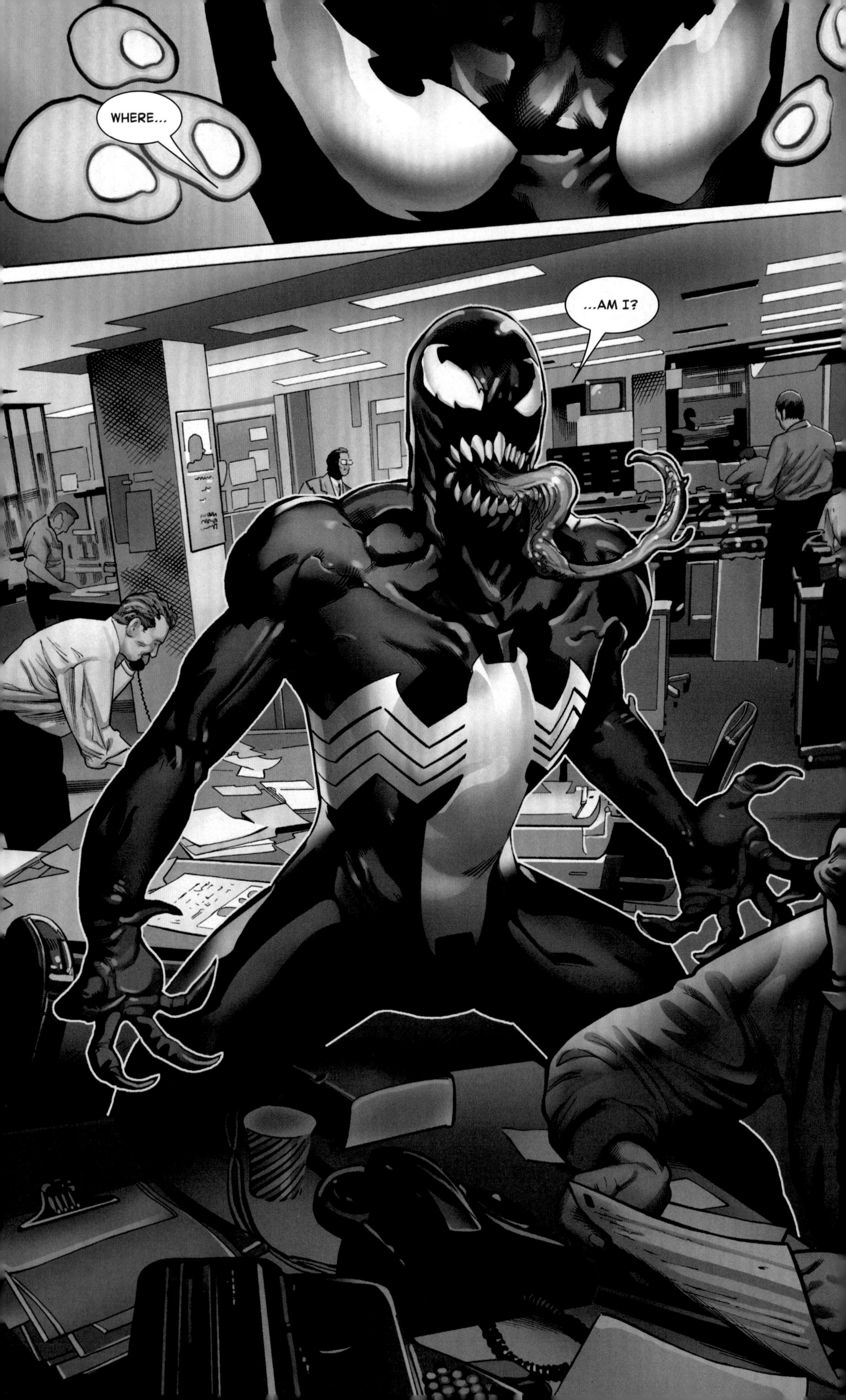
WHERE...
...AM I?

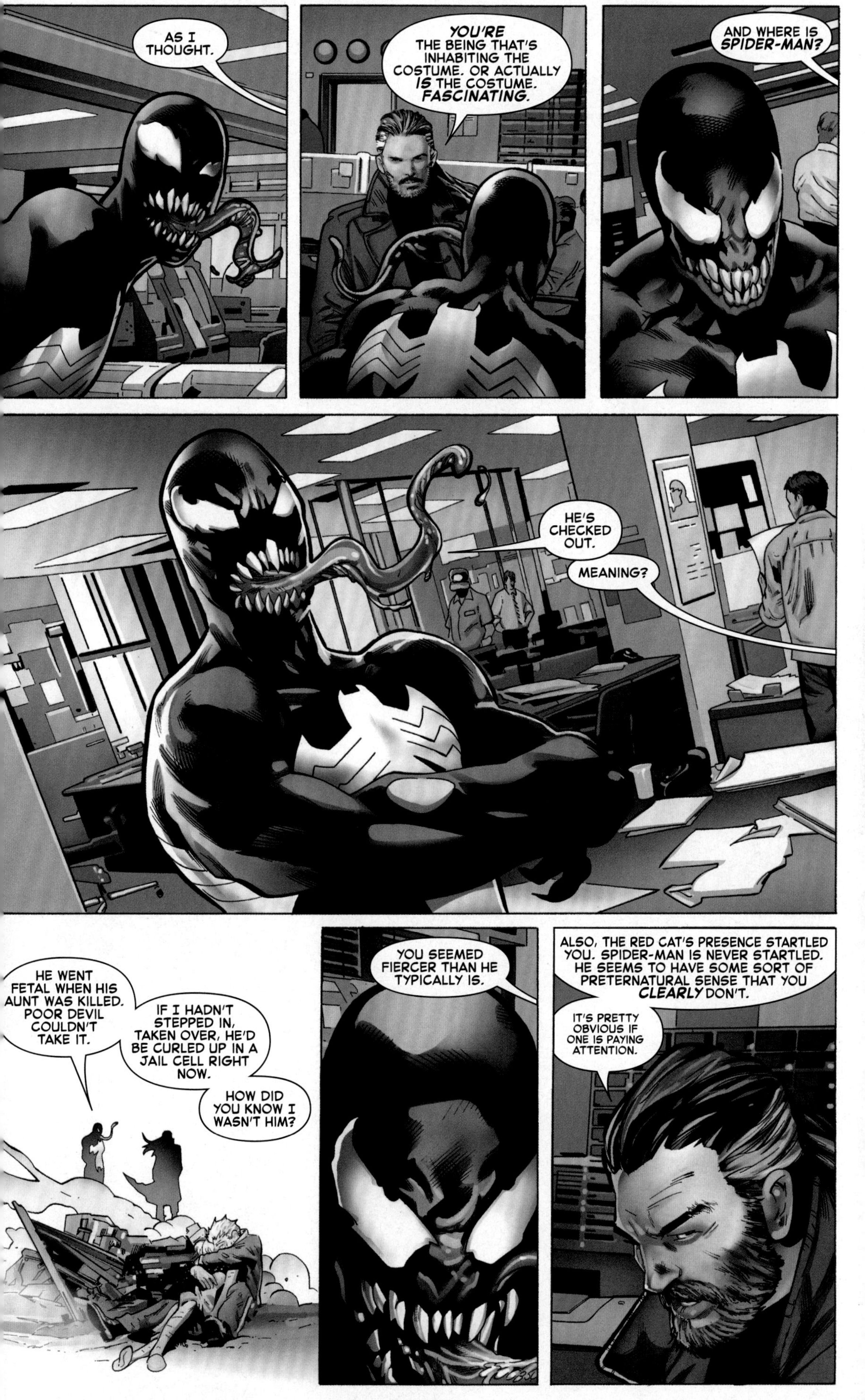
AS I THOUGHT.
YOU'RE THE BEING THAT'S INHABITING THE COSTUME. OR ACTUALLY IS THE COSTUME. FASCINATING.
AND WHERE IS SPIDER-MAN?
HE'S CHECKED OUT.
MEANING?
HE WENT FETAL WHEN HIS AUNT WAS KILLED. POOR DEVIL COULDN'T TAKE IT.
IF I HADN'T STEPPED IN, TAKEN OVER, HE'D BE CURLED UP IN A JAIL CELL RIGHT NOW.
HOW DID YOU KNOW I WASN'T HIM?
YOU SEEMED FIERCER THAN HE TYPICALLY IS.
ALSO, THE RED CAT'S PRESENCE STARTLED YOU. SPIDER-MAN IS NEVER STARTLED. HE SEEMS TO HAVE SOME SORT OF PRETERNATURAL SENSE THAT YOU CLEARLY DON'T.
IT'S PRETTY OBVIOUS IF ONE IS PAYING ATTENTION.

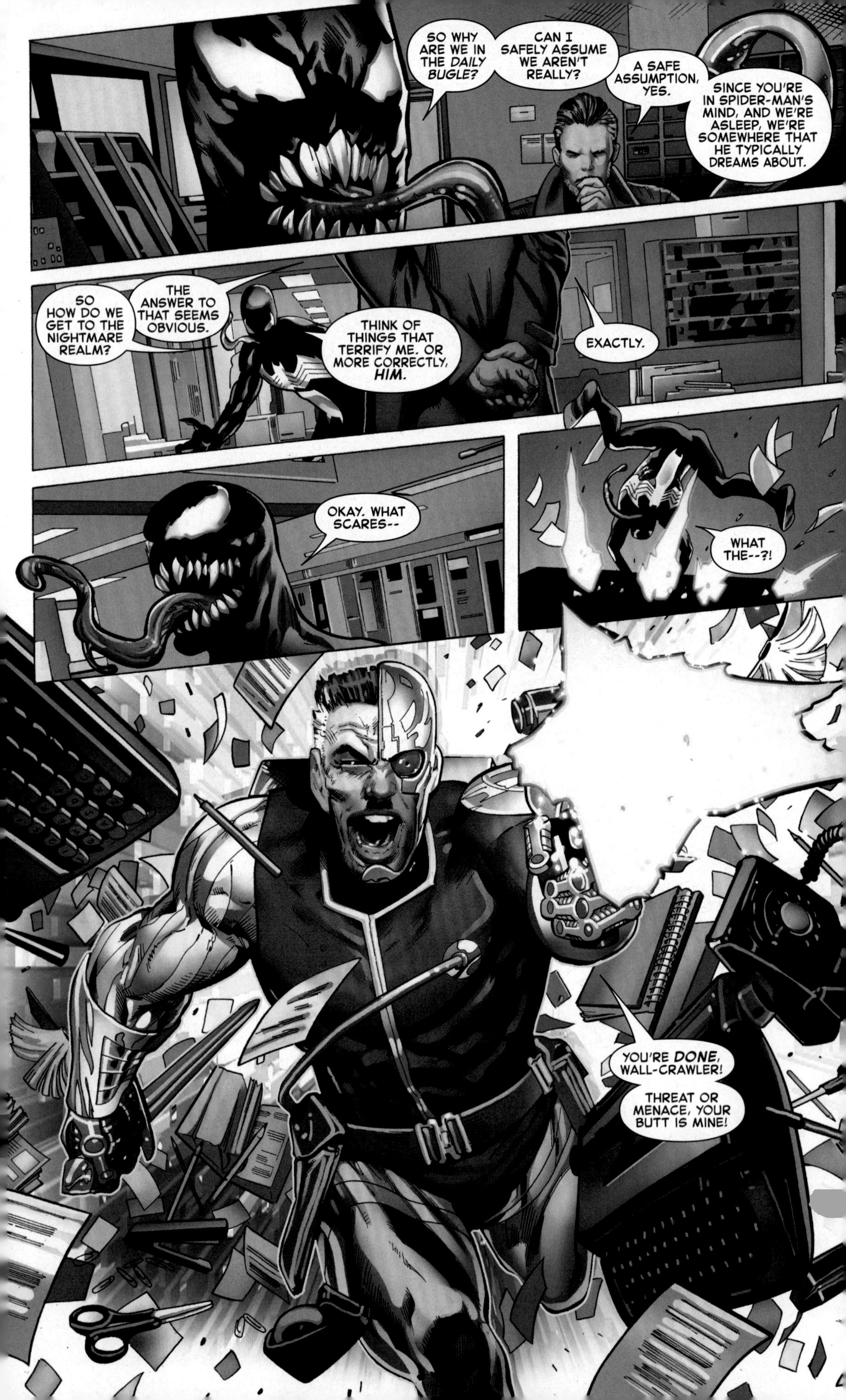
SO WHY ARE WE IN THE *DAILY BUGLE*?
CAN I SAFELY ASSUME WE AREN'T REALLY?
A SAFE ASSUMPTION, YES.
SINCE YOU'RE IN SPIDER-MAN'S MIND, AND WE'RE ASLEEP, WE'RE SOMEWHERE THAT HE TYPICALLY DREAMS ABOUT.
SO HOW DO WE GET TO THE NIGHTMARE REALM?
THE ANSWER TO THAT SEEMS OBVIOUS.
THINK OF THINGS THAT TERRIFY ME. OR MORE CORRECTLY, **HIM**.
EXACTLY.
OKAY. WHAT SCARES--
WHAT THE--?!
YOU'RE **DONE**, WALL-CRAWLER!
THREAT OR MENACE, YOUR BUTT IS MINE!

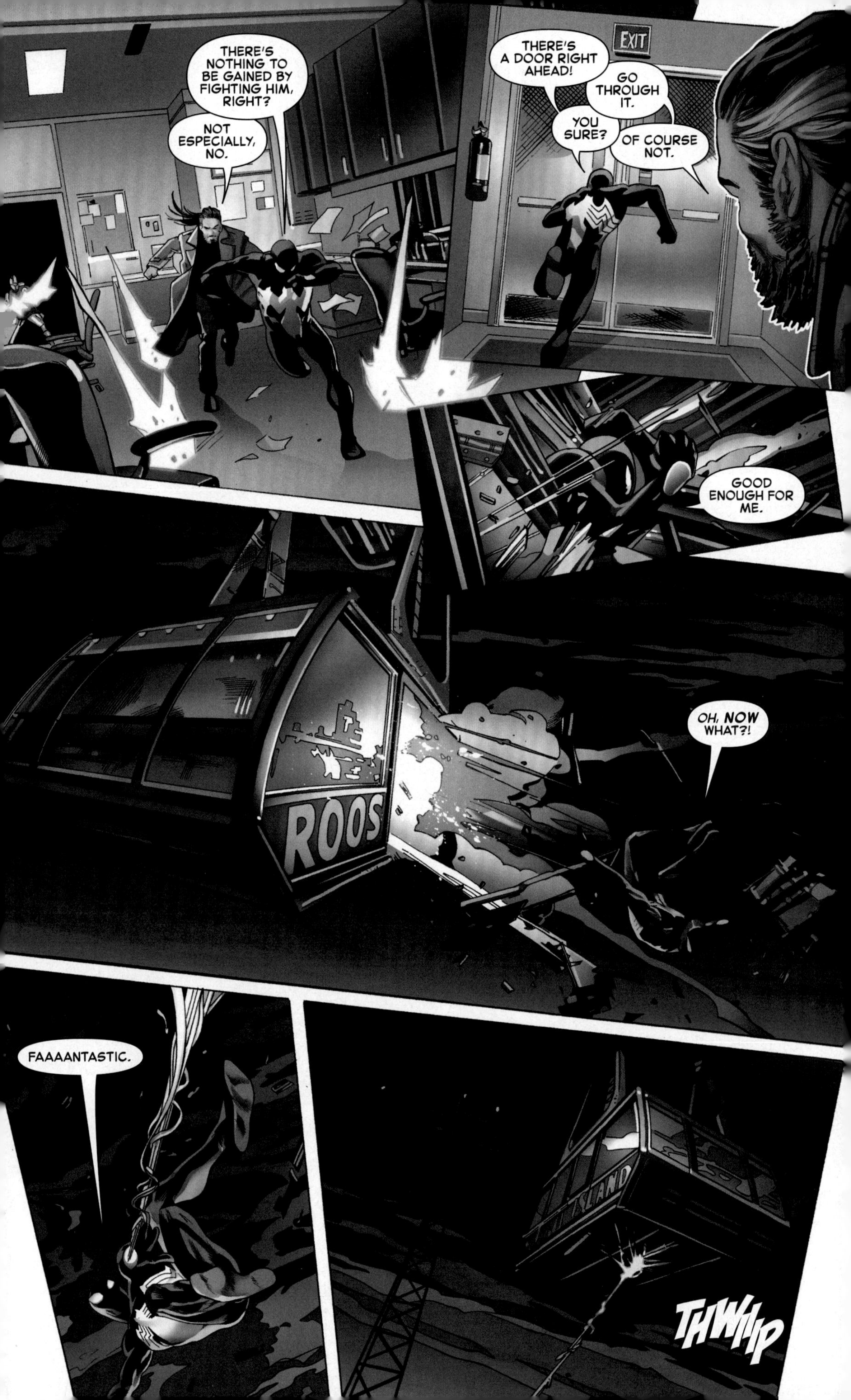
THERE'S NOTHING TO BE GAINED BY FIGHTING HIM, RIGHT?
NOT ESPECIALLY, NO.
EXIT
THERE'S A DOOR RIGHT AHEAD!
GO THROUGH IT.
YOU SURE?
OF COURSE NOT.
GOOD ENOUGH FOR ME.
ROOS
OH, NOW WHAT?!
FAAAANTASTIC.
THWIP

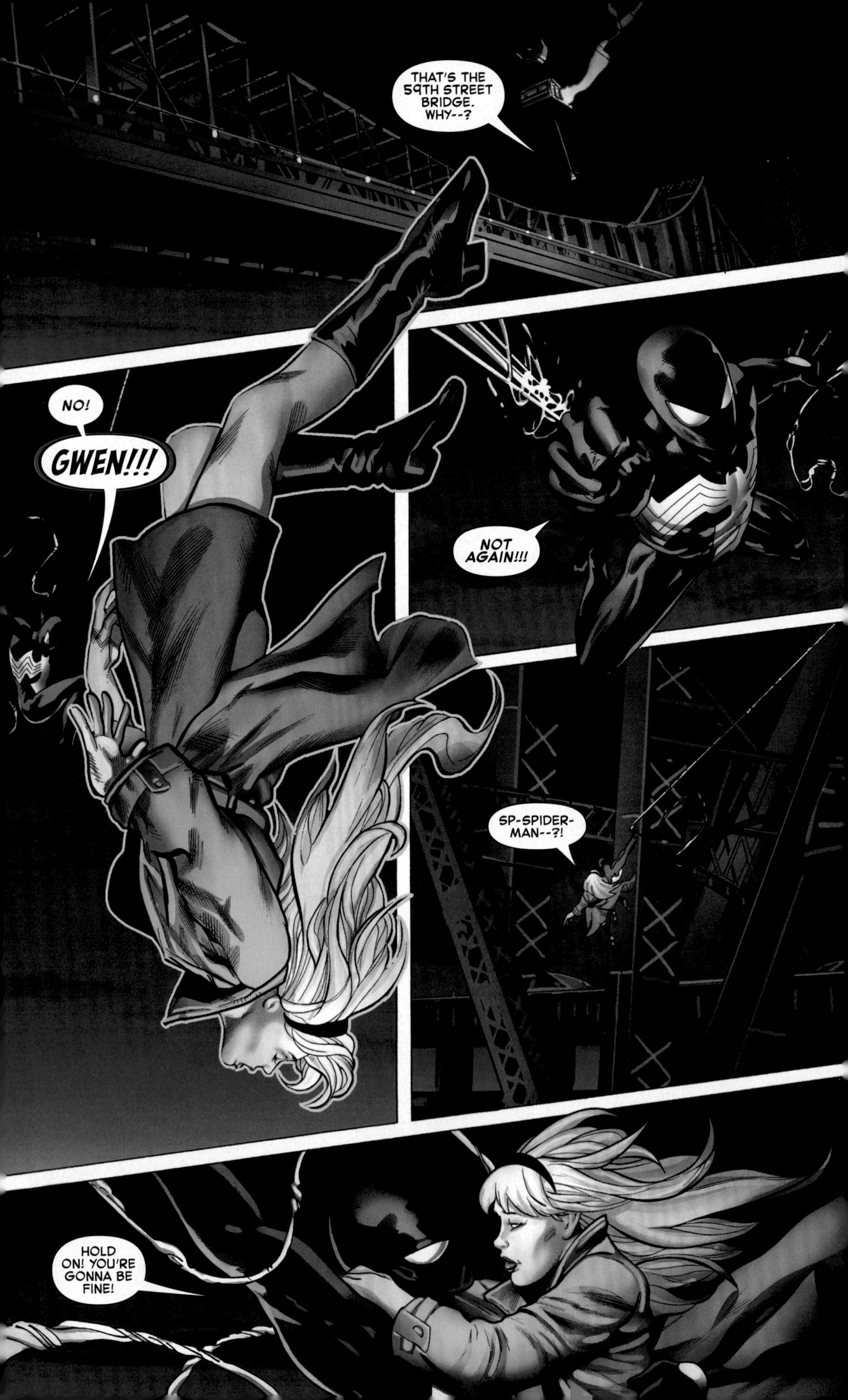
THAT'S THE 59TH STREET BRIDGE. WHY--?
NO!
GWEN!!!
NOT AGAIN!!!
SP-SPIDER-MAN--?!
HOLD ON! YOU'RE GONNA BE FINE!

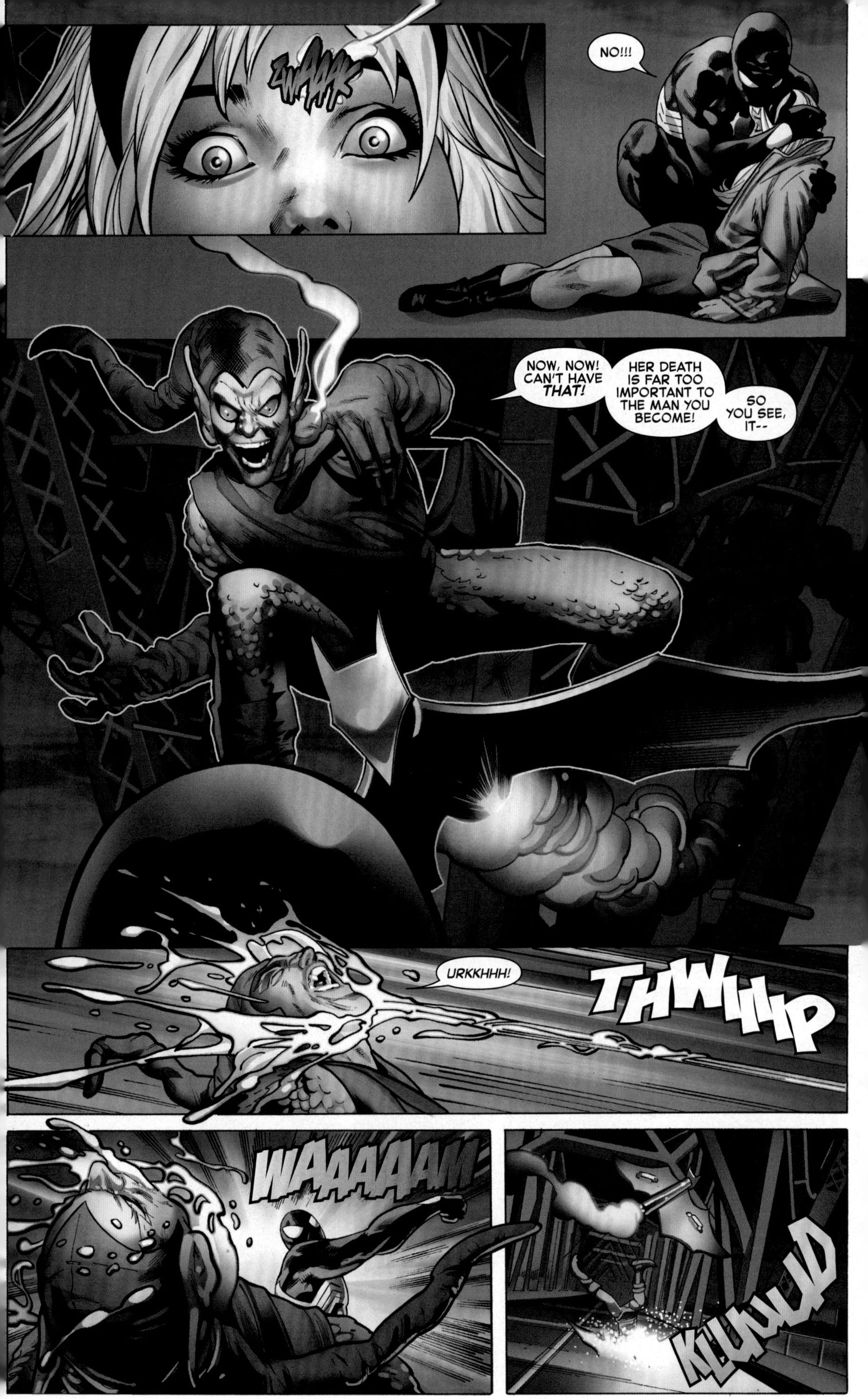
ZWAAAK
NO!!!
NOW, NOW! CAN'T HAVE THAT!
HER DEATH IS FAR TOO IMPORTANT TO THE MAN YOU BECOME!
SO YOU SEE, IT--
URKKHHH!
THWHHP
WAAAAAAM
KLUUUD

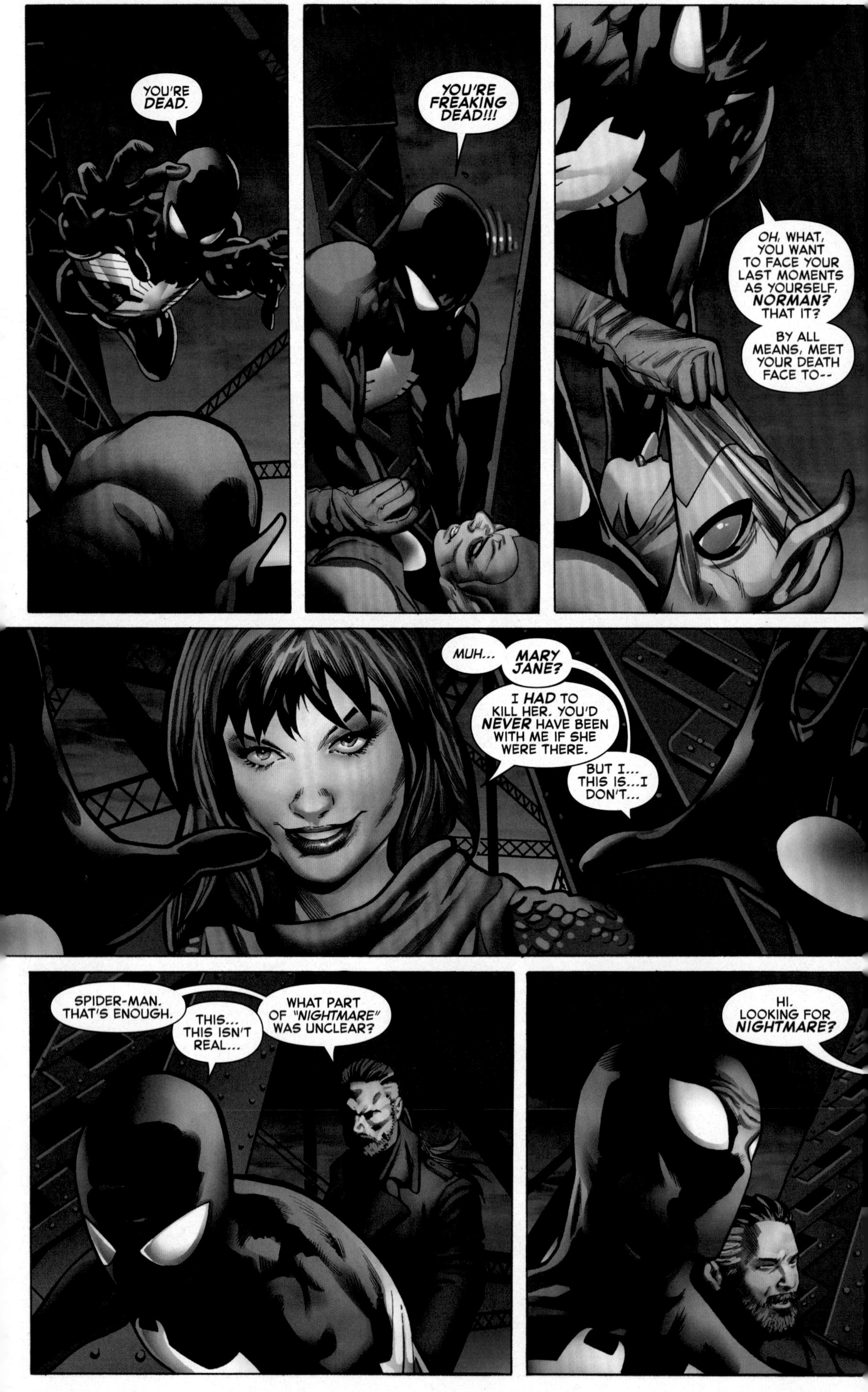
YOU'RE DEAD.
YOU'RE FREAKING DEAD!!!
OH, WHAT, YOU WANT TO FACE YOUR LAST MOMENTS AS YOURSELF, NORMAN? THAT IT?
BY ALL MEANS, MEET YOUR DEATH FACE TO--
MUH... MARY JANE?
I HAD TO KILL HER. YOU'D NEVER HAVE BEEN WITH ME IF SHE WERE THERE.
BUT I... THIS IS...I DON'T...
SPIDER-MAN. THAT'S ENOUGH.
THIS... THIS ISN'T REAL...
WHAT PART OF "NIGHTMARE" WAS UNCLEAR?
HI. LOOKING FOR NIGHTMARE?

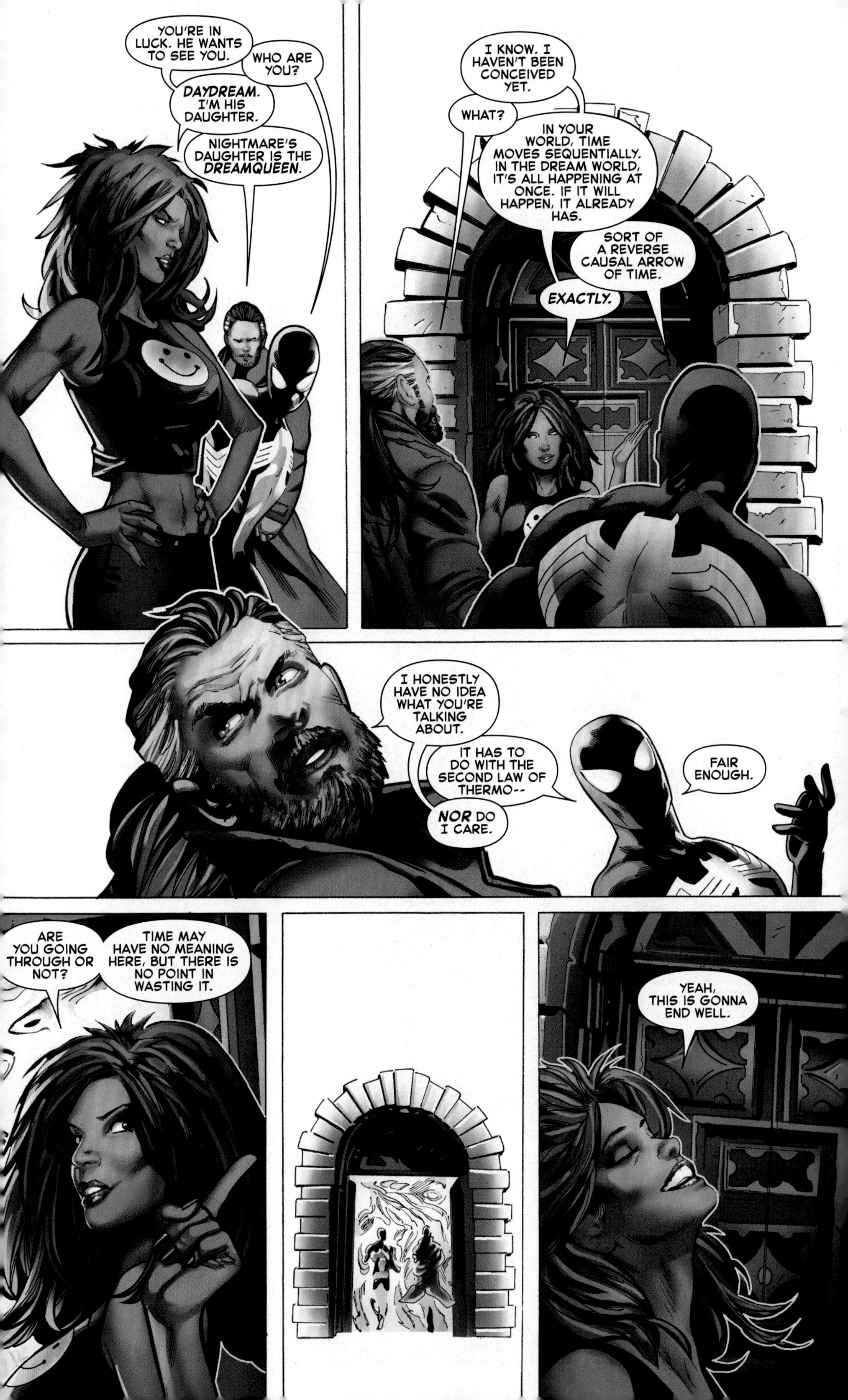
YOU'RE IN LUCK. HE WANTS TO SEE YOU.
WHO ARE YOU?
DAYDREAM. I'M HIS DAUGHTER.
NIGHTMARE'S DAUGHTER IS THE DREAMQUEEN.
I KNOW. I HAVEN'T BEEN CONCEIVED YET.
WHAT?
IN YOUR WORLD, TIME MOVES SEQUENTIALLY. IN THE DREAM WORLD, IT'S ALL HAPPENING AT ONCE. IF IT WILL HAPPEN, IT ALREADY HAS.
SORT OF A REVERSE CAUSAL ARROW OF TIME.
EXACTLY.
I HONESTLY HAVE NO IDEA WHAT YOU'RE TALKING ABOUT.
IT HAS TO DO WITH THE SECOND LAW OF THERMO--
NOR DO I CARE.
FAIR ENOUGH.
ARE YOU GOING THROUGH OR NOT?
TIME MAY HAVE NO MEANING HERE, BUT THERE IS NO POINT IN WASTING IT.
YEAH, THIS IS GONNA END WELL.

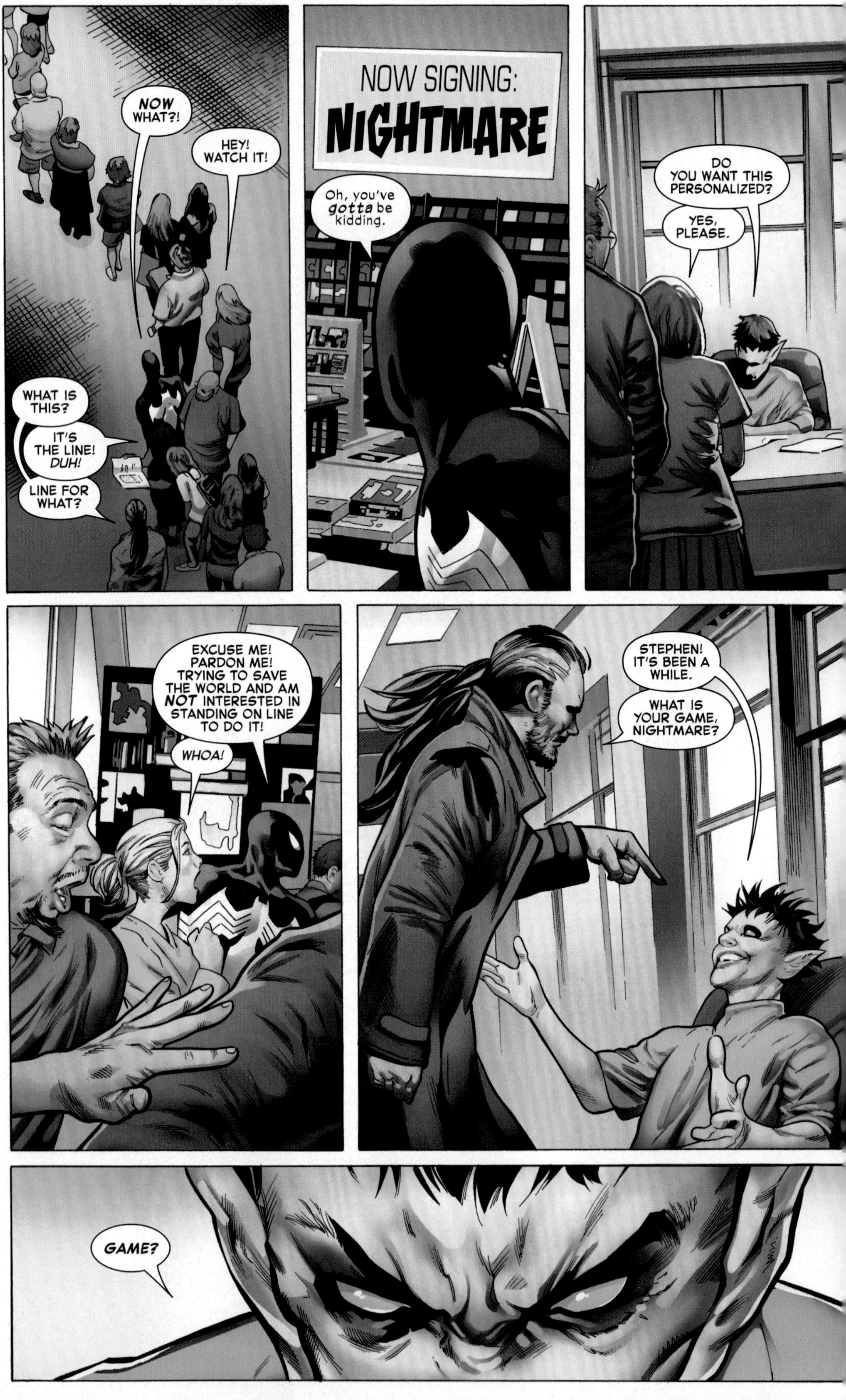
NOW WHAT?!
HEY! WATCH IT!
WHAT IS THIS?
IT'S THE LINE! DUH!
LINE FOR WHAT?
NOW SIGNING: NIGHTMARE
Oh, you've gotta be kidding.
DO YOU WANT THIS PERSONALIZED?
YES, PLEASE.
EXCUSE ME! PARDON ME! TRYING TO SAVE THE WORLD AND AM NOT INTERESTED IN STANDING ON LINE TO DO IT!
WHOA!
STEPHEN! IT'S BEEN A WHILE.
WHAT IS YOUR GAME, NIGHTMARE?
GAME?

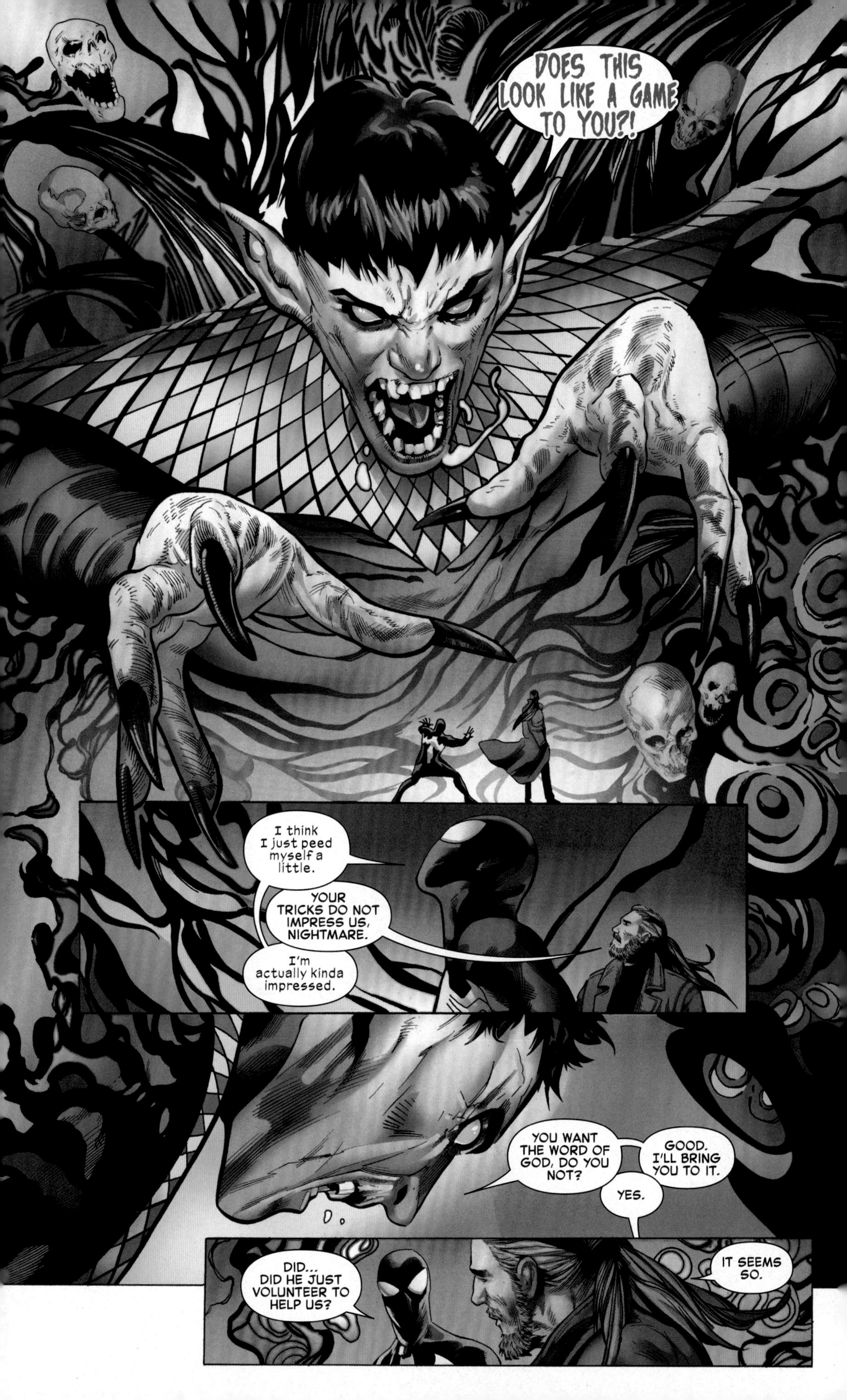

DOES THIS LOOK LIKE A GAME TO YOU?!
I think I just peed myself a little.
YOUR TRICKS DO NOT IMPRESS US, NIGHTMARE.
I'm actually kinda impressed.
YOU WANT THE WORD OF GOD, DO YOU NOT?
YES.
GOOD. I'LL BRING YOU TO IT.
DID... DID HE JUST VOLUNTEER TO HELP US?
IT SEEMS SO.

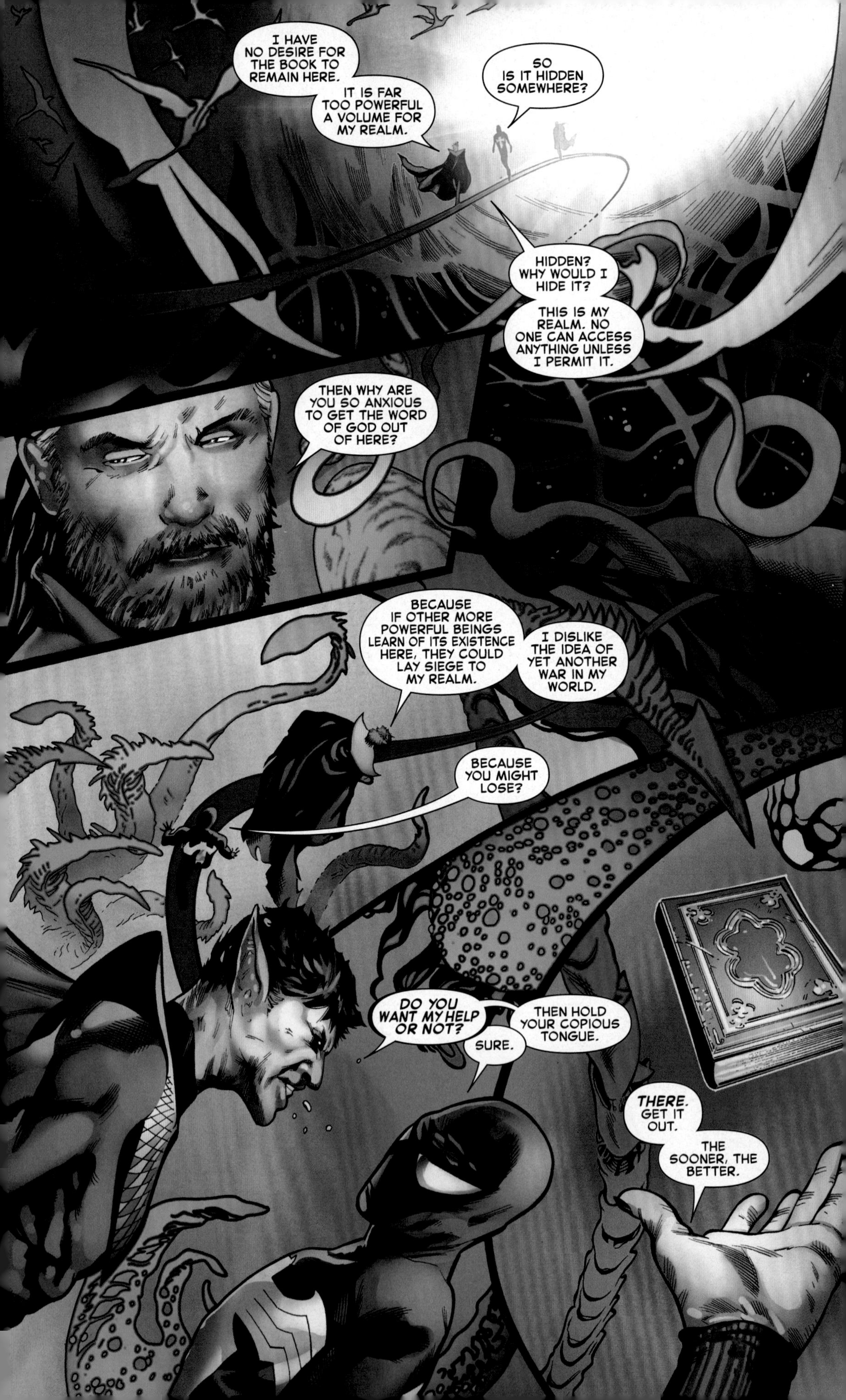
I HAVE NO DESIRE FOR THE BOOK TO REMAIN HERE.
IT IS FAR TOO POWERFUL A VOLUME FOR MY REALM.
SO IS IT HIDDEN SOMEWHERE?
HIDDEN? WHY WOULD I HIDE IT?
THIS IS MY REALM. NO ONE CAN ACCESS ANYTHING UNLESS I PERMIT IT.
THEN WHY ARE YOU SO ANXIOUS TO GET THE WORD OF GOD OUT OF HERE?
BECAUSE IF OTHER MORE POWERFUL BEINGS LEARN OF ITS EXISTENCE HERE, THEY COULD LAY SIEGE TO MY REALM.
I DISLIKE THE IDEA OF YET ANOTHER WAR IN MY WORLD.
BECAUSE YOU MIGHT LOSE?
DO YOU WANT MY HELP OR NOT?
SURE.
THEN HOLD YOUR COPIOUS TONGUE.
THERE. GET IT OUT.
THE SOONER, THE BETTER.

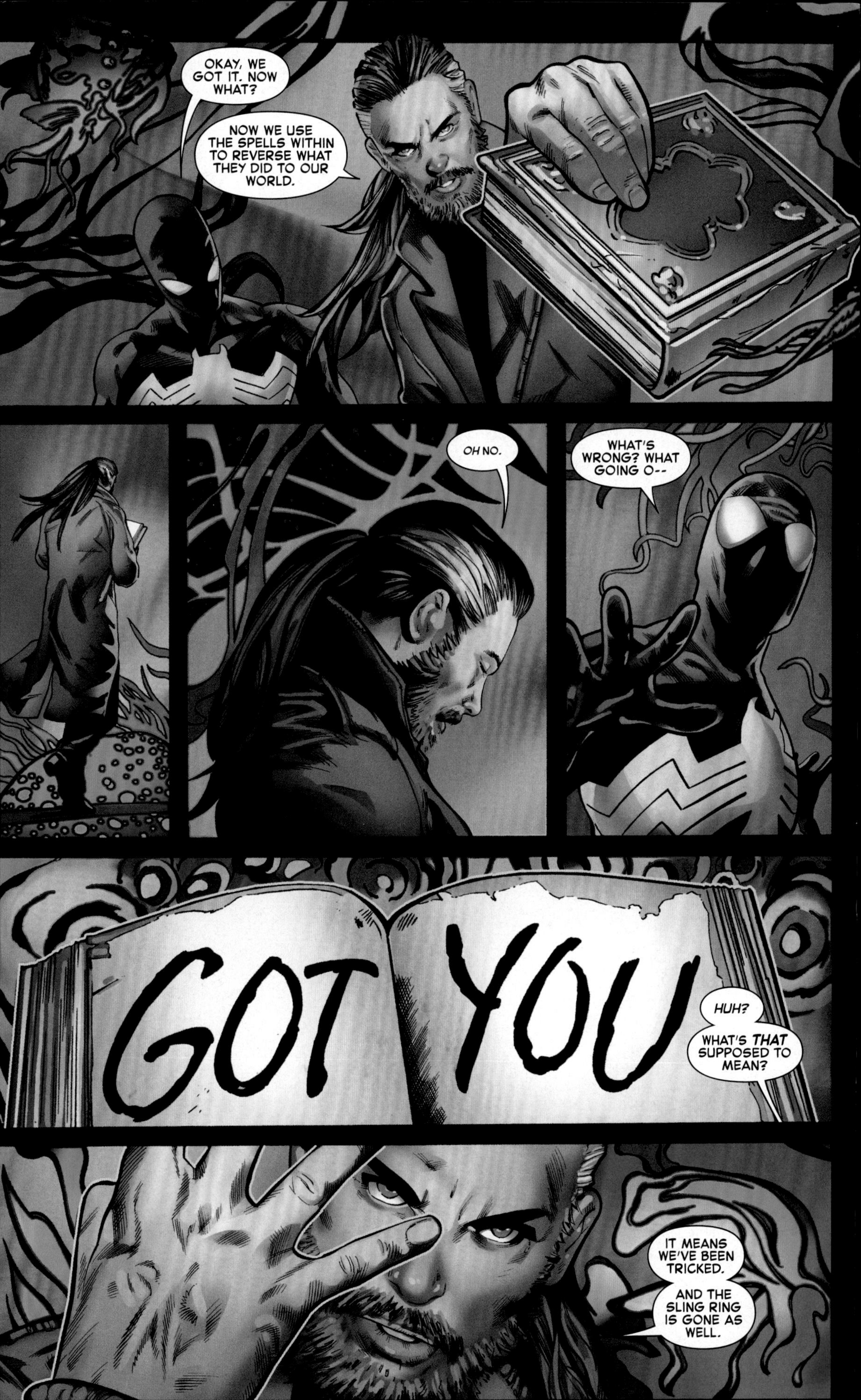
OKAY, WE GOT IT. NOW WHAT?
NOW WE USE THE SPELLS WITHIN TO REVERSE WHAT THEY DID TO OUR WORLD.
OH NO.
WHAT'S WRONG? WHAT GOING O--
GOT YOU
HUH?
WHAT'S THAT SUPPOSED TO MEAN?
IT MEANS WE'VE BEEN TRICKED.
AND THE SLING RING IS GONE AS WELL.

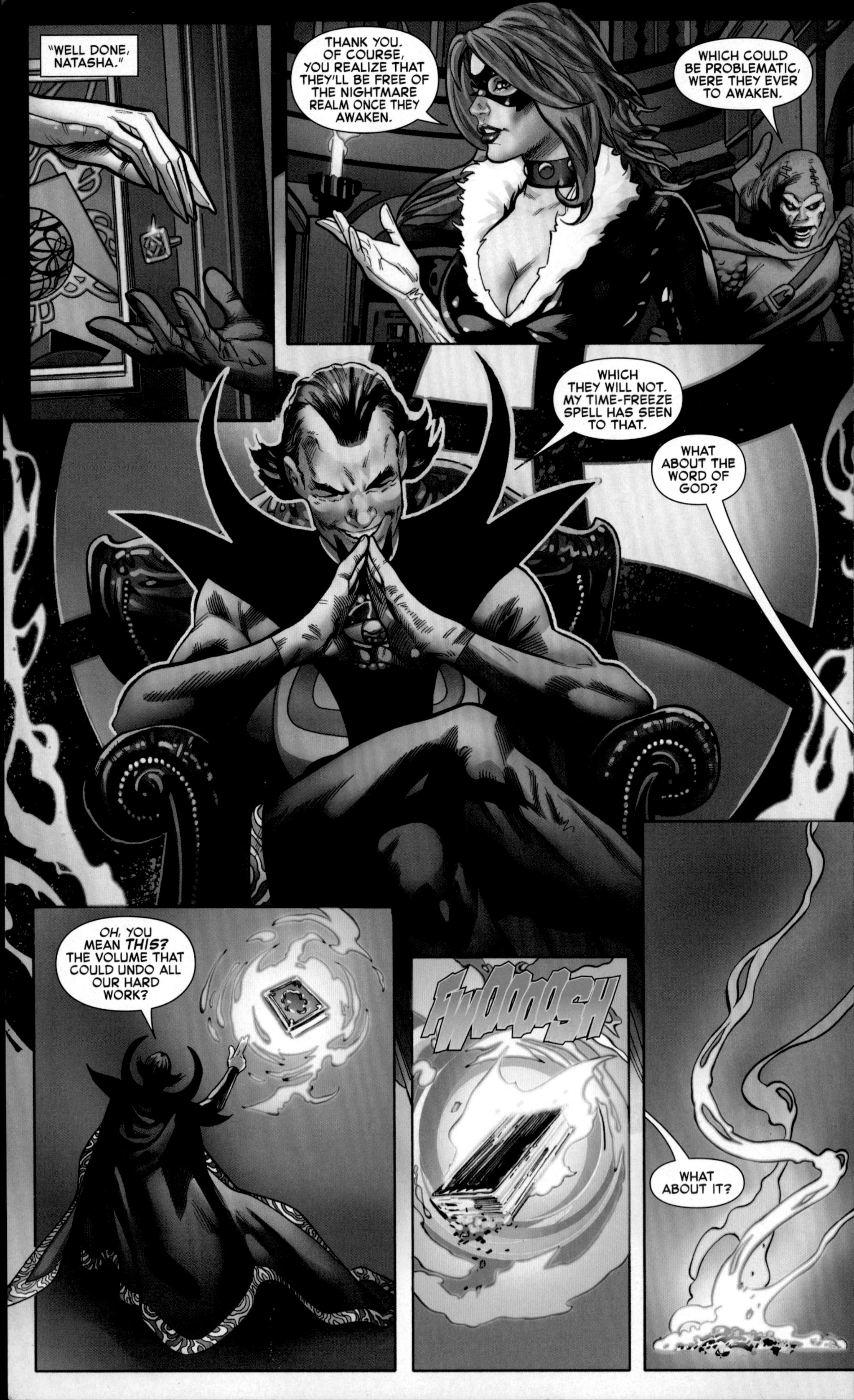
"WELL DONE, NATASHA."
THANK YOU. OF COURSE, YOU REALIZE THAT THEY'LL BE FREE OF THE NIGHTMARE REALM ONCE THEY AWAKEN.
WHICH COULD BE PROBLEMATIC, WERE THEY EVER TO AWAKEN.
WHICH THEY WILL NOT. MY TIME-FREEZE SPELL HAS SEEN TO THAT.
WHAT ABOUT THE WORD OF GOD?
OH, YOU MEAN *THIS?* THE VOLUME THAT COULD UNDO ALL OUR HARD WORK?
FWOOOOSH
WHAT ABOUT IT?

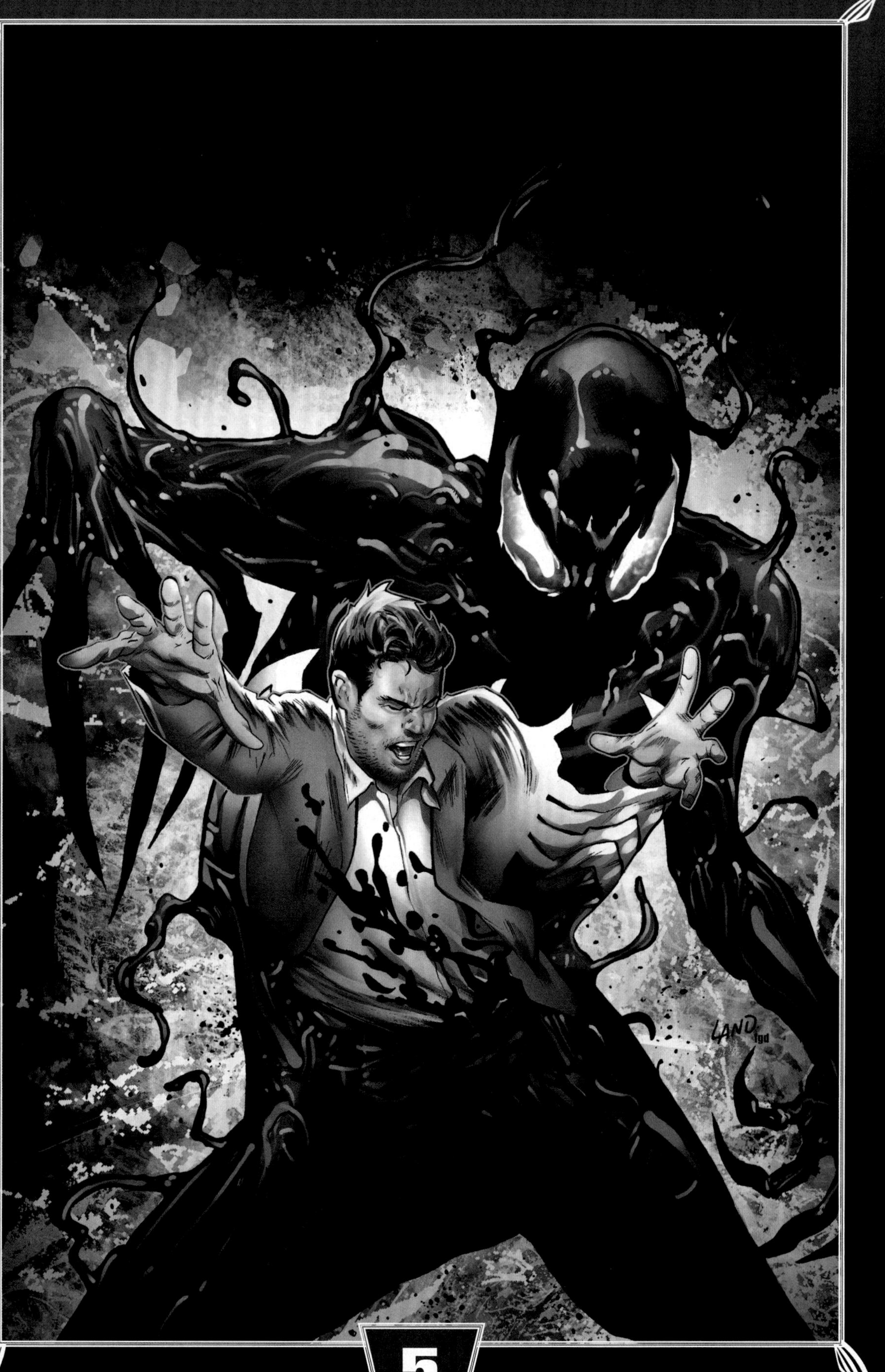

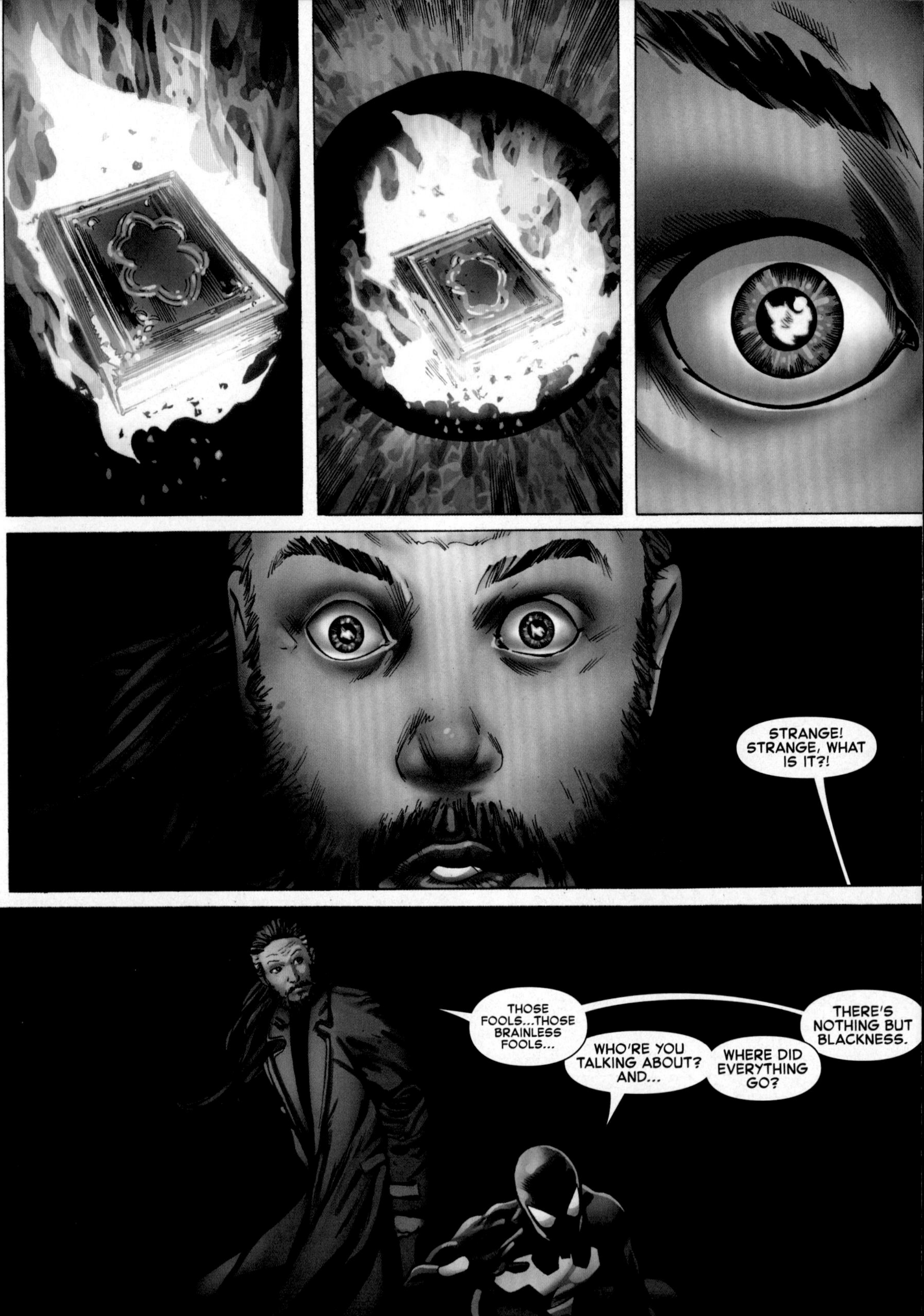
STRANGE! STRANGE, WHAT IS IT?!
THOSE FOOLS...THOSE BRAINLESS FOOLS...
WHO'RE YOU TALKING ABOUT? AND...
WHERE DID EVERYTHING GO?
THERE'S NOTHING BUT BLACKNESS.

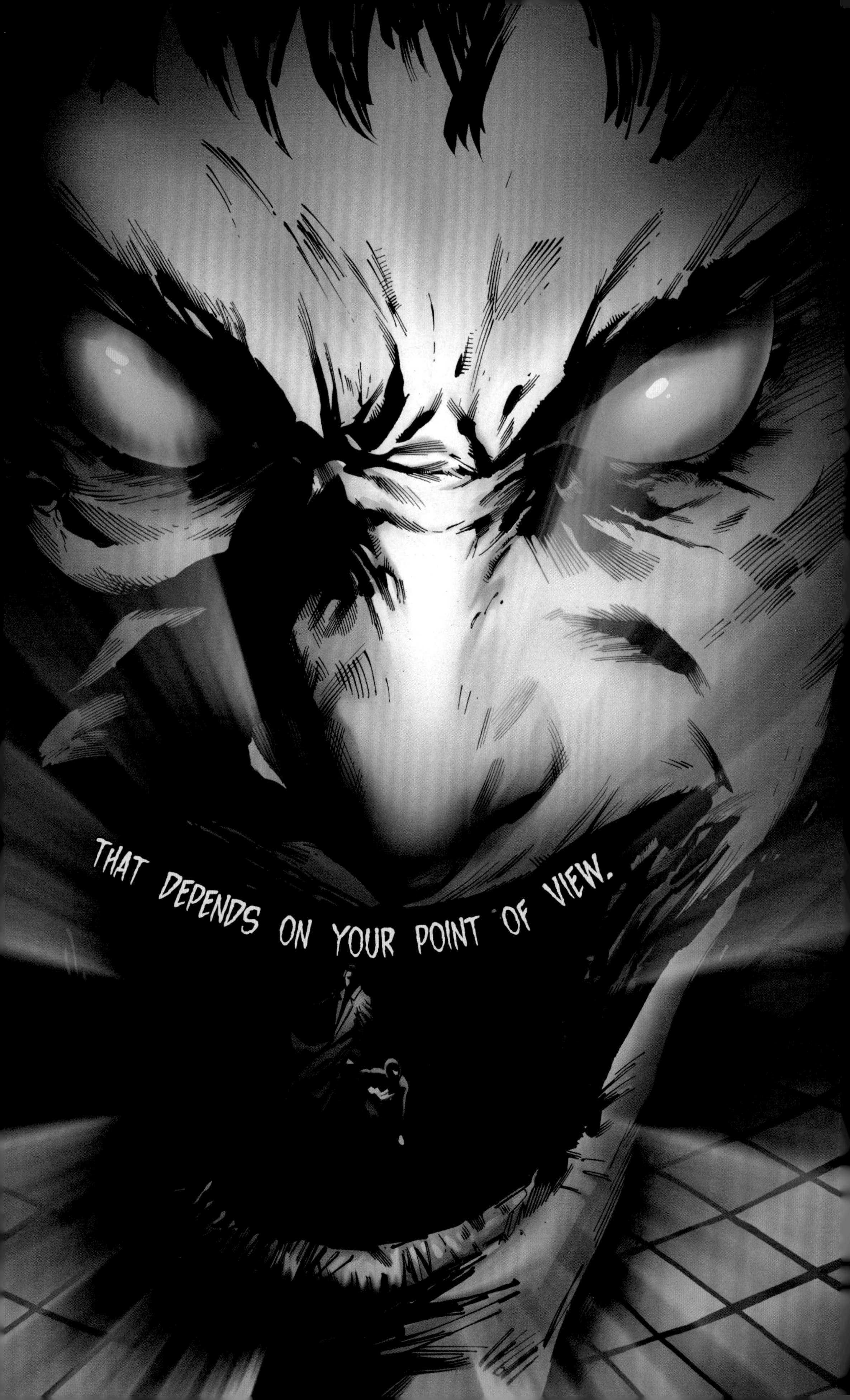
THAT DEPENDS ON YOUR POINT OF VIEW.

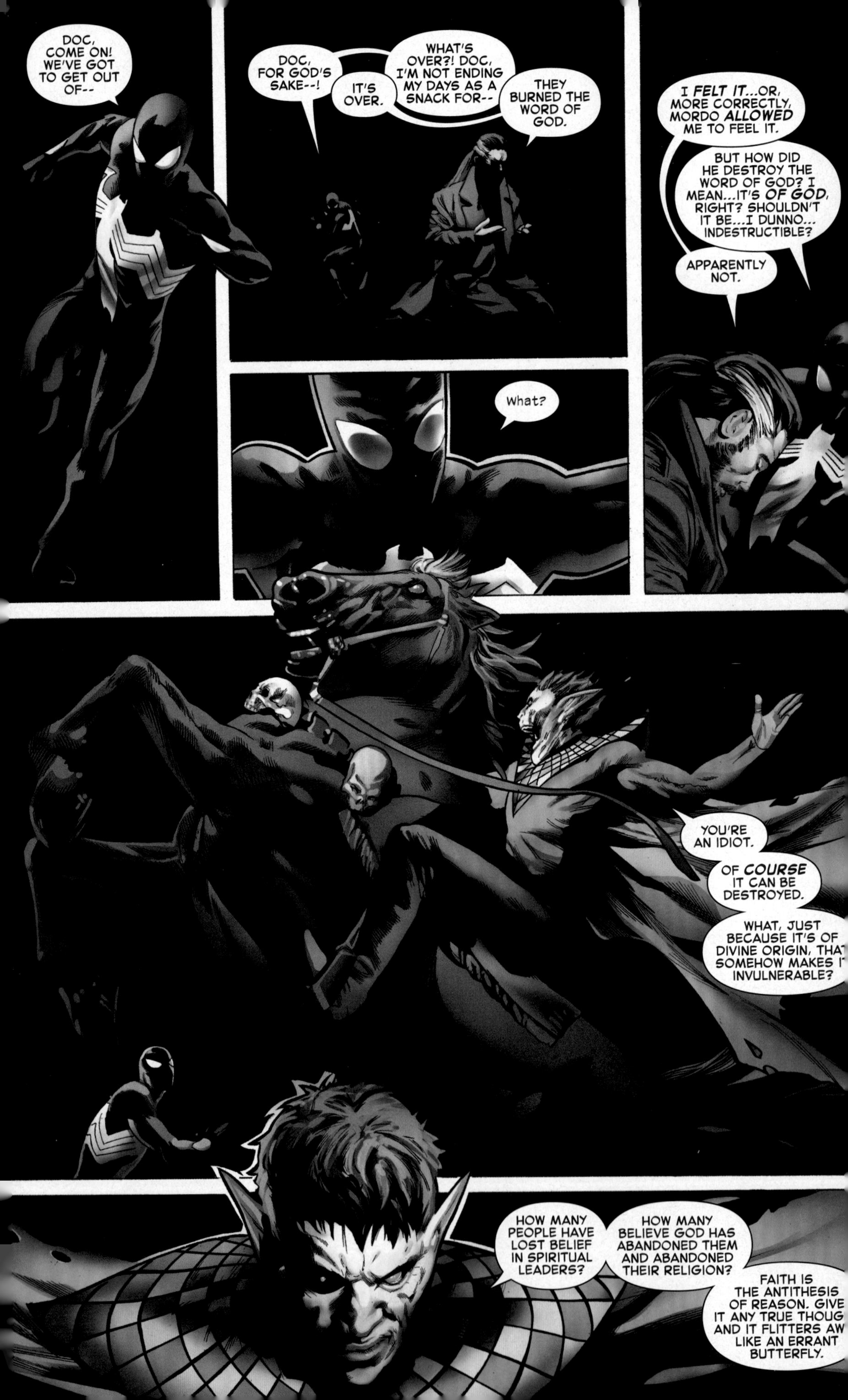

DOC, COME ON! WE'VE GOT TO GET OUT OF--
DOC, FOR GOD'S SAKE--!
IT'S OVER.
WHAT'S OVER?! DOC, I'M NOT ENDING MY DAYS AS A SNACK FOR--
THEY BURNED THE WORD OF GOD.
What?
I FELT IT...OR, MORE CORRECTLY, MORDO ALLOWED ME TO FEEL IT.
BUT HOW DID HE DESTROY THE WORD OF GOD? I MEAN...IT'S OF GOD, RIGHT? SHOULDN'T IT BE...I DUNNO... INDESTRUCTIBLE?
APPARENTLY NOT.
YOU'RE AN IDIOT.
OF COURSE IT CAN BE DESTROYED.
WHAT, JUST BECAUSE IT'S OF DIVINE ORIGIN, THAT SOMEHOW MAKES IT INVULNERABLE?
HOW MANY PEOPLE HAVE LOST BELIEF IN SPIRITUAL LEADERS?
HOW MANY BELIEVE GOD HAS ABANDONED THEM AND ABANDONED THEIR RELIGION?
FAITH IS THE ANTITHESIS OF REASON. GIVE IT ANY TRUE THOUG AND IT FLITTERS AW LIKE AN ERRANT BUTTERFLY.

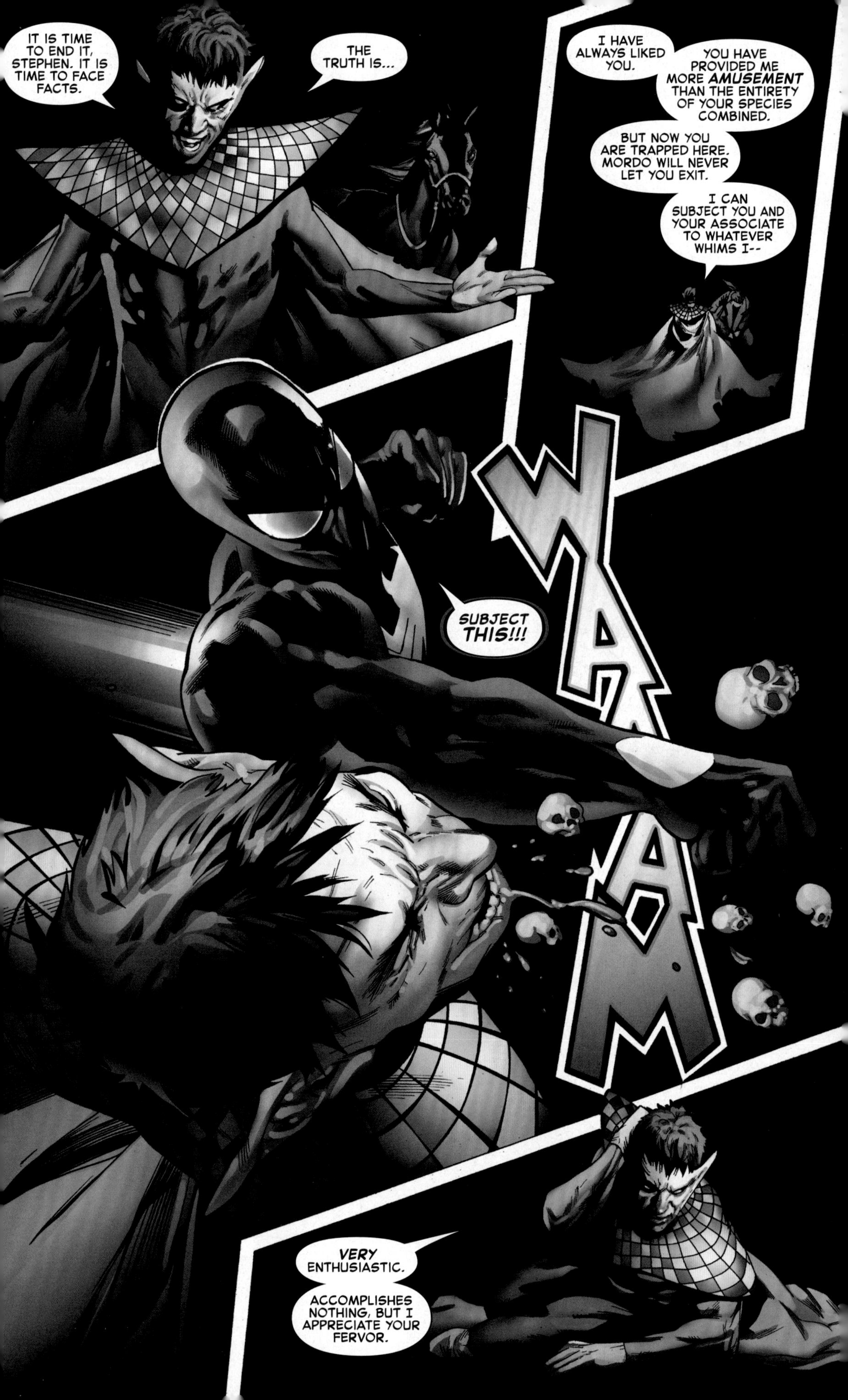
IT IS TIME TO END IT, STEPHEN. IT IS TIME TO FACE FACTS.
THE TRUTH IS...
I HAVE ALWAYS LIKED YOU.
YOU HAVE PROVIDED ME MORE AMUSEMENT THAN THE ENTIRETY OF YOUR SPECIES COMBINED.
BUT NOW YOU ARE TRAPPED HERE. MORDO WILL NEVER LET YOU EXIT.
I CAN SUBJECT YOU AND YOUR ASSOCIATE TO WHATEVER WHIMS I--
SUBJECT THIS!!!
WHAAAM
VERY ENTHUSIASTIC.
ACCOMPLISHES NOTHING, BUT I APPRECIATE YOUR FERVOR.

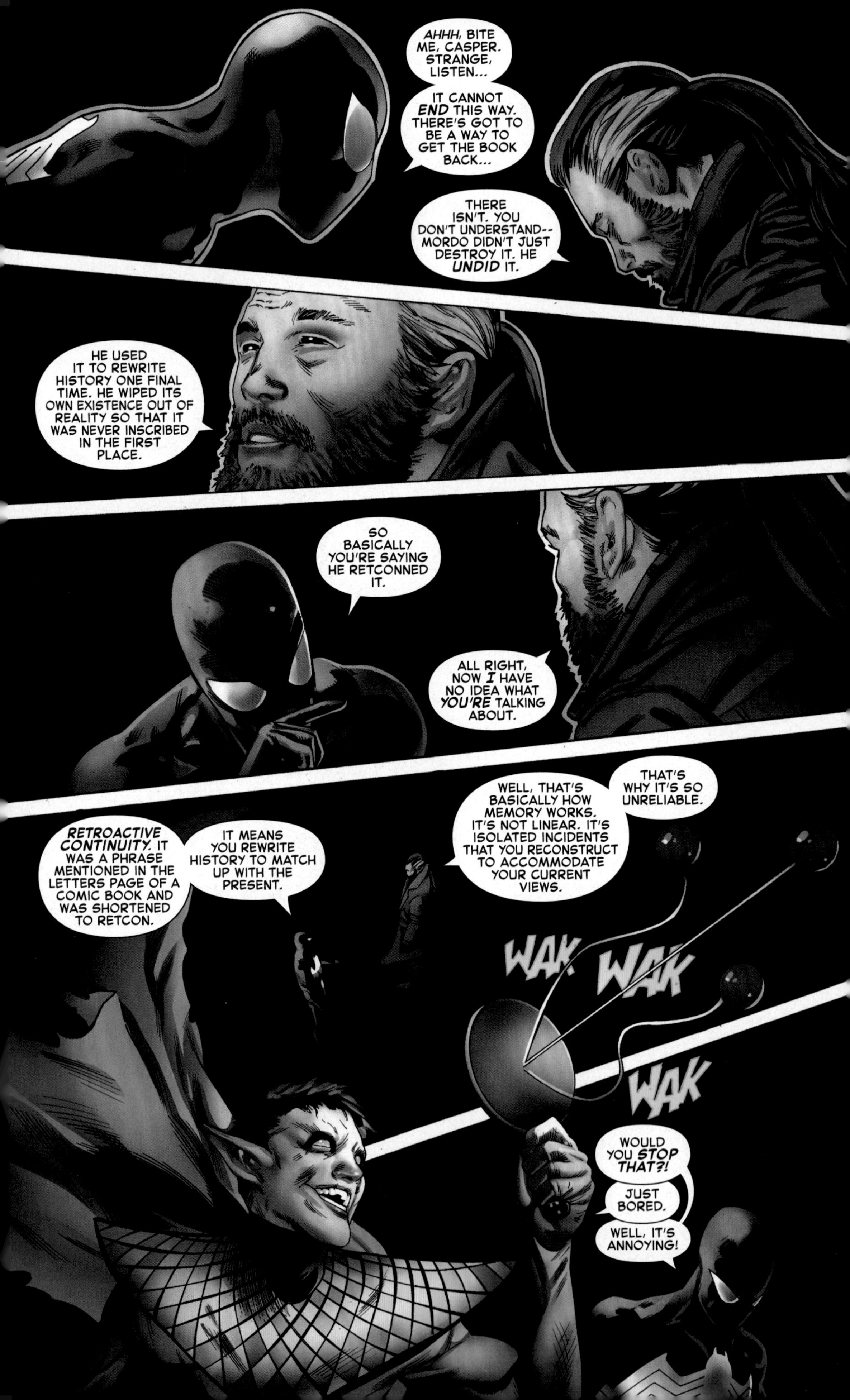
AHHH, BITE ME, CASPER. STRANGE, LISTEN...
IT CANNOT END THIS WAY. THERE'S GOT TO BE A WAY TO GET THE BOOK BACK...
THERE ISN'T. YOU DON'T UNDERSTAND-- MORDO DIDN'T JUST DESTROY IT. HE UNDID IT.
HE USED IT TO REWRITE HISTORY ONE FINAL TIME. HE WIPED ITS OWN EXISTENCE OUT OF REALITY SO THAT IT WAS NEVER INSCRIBED IN THE FIRST PLACE.
SO BASICALLY YOU'RE SAYING HE RETCONNED IT.
ALL RIGHT, NOW I HAVE NO IDEA WHAT YOU'RE TALKING ABOUT.
RETROACTIVE CONTINUITY. IT WAS A PHRASE MENTIONED IN THE LETTERS PAGE OF A COMIC BOOK AND WAS SHORTENED TO RETCON.
IT MEANS YOU REWRITE HISTORY TO MATCH UP WITH THE PRESENT.
WELL, THAT'S BASICALLY HOW MEMORY WORKS. IT'S NOT LINEAR. IT'S ISOLATED INCIDENTS THAT YOU RECONSTRUCT TO ACCOMMODATE YOUR CURRENT VIEWS.
THAT'S WHY IT'S SO UNRELIABLE.
WAK WAK
WAK
WOULD YOU STOP THAT?!
JUST BORED.
WELL, IT'S ANNOYING!

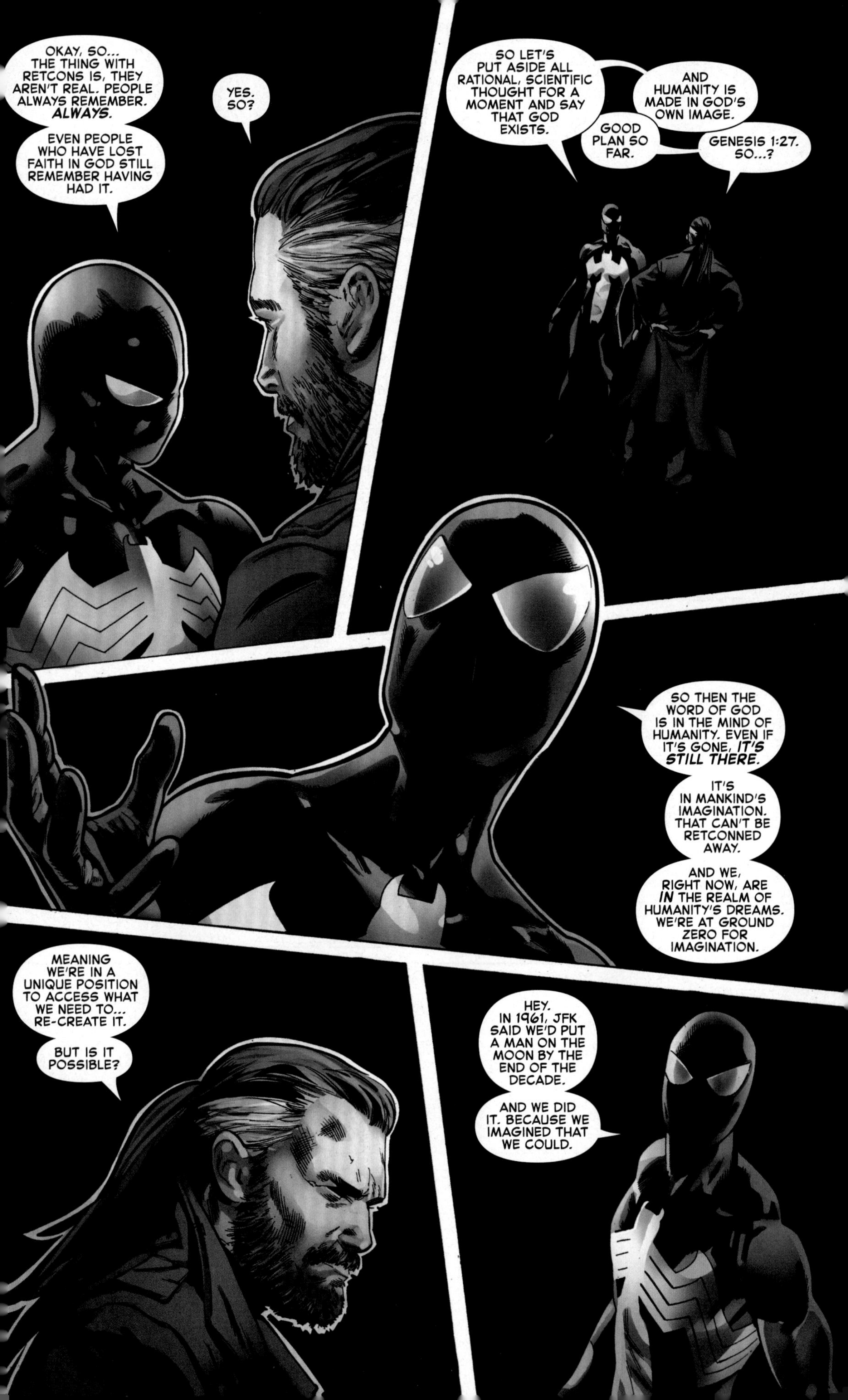
OKAY, SO... THE THING WITH RETCONS IS, THEY AREN'T REAL. PEOPLE ALWAYS REMEMBER. ALWAYS.
EVEN PEOPLE WHO HAVE LOST FAITH IN GOD STILL REMEMBER HAVING HAD IT.
YES. SO?
SO LET'S PUT ASIDE ALL RATIONAL, SCIENTIFIC THOUGHT FOR A MOMENT AND SAY THAT GOD EXISTS.
GOOD PLAN SO FAR.
AND HUMANITY IS MADE IN GOD'S OWN IMAGE.
GENESIS 1:27. SO...?
SO THEN THE WORD OF GOD IS IN THE MIND OF HUMANITY. EVEN IF IT'S GONE, IT'S STILL THERE.
IT'S IN MANKIND'S IMAGINATION. THAT CAN'T BE RETCONNED AWAY.
AND WE, RIGHT NOW, ARE IN THE REALM OF HUMANITY'S DREAMS. WE'RE AT GROUND ZERO FOR IMAGINATION.
MEANING WE'RE IN A UNIQUE POSITION TO ACCESS WHAT WE NEED TO... RE-CREATE IT.
BUT IS IT POSSIBLE?
HEY. IN 1961, JFK SAID WE'D PUT A MAN ON THE MOON BY THE END OF THE DECADE.
AND WE DID IT. BECAUSE WE IMAGINED THAT WE COULD.

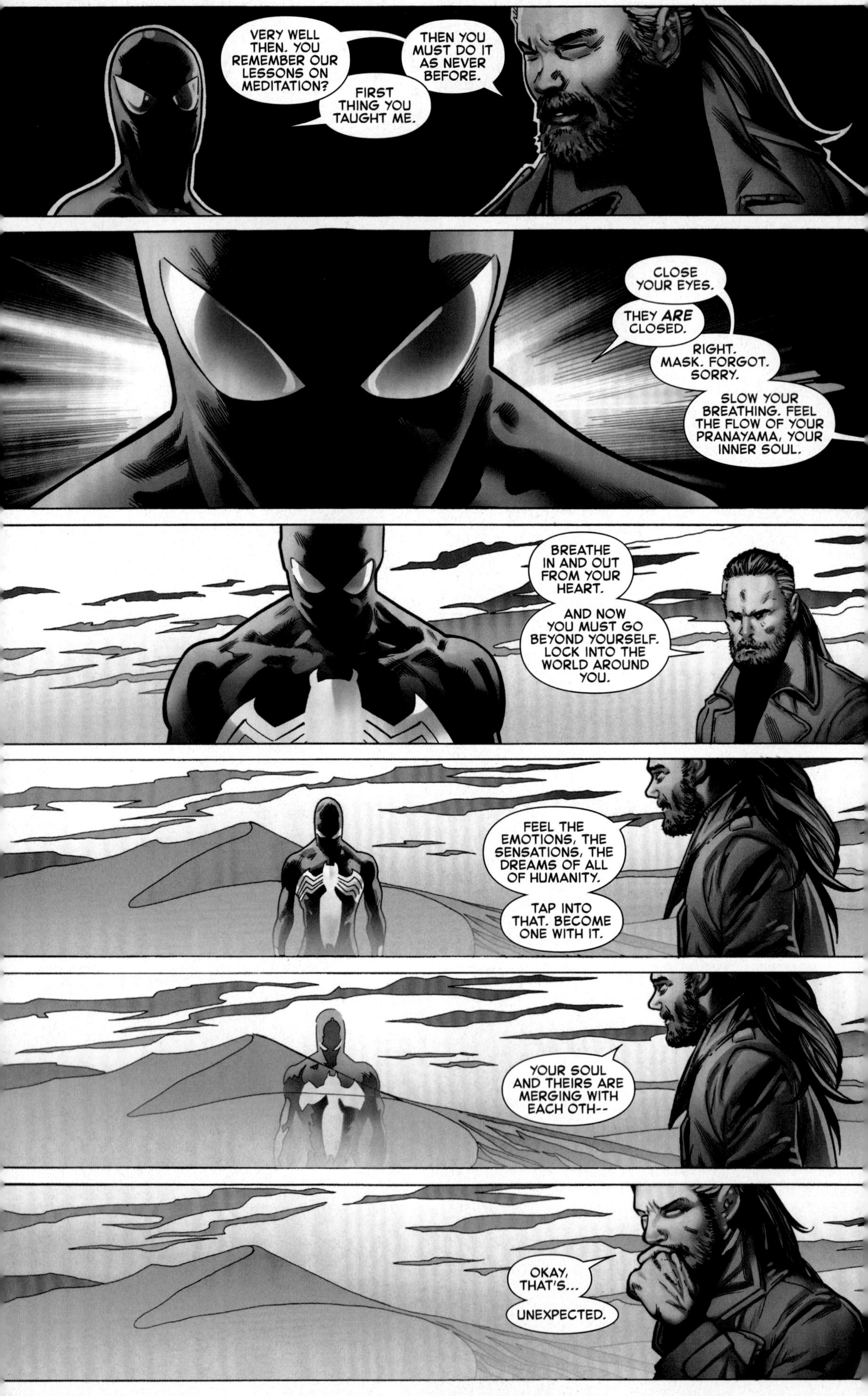
VERY WELL THEN. YOU REMEMBER OUR LESSONS ON MEDITATION?
FIRST THING YOU TAUGHT ME.
THEN YOU MUST DO IT AS NEVER BEFORE.
CLOSE YOUR EYES.
THEY ARE CLOSED.
RIGHT. MASK. FORGOT. SORRY.
SLOW YOUR BREATHING. FEEL THE FLOW OF YOUR PRANAYAMA, YOUR INNER SOUL.
BREATHE IN AND OUT FROM YOUR HEART.
AND NOW YOU MUST GO BEYOND YOURSELF. LOCK INTO THE WORLD AROUND YOU.
FEEL THE EMOTIONS, THE SENSATIONS, THE DREAMS OF ALL OF HUMANITY.
TAP INTO THAT. BECOME ONE WITH IT.
YOUR SOUL AND THEIRS ARE MERGING WITH EACH OTH--
OKAY, THAT'S...
UNEXPECTED.

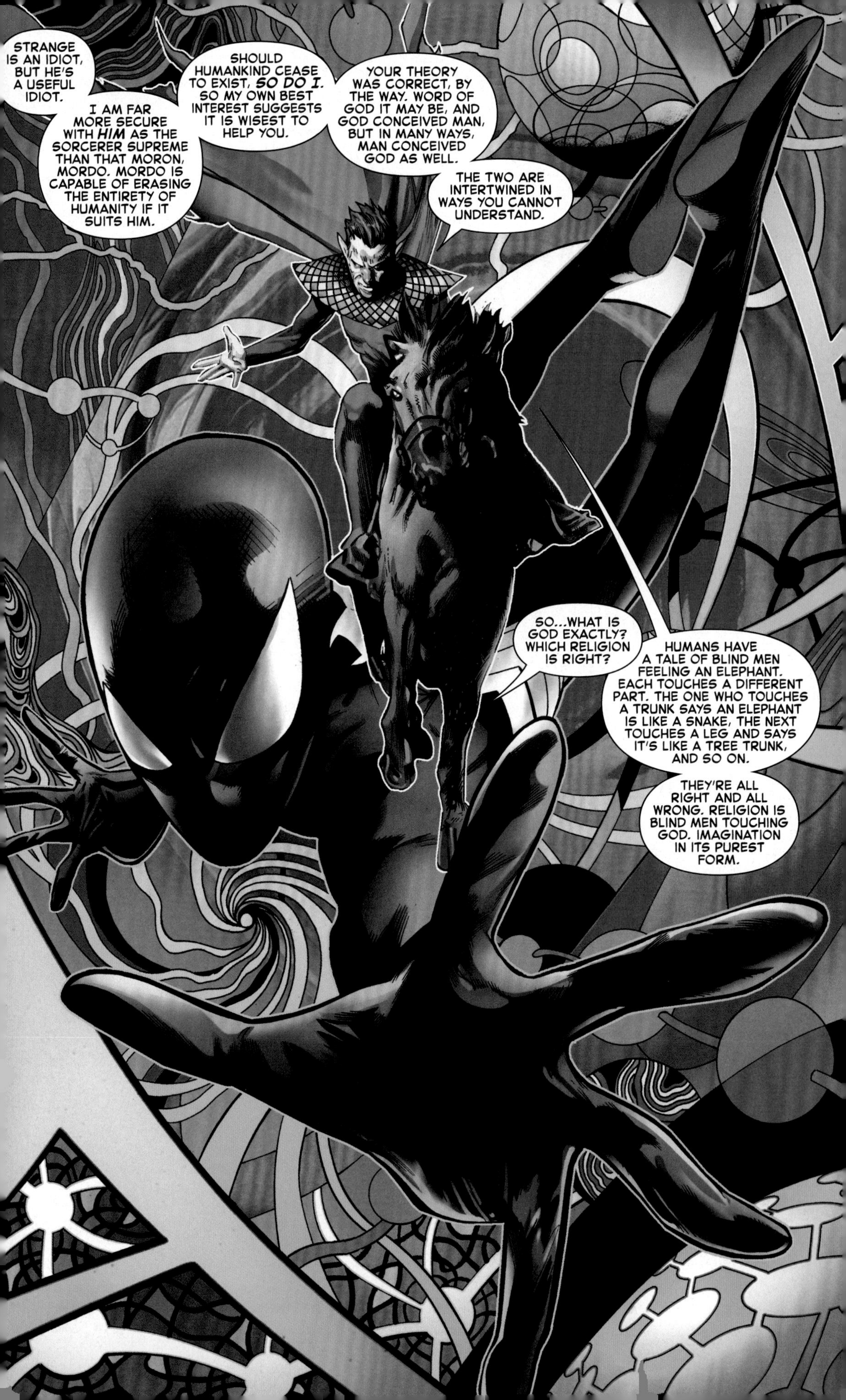
STRANGE IS AN IDIOT, BUT HE'S A USEFUL IDIOT.
I AM FAR MORE SECURE WITH *HIM* AS THE SORCERER SUPREME THAN THAT MORON, MORDO. MORDO IS CAPABLE OF ERASING THE ENTIRETY OF HUMANITY IF IT SUITS HIM.
SHOULD HUMANKIND CEASE TO EXIST, *SO DO I.* SO MY OWN BEST INTEREST SUGGESTS IT IS WISEST TO HELP YOU.
YOUR THEORY WAS CORRECT, BY THE WAY. WORD OF GOD IT MAY BE, AND GOD CONCEIVED MAN, BUT IN MANY WAYS, MAN CONCEIVED GOD AS WELL.
THE TWO ARE INTERTWINED IN WAYS YOU CANNOT UNDERSTAND.
SO...WHAT IS GOD EXACTLY? WHICH RELIGION IS RIGHT?
HUMANS HAVE A TALE OF BLIND MEN FEELING AN ELEPHANT. EACH TOUCHES A DIFFERENT PART. THE ONE WHO TOUCHES A TRUNK SAYS AN ELEPHANT IS LIKE A SNAKE, THE NEXT TOUCHES A LEG AND SAYS IT'S LIKE A TREE TRUNK, AND SO ON.
THEY'RE ALL RIGHT AND ALL WRONG. RELIGION IS BLIND MEN TOUCHING GOD. IMAGINATION IN ITS PUREST FORM.

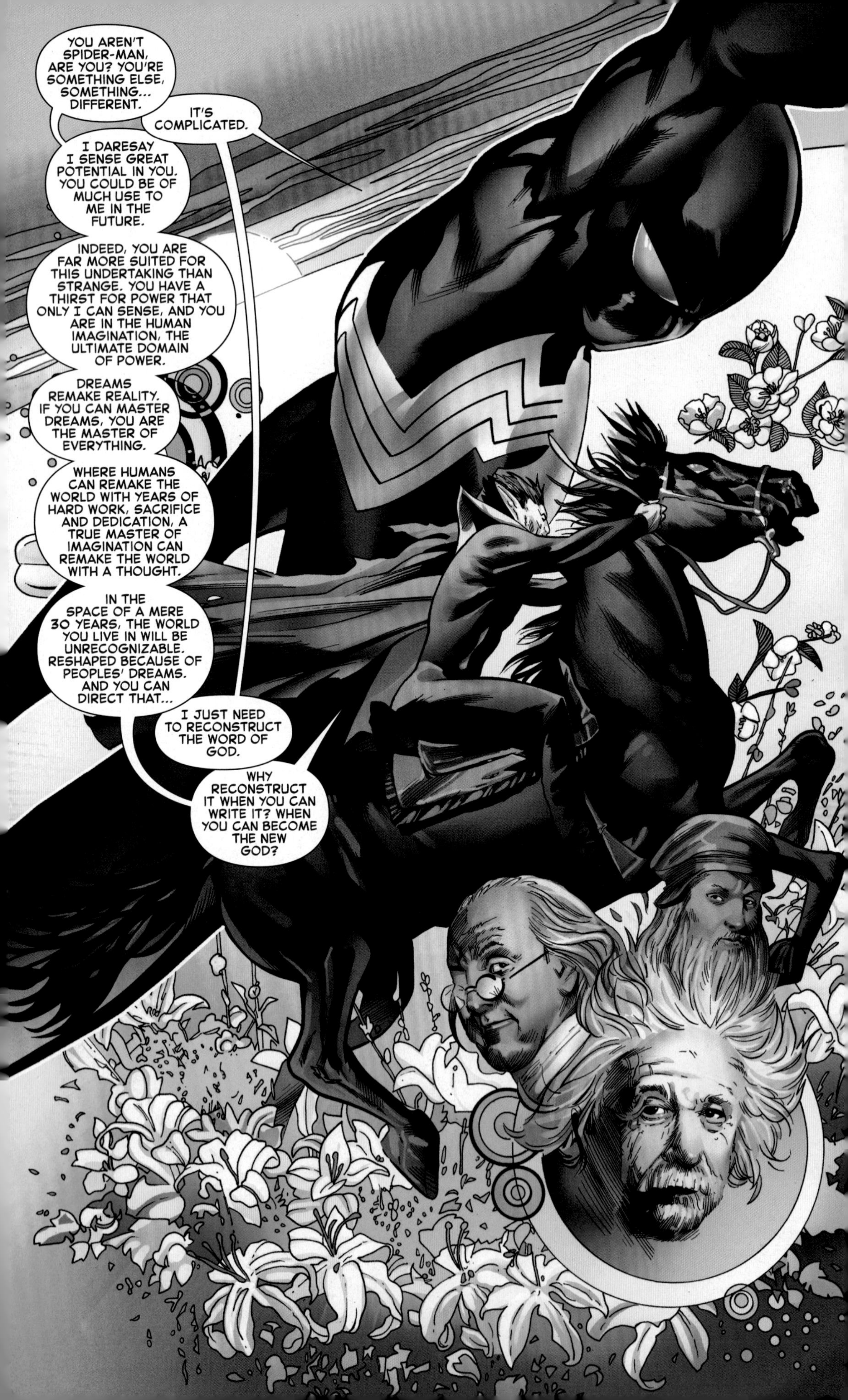
YOU AREN'T SPIDER-MAN, ARE YOU? YOU'RE SOMETHING ELSE, SOMETHING... DIFFERENT.
IT'S COMPLICATED.
I DARESAY I SENSE GREAT POTENTIAL IN YOU. YOU COULD BE OF MUCH USE TO ME IN THE FUTURE.
INDEED, YOU ARE FAR MORE SUITED FOR THIS UNDERTAKING THAN STRANGE. YOU HAVE A THIRST FOR POWER THAT ONLY I CAN SENSE, AND YOU ARE IN THE HUMAN IMAGINATION, THE ULTIMATE DOMAIN OF POWER.
DREAMS REMAKE REALITY. IF YOU CAN MASTER DREAMS, YOU ARE THE MASTER OF EVERYTHING.
WHERE HUMANS CAN REMAKE THE WORLD WITH YEARS OF HARD WORK, SACRIFICE AND DEDICATION, A TRUE MASTER OF IMAGINATION CAN REMAKE THE WORLD WITH A THOUGHT.
IN THE SPACE OF A MERE 30 YEARS, THE WORLD YOU LIVE IN WILL BE UNRECOGNIZABLE. RESHAPED BECAUSE OF PEOPLES' DREAMS. AND YOU CAN DIRECT THAT...
I JUST NEED TO RECONSTRUCT THE WORD OF GOD.
WHY RECONSTRUCT IT WHEN YOU CAN WRITE IT? WHEN YOU CAN BECOME THE NEW GOD?

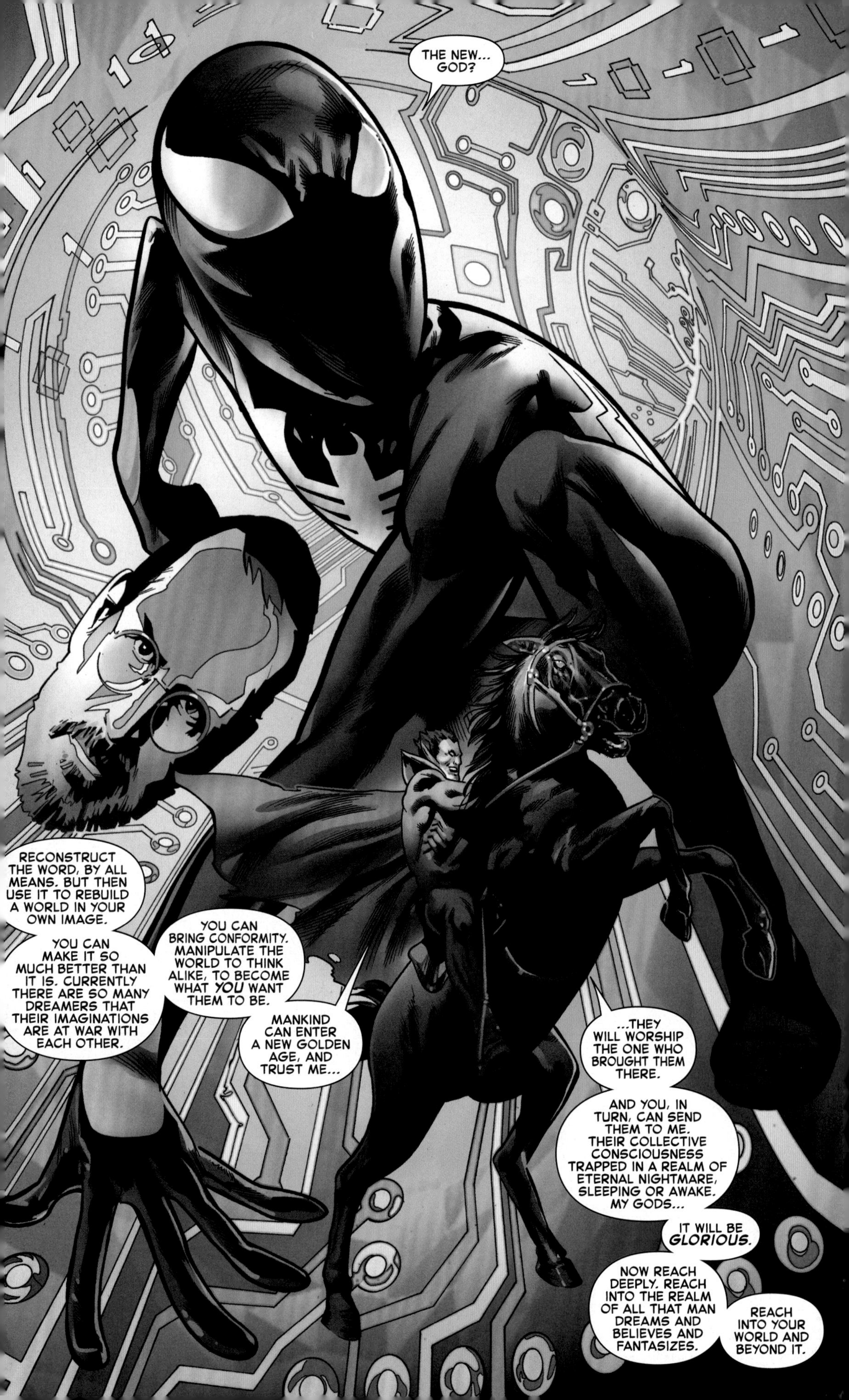
THE NEW... GOD?
RECONSTRUCT THE WORD, BY ALL MEANS. BUT THEN USE IT TO REBUILD A WORLD IN YOUR OWN IMAGE.
YOU CAN MAKE IT SO MUCH BETTER THAN IT IS. CURRENTLY THERE ARE SO MANY DREAMERS THAT THEIR IMAGINATIONS ARE AT WAR WITH EACH OTHER.
YOU CAN BRING CONFORMITY. MANIPULATE THE WORLD TO THINK ALIKE, TO BECOME WHAT *YOU* WANT THEM TO BE.
MANKIND CAN ENTER A NEW GOLDEN AGE, AND TRUST ME...
...THEY WILL WORSHIP THE ONE WHO BROUGHT THEM THERE.
AND YOU, IN TURN, CAN SEND THEM TO ME. THEIR COLLECTIVE CONSCIOUSNESS TRAPPED IN A REALM OF ETERNAL NIGHTMARE, SLEEPING OR AWAKE. MY GODS...
IT WILL BE ***GLORIOUS.***
NOW REACH DEEPLY. REACH INTO THE REALM OF ALL THAT MAN DREAMS AND BELIEVES AND FANTASIZES.
REACH INTO YOUR WORLD AND BEYOND IT.

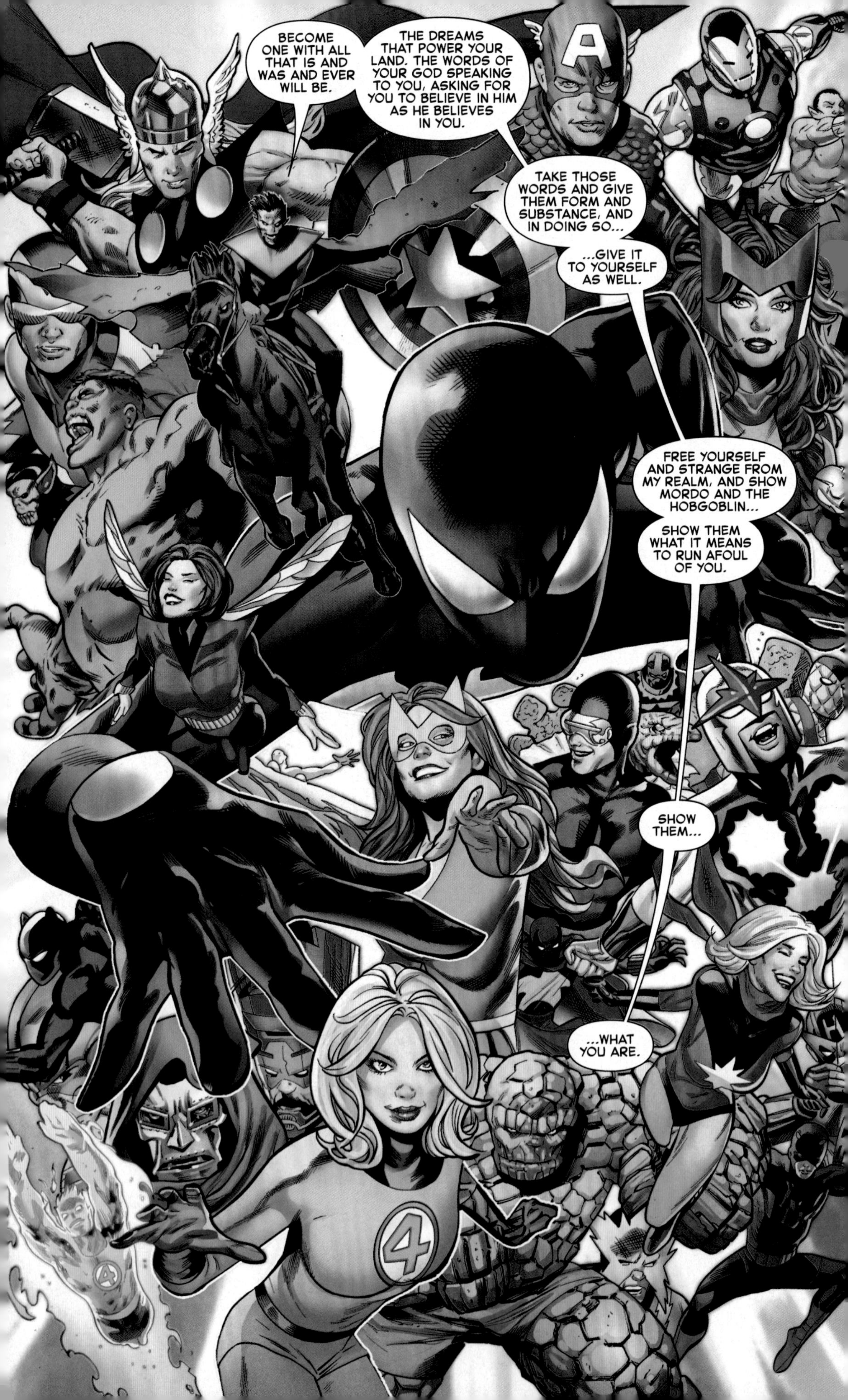
BECOME ONE WITH ALL THAT IS AND WAS AND EVER WILL BE.
THE DREAMS THAT POWER YOUR LAND. THE WORDS OF YOUR GOD SPEAKING TO YOU, ASKING FOR YOU TO BELIEVE IN HIM AS HE BELIEVES IN YOU.
TAKE THOSE WORDS AND GIVE THEM FORM AND SUBSTANCE, AND IN DOING SO...
...GIVE IT TO YOURSELF AS WELL.
FREE YOURSELF AND STRANGE FROM MY REALM, AND SHOW MORDO AND THE HOBGOBLIN...
SHOW THEM WHAT IT MEANS TO RUN AFOUL OF YOU.
SHOW THEM...
...WHAT YOU ARE.

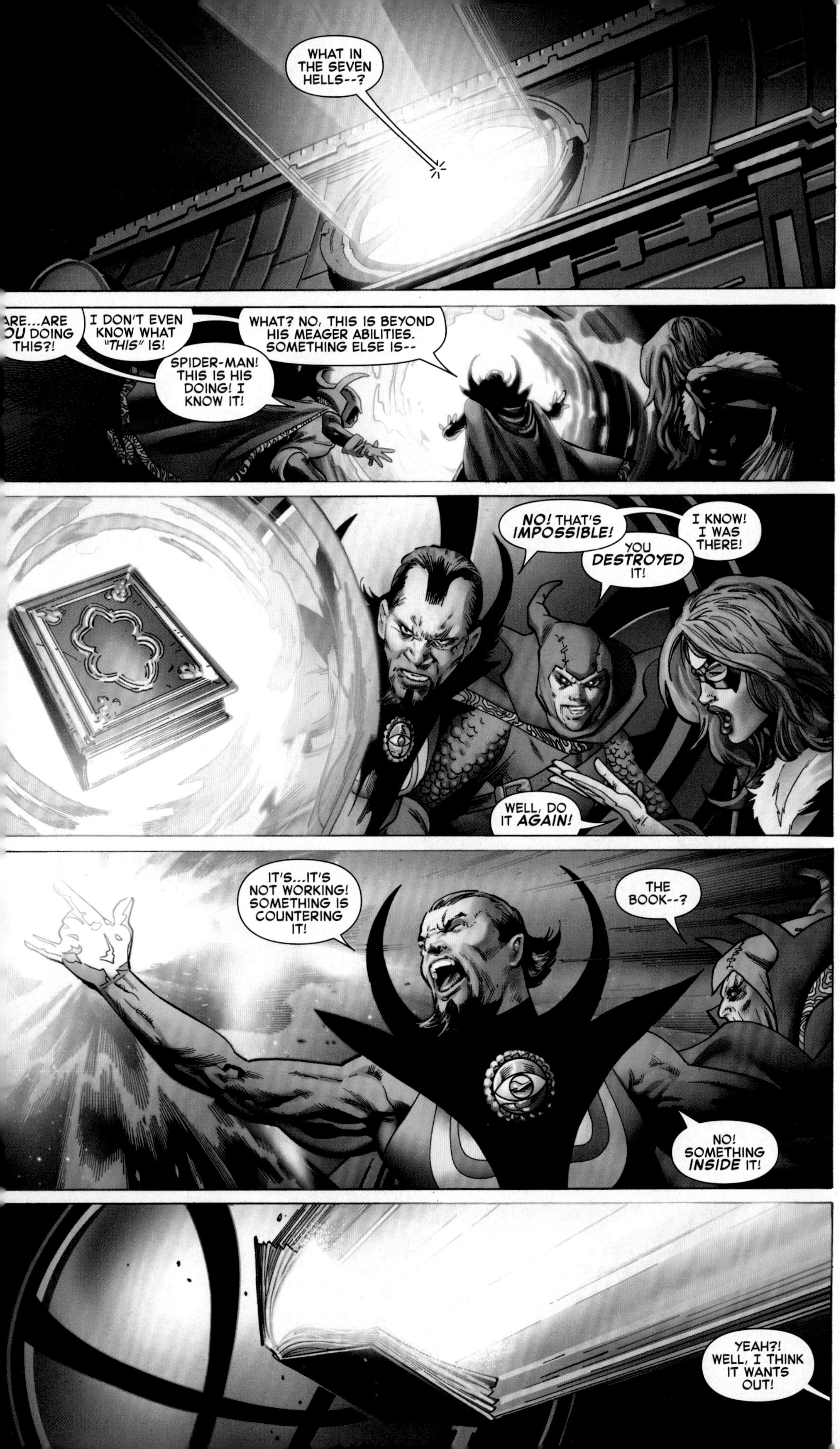
WHAT IN THE SEVEN HELLS--?
ARE...ARE OU DOING THIS?!
I DON'T EVEN KNOW WHAT "THIS" IS!
SPIDER-MAN! THIS IS HIS DOING! I KNOW IT!
WHAT? NO, THIS IS BEYOND HIS MEAGER ABILITIES. SOMETHING ELSE IS--
NO! THAT'S IMPOSSIBLE!
YOU DESTROYED IT!
I KNOW! I WAS THERE!
WELL, DO IT AGAIN!
IT'S...IT'S NOT WORKING! SOMETHING IS COUNTERING IT!
THE BOOK--?
NO! SOMETHING INSIDE IT!
YEAH?! WELL, I THINK IT WANTS OUT!

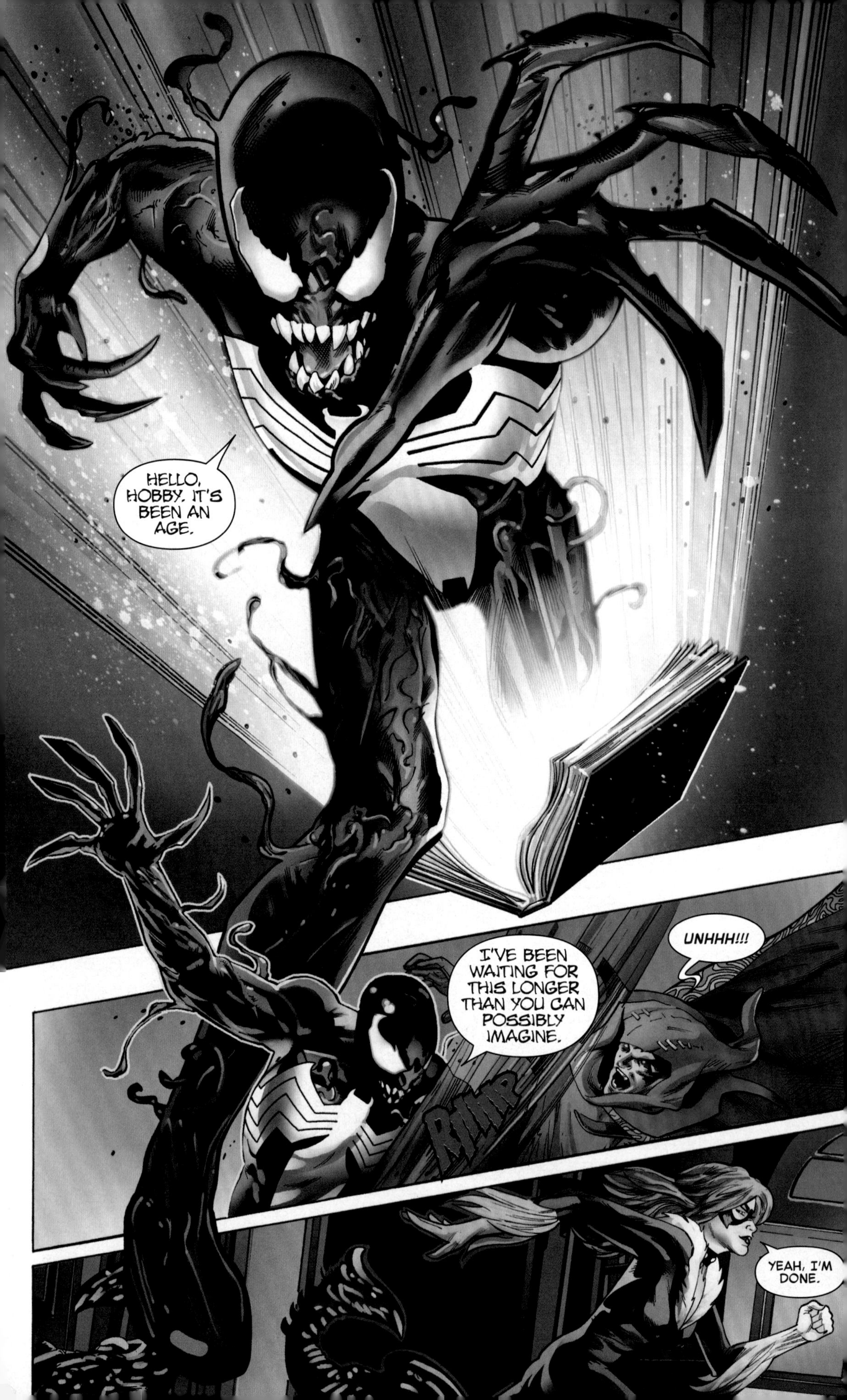
HELLO, HOBBY. IT'S BEEN AN AGE.
I'VE BEEN WAITING FOR THIS LONGER THAN YOU CAN POSSIBLY IMAGINE.
UNHHH!!!
YEAH, I'M DONE.

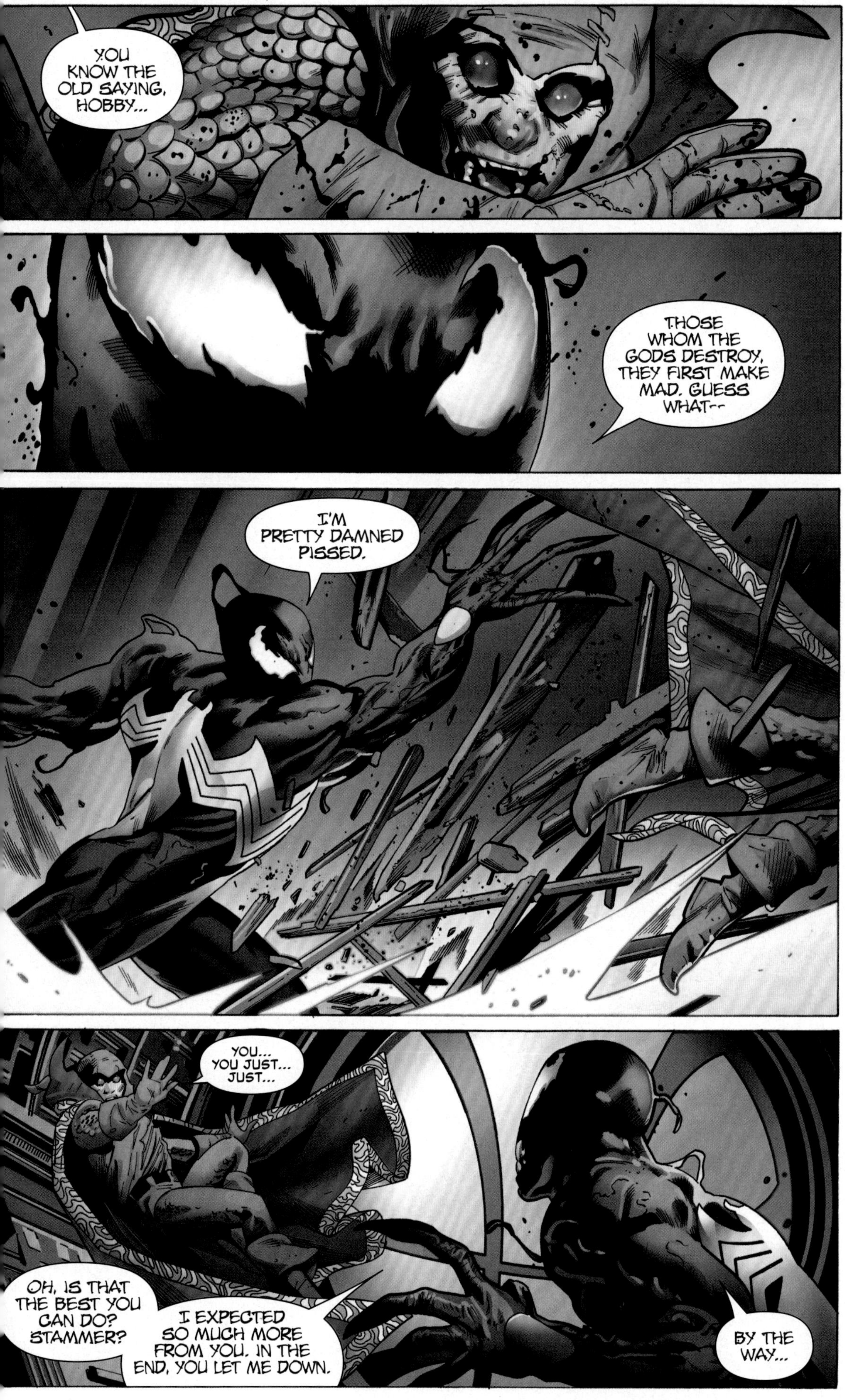
YOU KNOW THE OLD SAYING, HOBBY...
THOSE WHOM THE GODS DESTROY, THEY FIRST MAKE MAD. GUESS WHAT--
I'M PRETTY DAMNED PISSED.
YOU... YOU JUST... JUST...
OH, IS THAT THE BEST YOU CAN DO? STAMMER?
I EXPECTED SO MUCH MORE FROM YOU. IN THE END, YOU LET ME DOWN.
BY THE WAY...

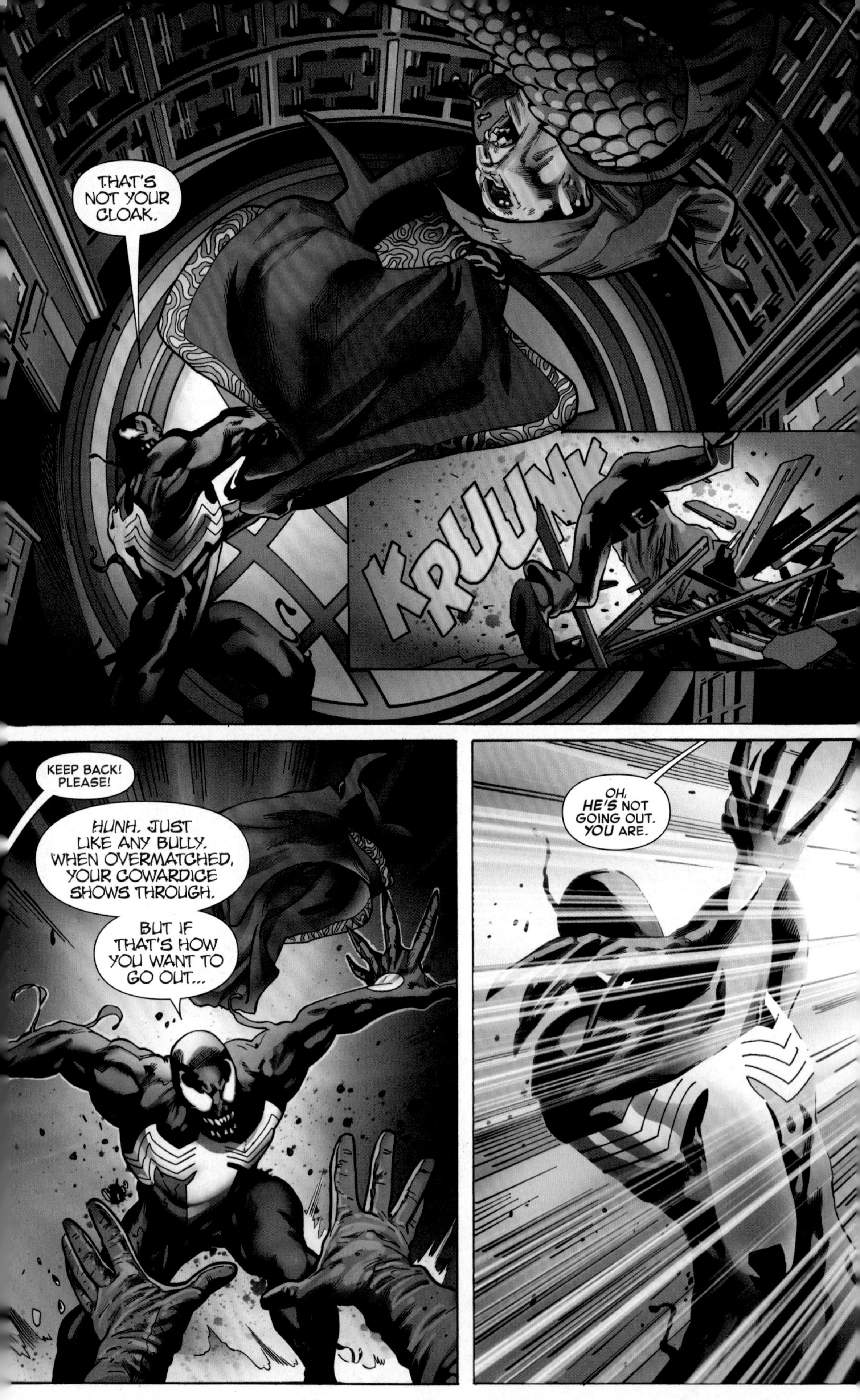

THAT'S NOT YOUR CLOAK.
KRUUNK
KEEP BACK! PLEASE!
HUNH. JUST LIKE ANY BULLY. WHEN OVERMATCHED, YOUR COWARDICE SHOWS THROUGH.
BUT IF THAT'S HOW YOU WANT TO GO OUT...
OH, HE'S NOT GOING OUT. YOU ARE.

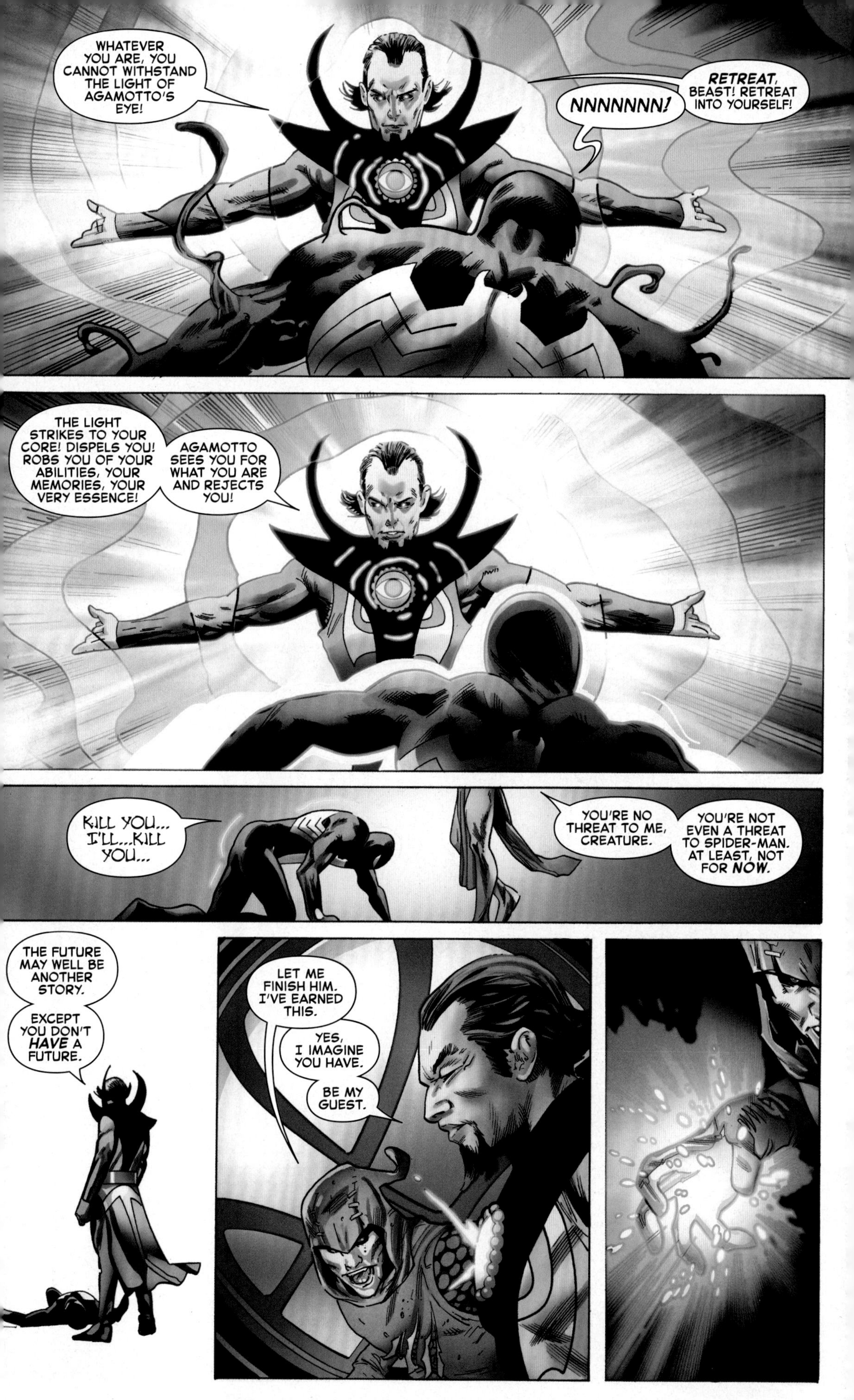
WHATEVER YOU ARE, YOU CANNOT WITHSTAND THE LIGHT OF AGAMOTTO'S EYE!
NNNNNNN!
RETREAT, BEAST! RETREAT INTO YOURSELF!
THE LIGHT STRIKES TO YOUR CORE! DISPELS YOU! ROBS YOU OF YOUR ABILITIES, YOUR MEMORIES, YOUR VERY ESSENCE!
AGAMOTTO SEES YOU FOR WHAT YOU ARE AND REJECTS YOU!
KILL YOU... I'LL...KILL YOU...
YOU'RE NO THREAT TO ME, CREATURE.
YOU'RE NOT EVEN A THREAT TO SPIDER-MAN. AT LEAST, NOT FOR NOW.
THE FUTURE MAY WELL BE ANOTHER STORY.
EXCEPT YOU DON'T HAVE A FUTURE.
LET ME FINISH HIM. I'VE EARNED THIS.
YES, I IMAGINE YOU HAVE.
BE MY GUEST.

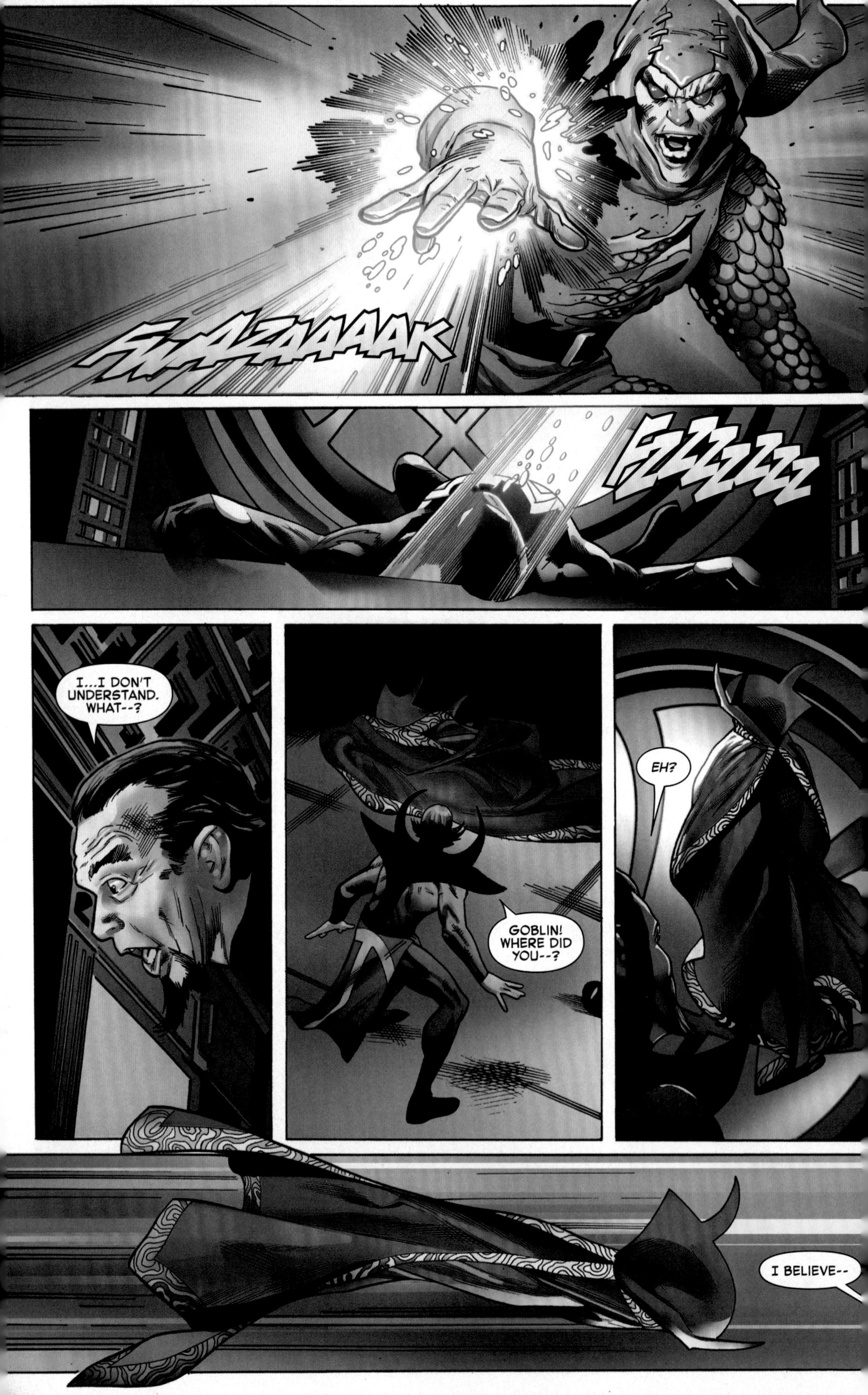
FWAZAAAAK
FZZZZZZZ
I...I DON'T UNDERSTAND. WHAT--?
GOBLIN! WHERE DID YOU--?
EH?
I BELIEVE--

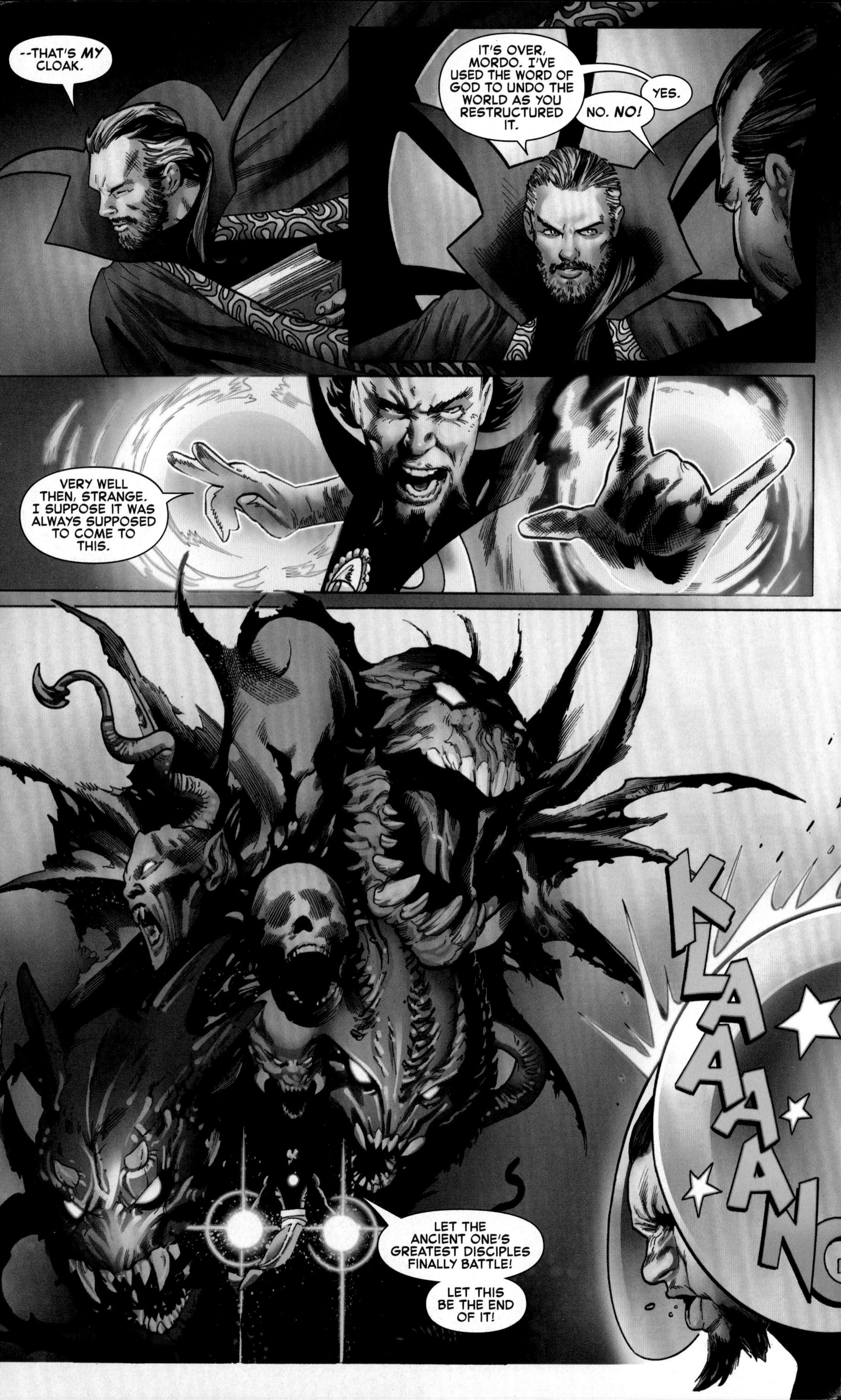
--THAT'S MY CLOAK.
IT'S OVER, MORDO. I'VE USED THE WORD OF GOD TO UNDO THE WORLD AS YOU RESTRUCTURED IT.
YES.
NO. NO!
VERY WELL THEN, STRANGE. I SUPPOSE IT WAS ALWAYS SUPPOSED TO COME TO THIS.
LET THE ANCIENT ONE'S GREATEST DISCIPLES FINALLY BATTLE!
LET THIS BE THE END OF IT!
KLAAAANG

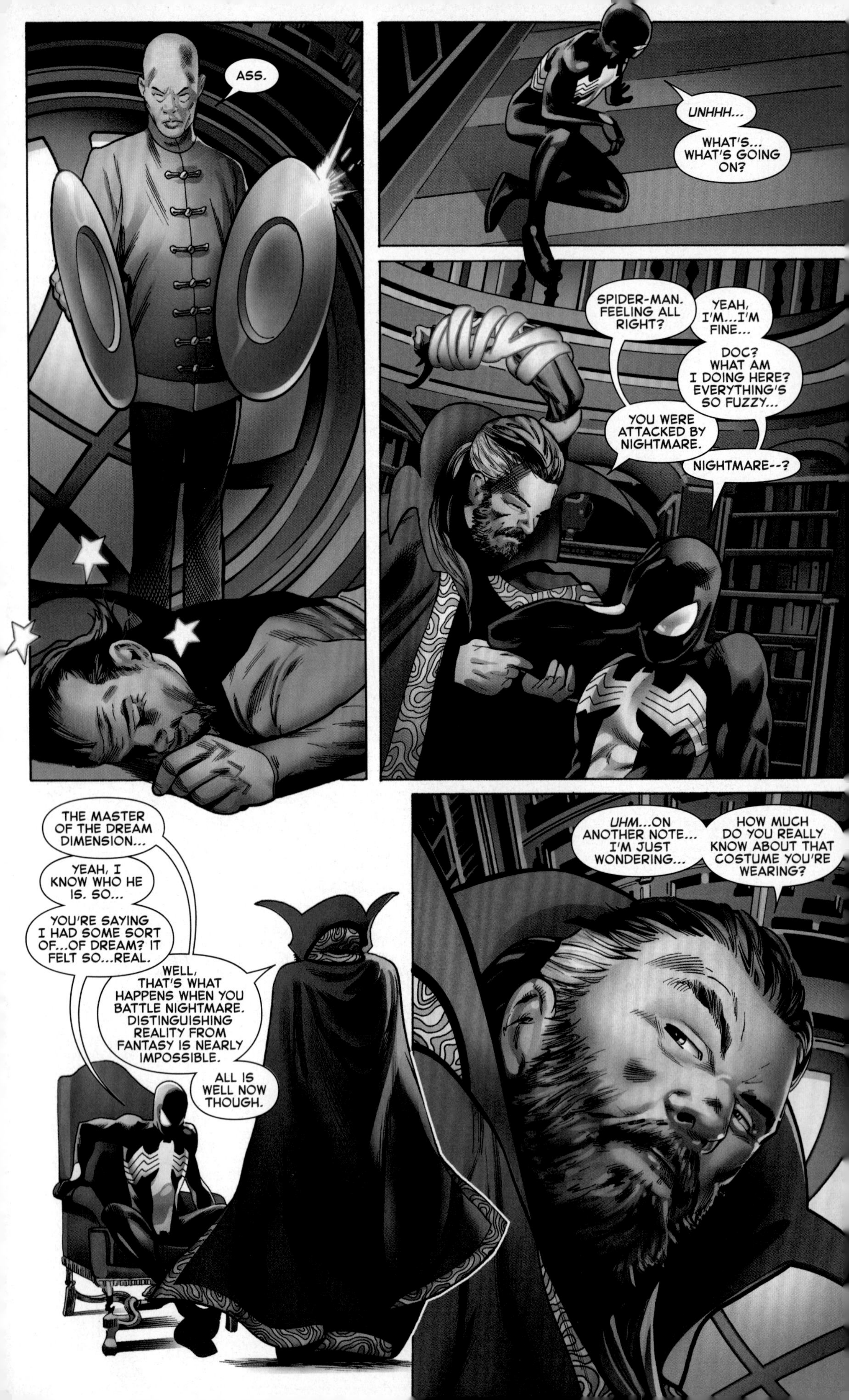
ASS.
UNHHH...
WHAT'S... WHAT'S GOING ON?
SPIDER-MAN. FEELING ALL RIGHT?
YEAH, I'M...I'M FINE...
DOC? WHAT AM I DOING HERE? EVERYTHING'S SO FUZZY...
YOU WERE ATTACKED BY NIGHTMARE.
NIGHTMARE--?
THE MASTER OF THE DREAM DIMENSION...
YEAH, I KNOW WHO HE IS. SO...
YOU'RE SAYING I HAD SOME SORT OF...OF DREAM? IT FELT SO...REAL.
WELL, THAT'S WHAT HAPPENS WHEN YOU BATTLE NIGHTMARE. DISTINGUISHING REALITY FROM FANTASY IS NEARLY IMPOSSIBLE.
ALL IS WELL NOW THOUGH.
UHM...ON ANOTHER NOTE... I'M JUST WONDERING...
HOW MUCH DO YOU REALLY KNOW ABOUT THAT COSTUME YOU'RE WEARING?

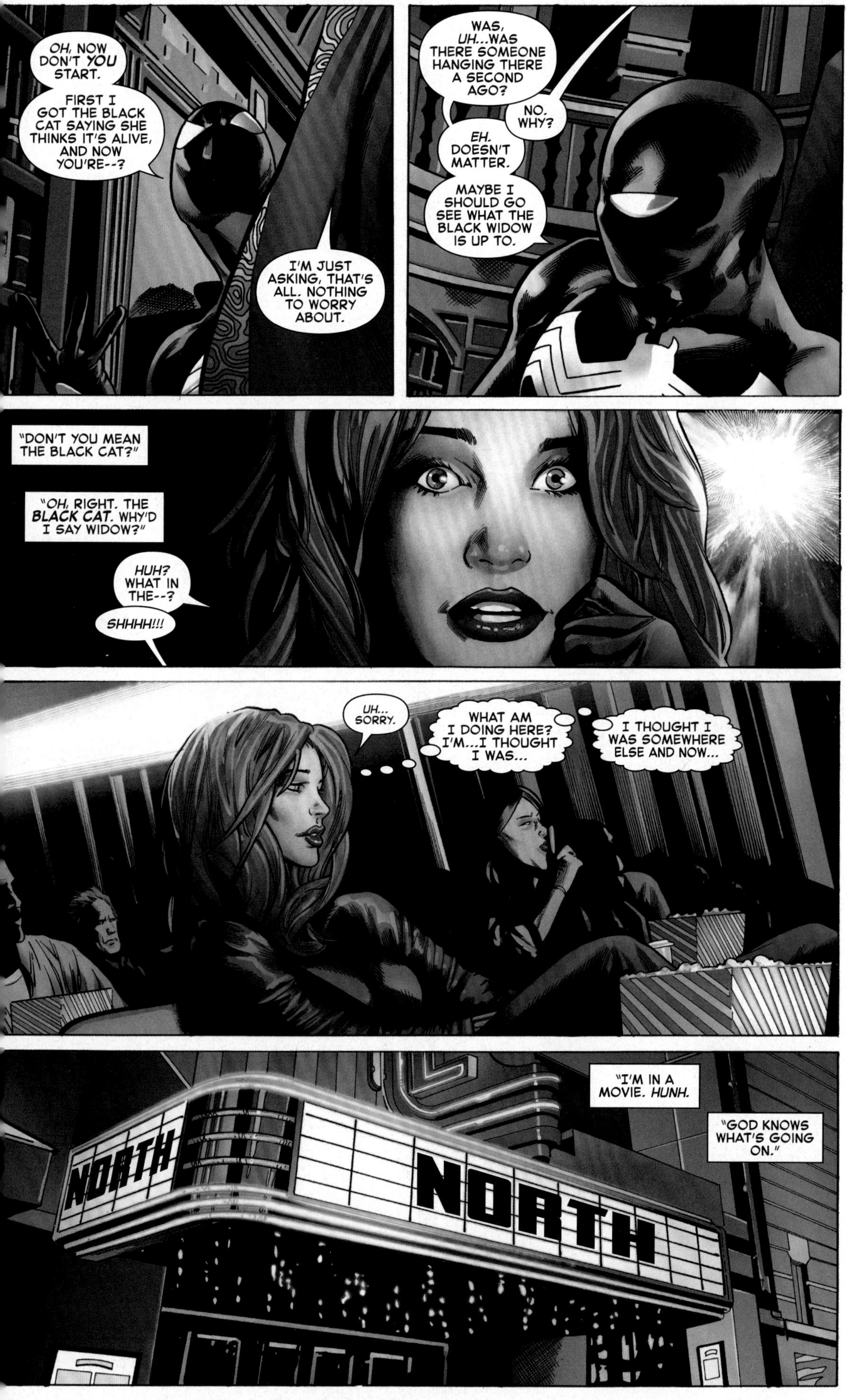
OH, NOW DON'T YOU START.
FIRST I GOT THE BLACK CAT SAYING SHE THINKS IT'S ALIVE, AND NOW YOU'RE--?
I'M JUST ASKING, THAT'S ALL. NOTHING TO WORRY ABOUT.
WAS, UH...WAS THERE SOMEONE HANGING THERE A SECOND AGO?
NO. WHY?
EH. DOESN'T MATTER.
MAYBE I SHOULD GO SEE WHAT THE BLACK WIDOW IS UP TO.
"DON'T YOU MEAN THE BLACK CAT?"
"OH, RIGHT. THE BLACK CAT. WHY'D I SAY WIDOW?"
HUH? WHAT IN THE--?
SHHHH!!!
UH... SORRY.
WHAT AM I DOING HERE? I'M...I THOUGHT I WAS...
I THOUGHT I WAS SOMEWHERE ELSE AND NOW...
"I'M IN A MOVIE. HUNH.
"GOD KNOWS WHAT'S GOING ON."
NORTH
NORTH

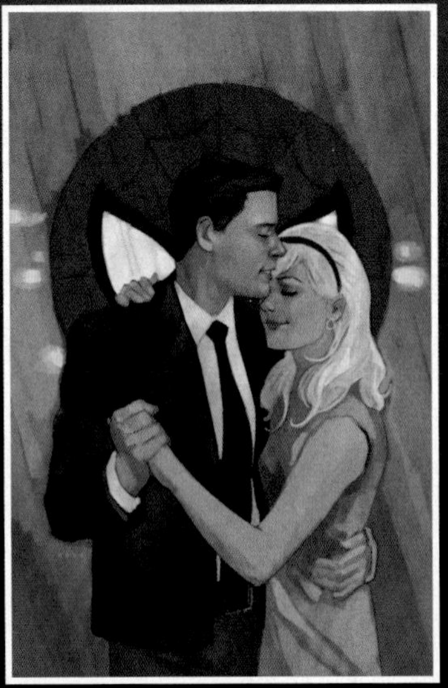

#3 GWEN STACY VARIANT BY
PHIL NOTO

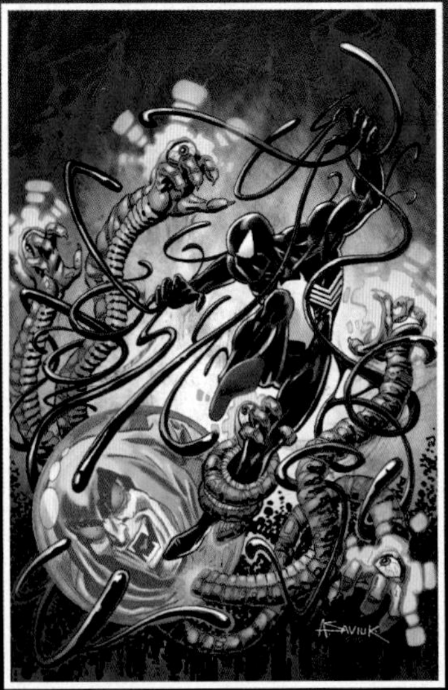

#4 VARIANT BY
ALEX SAVIUK & CHRIS SOTOMAYOR

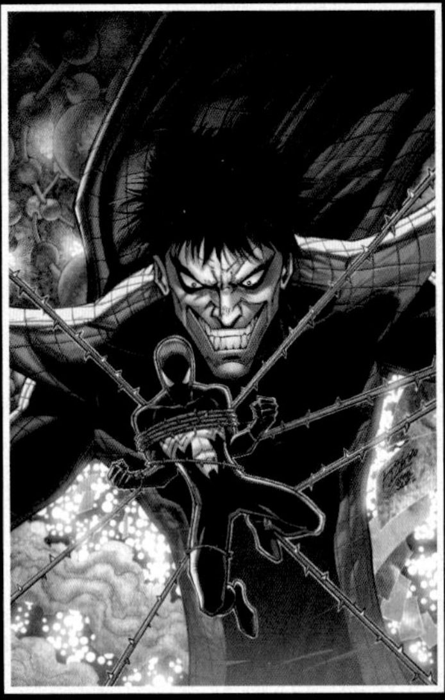

#4 VARIANT BY
RON LIM & ISRAEL SILVA

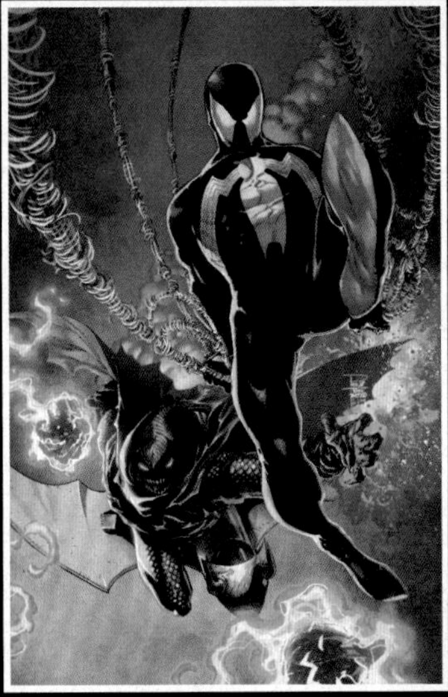

#4 VARIANT BY
PHILIP TAN & JAY DAVID RAMOS

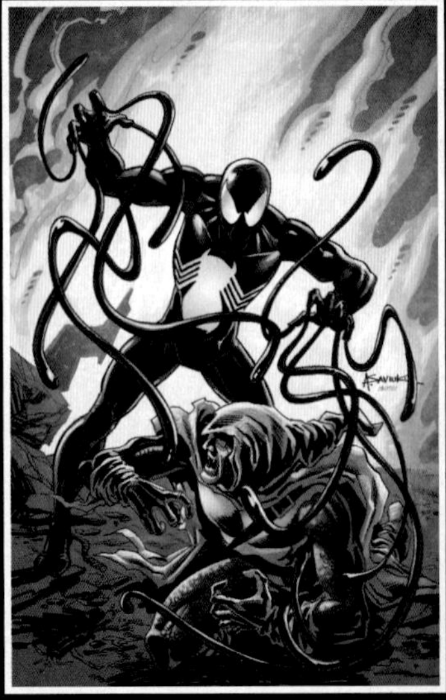

#5 VARIANT BY
ALEX SAVIUK & CHRIS SOTOMAYOR

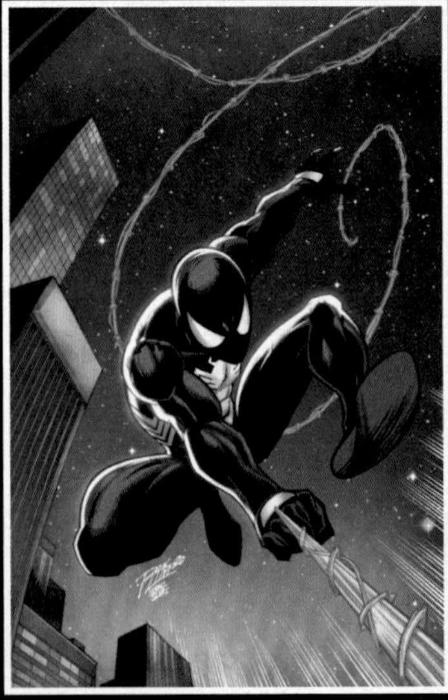

#5 VARIANT BY
RON LIM & ISRAEL SILVA

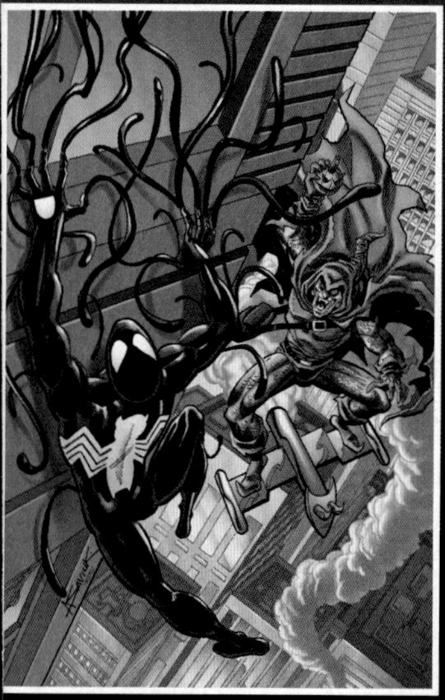

#2 VARIANT BY
ALEX SAVIUK & **CHRIS SOTOMAYOR**

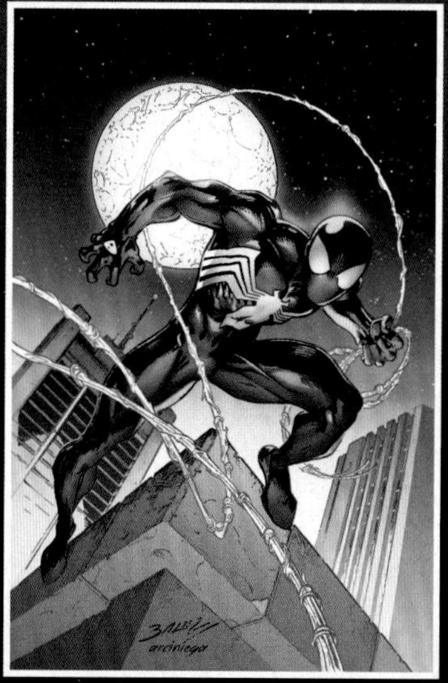

#2 VARIANT BY
MARK BAGLEY & **ERICK ARCINIEGA**

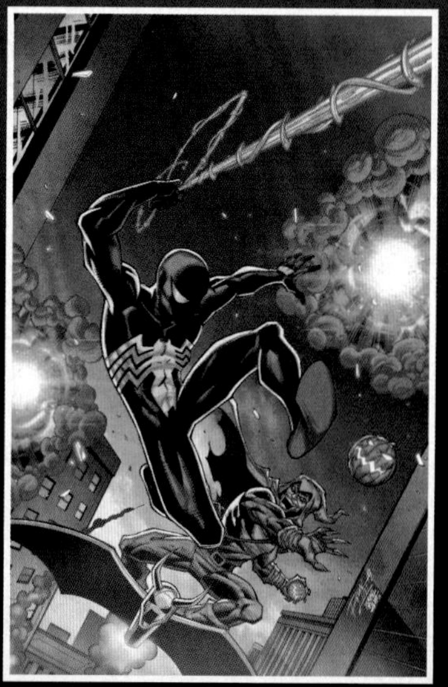

#2 VARIANT BY
RON LIM & **ISRAEL SILVA**

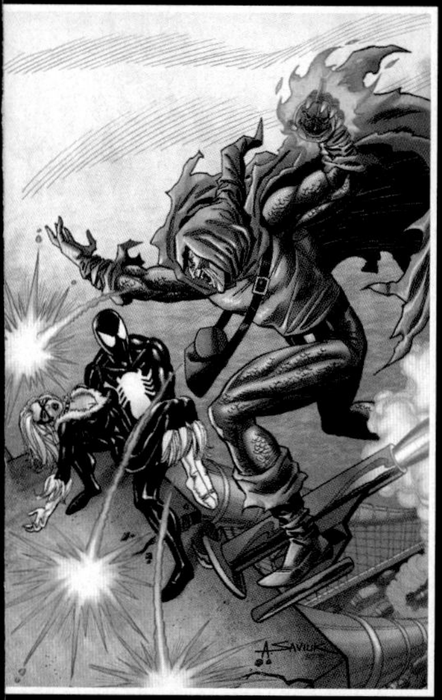

#3 VARIANT BY
ALEX SAVIUK & **CHRIS SOTOMAYOR**

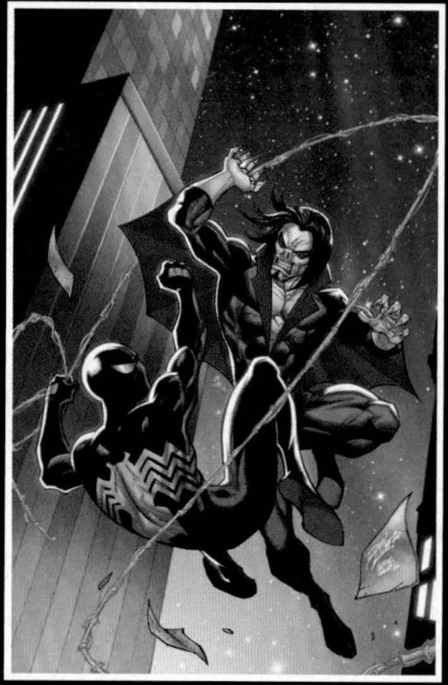

#3 VARIANT BY
RON LIM & **ISRAEL SILVA**

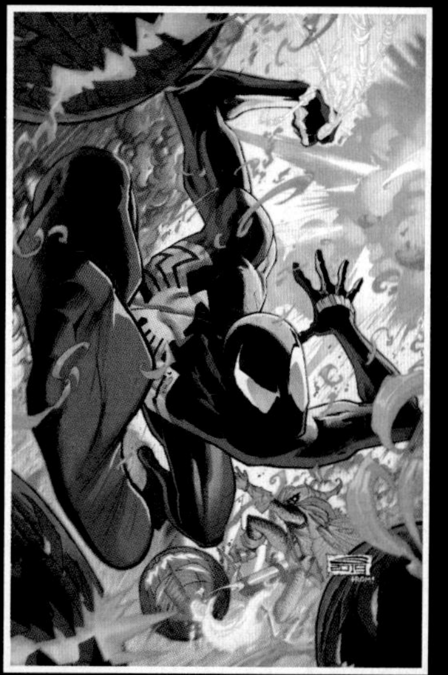

#3 VARIANT BY
GERARDO SANDOVAL &
ROMULO FAJARDO JR.

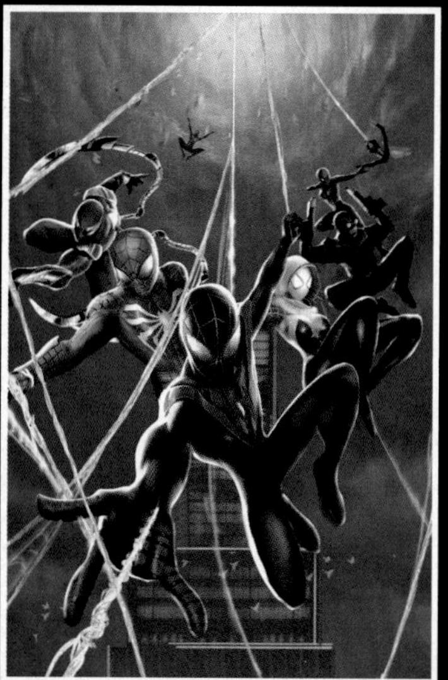

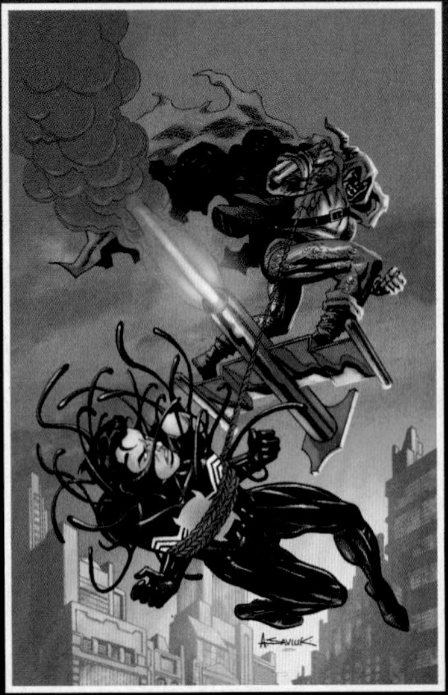

#1 VARIANT BY
ALEX SAVIUK & CHRIS SOTOMAYOR

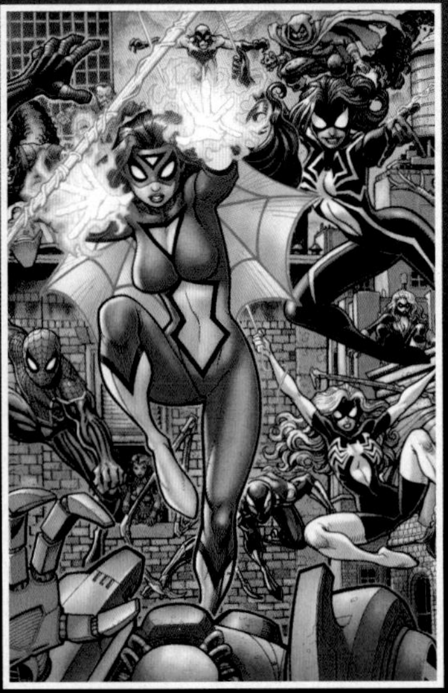

#1 CONNECTING VARIANT BY
ARTHUR ADAMS & EDGAR DELGADO

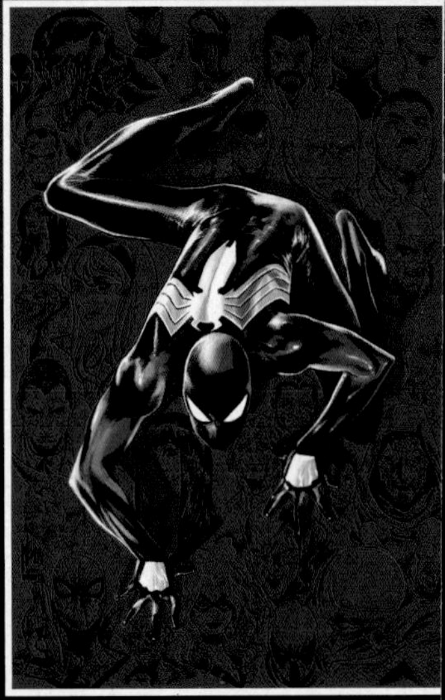

#1 YOUNG GUNS VARIANT BY
MARCO CHECCHETTO

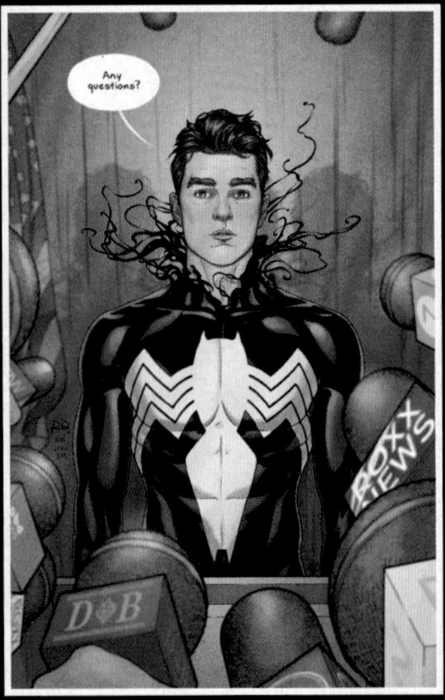
Any questions?

#1 YOUNG GUNS VARIANT BY
RUSSELL DAUTERMAN & MATTHEW WILSON

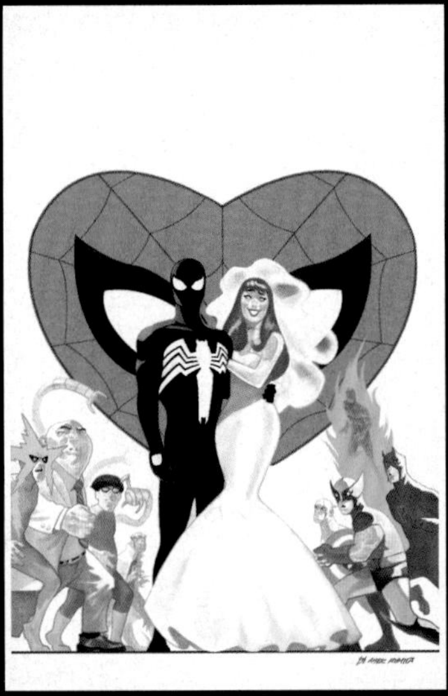

#1 YOUNG GUNS VARIANT BY
MIKE DEL MUNDO

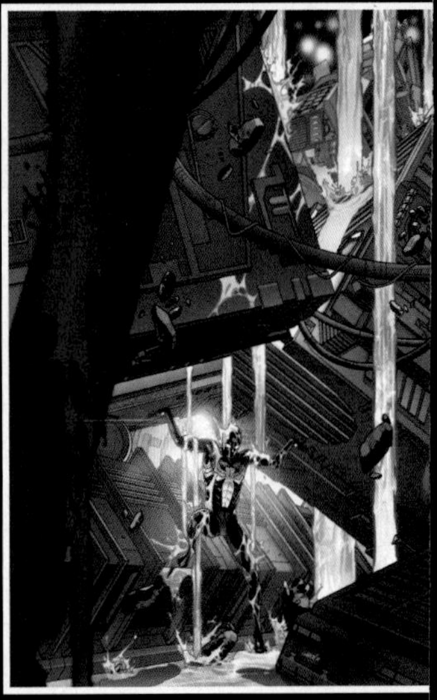

#1 YOUNG GUNS VARIANT BY
JAVIER GARRÓN & DAVID CURIEL

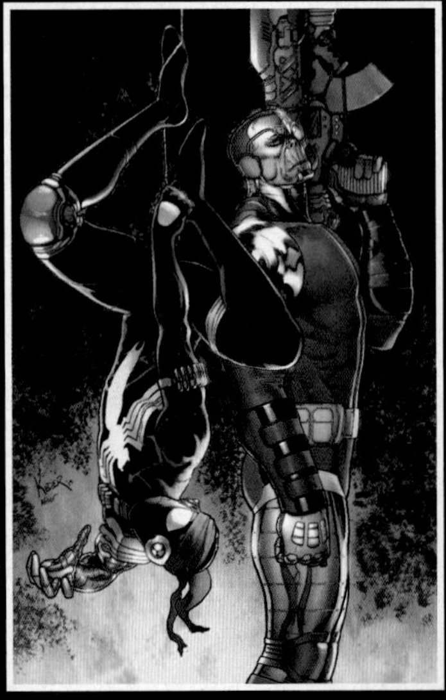

#1 YOUNG GUNS VARIANT BY
AARON KUDER & JASON KEITH

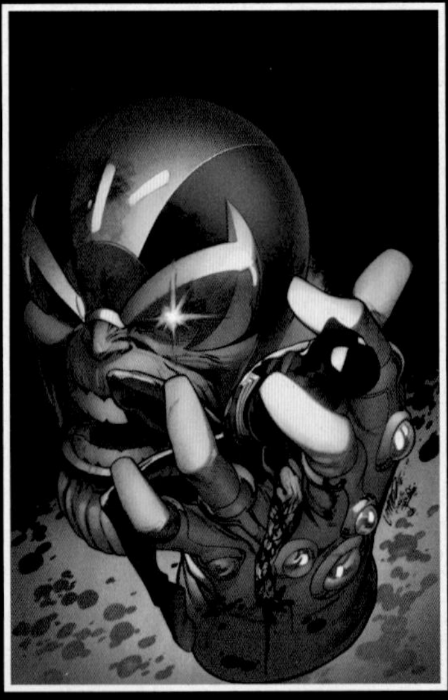

#1 YOUNG GUNS VARIANT BY
PEPE LARRAZ & MARTE GRACIA

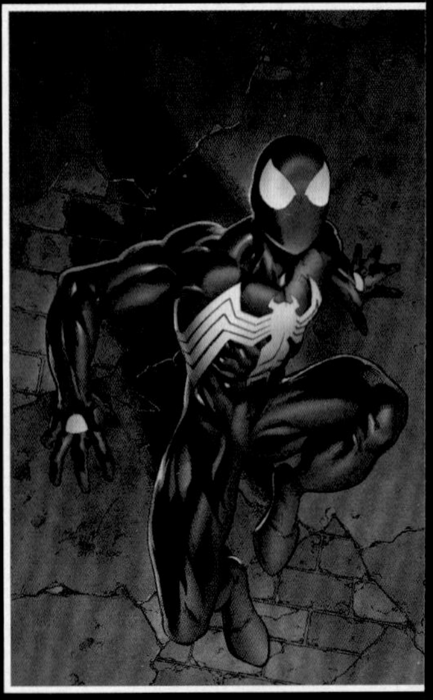

#1 VARIANT BY
MARK BAGLEY & ERICK ARCINIEGA